NIMBY is Beautiful

NIMBY is Beautiful

Cases of Local Activism and Environmental Innovation Around the World

Edited by
Carol Hager and Mary Alice Haddad

Published by
Berghahn Books
www.berghahnbooks.com

Library of Congress Cataloging-in-Publication Data

NIMBY is beautiful : cases of local activism and environmental innovation around the world / edited by Carol Hager and Mary Alice Haddad.
pages cm
Includes index.
ISBN 978-1-78238-601-8 (hardback) —
ISBN 978-1-78238-602-5 (ebook)
1. Environmentalism—Case studies. 2. Environmental protection—Case studies. 3. NIMBY syndrome—Case studies. 4. Protest movements—Case studies. I. Hager, Carol J., 1958– editor of compilation. II. Haddad, Mary Alice, 1973- editor of compilation.
GE195.N56 2015
333.72—dc23

2014033539

British Library Cataloguing in Publication Data

A catalogue record for this book is available from the British Library

Printed on acid-free paper.

ISBN: 978-1-78238-601-8 hardback
ISBN: 978-1-78238-602-5 ebook

To the local communities around the world
that are fighting to make our planet a nicer place to live.
And to our children,
who remind us daily why the fight is so important.

Contents

Illustrations

Figures

Tables

Preface

The original contributors to this volume met in Berlin at a faculty seminar, sponsored by Studienforum Berlin e.V., entitled "Germany as a Model? The Environmental and Energy Strategy," during the summer of 2009. Among a diverse group of faculty that included humanists and natural scientists, a number of the political scientists found our experience in Berlin to be inspirational. We kept in touch over the next several years, proposing joint panels and collaborating on papers for conferences, including the Midwest Political Science Association Annual Meeting (2010) and the American Political Science Association Annual Meeting (2011).

By 2012 we realized that our research projects intersected in ways that could result in an interesting edited volume. That spring we met at a workshop, hosted by Carol Hager at Bryn Mawr College in Pennsylvania, to identify core themes and develop a tentative chapter outline. What struck us all, regardless of regional expertise, was the profound yet largely unacknowledged contribution of local protest to innovation, both in environmental protection and in governance. Our title, *NIMBY is Beautiful,* was suggested by Takashi Kanatsu at that meeting and became a focal point for all of the writing and discussions that followed.

As we expanded our geographical scope, our membership grew as well. In the fall of 2012 we held a second workshop, hosted by Mary Alice Haddad at Wesleyan University in Connecticut. By this time we had full chapter drafts, and we could feel our volume coming to life. We believe the genesis of this book gives it a unique perspective, grounded in common experience of a core case and refined through years of comparative discussion and debate. It is an example of the intellectual synergy that can occur when curious people with different areas of expertise ask a common question.

All books, and edited volumes in particular, are the culmination of the efforts of many individuals and institutions. We would like to offer our sincere thanks to those who have helped us along the way. In particular, we are indebted to Hanns-D. Jacobsen of Studienforum Berlin, along with Gisela Jacobsen, Nathaniel Scheer, Annike Werner, and Andrew Ancygier, whose wonderful seminar created the opportunity for us to meet and offered the intellectual seeds not only for this volume, but for so many of our own independent research agendas. We would like to thank McGee Young, Patrick McKinlay, and James Workman, who contributed to our discussions and supported the project in ways large and small, even though they did not ultimately submit chapters to the volume. We would also like to acknowledge Bryn Mawr College and its Environmental Studies program, as well as Wesleyan University's College of the Environment, Allbritton Center for the Study of Public Life, and Department of Government. Without their financial support for the book workshops, this volume would not have been possible.

Introduction

A New Look at NIMBY

Carol Hager

Driving through southwestern Germany's Black Forest region, one encounters tranquil villages, idyllic pasturelands, and, if one is lucky enough to arrive in the fall, the spectacular colors of the fabled forest itself. It looks much as it did generations ago, but for a few distinctly modern touches. State-of-the-art wind turbines now dot the hillsides, and many of the characteristic Black Forest houses are adorned with solar panels. Driving down into the meadowlands near the Rhine, it is difficult for a visitor to imagine that this gentle landscape was once slated to become the smog belt of Europe.

In the early 1970s, the German, French, and Swiss governments planned to transform the Upper Rhine region into a massive industrial zone. Nuclear power plants, oil refineries, and chemical processing facilities would line the river from Basel to Frankfurt, squeezing out the vineyards and farms. Local planning authorities threw up their hands, complaining that they were consulted only after these facilities had been decided upon at higher levels of government, if they were consulted at all (*Der Spiegel* 1975). As natural landscapes dwindled, local populations began to rise up against the industrial build-out. Farmers and vintners, university students and clerics organized petition campaigns, filed legal actions, mobilized mass demonstrations, and finally resorted to site occupations in order to stop the construction. Dismissed by many as backward-looking NIMBY (Not In My Backyard) protesters, they stood their ground and began to push back, characterizing the large-scale development plans as unnecessary, technologically unsound, and environmentally and socially destructive.

Mass mobilization against nuclear power on the German side drew broad attention to the issue and started a national conversation about economic growth and energy policy goals. With time, as the concerns of the protesters were borne out, the state and national governments altered their plans. The protests, which policy makers had initially written off as NIMBY obstructionism, gave rise to a grassroots movement to develop decentralized, environmentally friendly alternatives to nuclear and fossil fuels. With help from the veterans of the anti-nuclear protests, this southwestern corner of Germany eventually achieved international renown for its innovations in solar technology. It is now proudly advertised as Germany's "solar region." Visitors from all over the world come here to learn about locally generated, environmentally sustainable energy.

As industrialization intensifies across the globe, local populations worldwide are mobilizing to protest environmental threats to their communities. Often, contrary to the negative stereotype of NIMBY, these movements achieve lasting change beyond the particular siting controversy. This is true across regions, types of political system, and levels of economic development. In this volume, we analyze cases of local protest in a variety of countries, including Germany, the United States, China, Russia, Japan, Taiwan, and Korea. These cases encompass a range of authority structures, including representative democracies, recently consolidated or consolidating democracies, and authoritarian governments. We find cases in which NIMBY leads to innovation irrespective of political or social context. The process begins with a serious environmental threat to the lives and livelihoods of local citizens. These citizens seek to redress the threat, but they find their access to the center of political power blocked. The blockage may result from a variety of factors, including corporatist design (Germany, Japan), the inability of the national government to implement policies effectively (China), or the dominance of particular private interests (USA), to name a few. Inaction from the state and blocked access to channels for political influence force local citizens to respond through NIMBY protests.

Local action is shaped initially by the political opportunity structure, but it can also reshape that structure. NIMBY protests can initiate a process of community learning in which important issues of citizen self-understanding, democratic politics, technical expertise, and issue framing are addressed, resulting in innovative solutions that can serve as models for others. In the end, NIMBY politics often leads to more general changes in the pattern of citizen-state relations and also to technological innovation, with positive results in terms of both environmental outcomes and participatory governance. By casting a wide net and finding such cases in a range of political settings, we demonstrate that these innovations are not limited to wealthy, advanced democracies, but are possible, and in fact are likely, to occur in poorer non- and semi-democratic countries as well.

We thus reject the common notion of NIMBY protests as particularistic, parochial, and short-lived. We argue instead that these protests often pursue more general aims and achieve positive, lasting influences on environmental policy and governance. Our volume stands out from other recent work for its geographical reach, its comparison of dissimilar political systems, and its theoretical emphasis on the positive impacts of political conflict. In some of our cases, such as the Chinese protesters' defense of the Nu River as a cultural asset rather than an energy source, local protest movements have aimed directly to pursue a competing notion of the public good (Plantan). In others, such as the German anti-nuclear protesters' development of new policy mechanisms for promoting renewable energy, local protest has resulted in innovations that have benefited not only the narrow community, but also the broader society (Hager).

Our purposes are to show that in many cases NIMBY conflict can be constructive, to explore the kinds of innovation that result from these conflicts, and ultimately to suggest explanations for how and why the innovations occur. We do not claim that NIMBY always results in broader societal change. Our claim is that such change occurs often enough, in a wide range of settings, to justify a re-interpretation of the significance of grassroots conflict.

In making this argument, we join a growing body of scholars offering a more nuanced view of NIMBY (Kraft and Clary 1991; McAvoy 1999; Wolsink 2006; Aldrich 2008; Devine-Wright 2010). We go a step farther than these scholars in showing how the grass roots itself can be the source of political, technological, and social innovation in the face of inaction at higher levels of governance. This is particularly important in contemporary politics, when national- and international-level political actors struggle to deal productively with pressing issues such as climate change.

We begin our comparative analysis with a review of the existing literature on NIMBY protest. We use perhaps the most common definition of NIMBY: the term describes protest organized by local citizens that centers, at least at first, on preventing an environmental harm in their community. In addition to local citizens, the participants may eventually include other actors such as journalists (Plantan), sympathetic local political officials (Kanatsu), or clergy (Hager). While the concept of NIMBY has evolved over time, there are fairly consistent underlying assumptions that have supported an overall negative view of the phenomenon. We describe those assumptions and explain how our case studies challenge each of them. We then introduce the individual chapters, explaining how our cases, taken together, support a new, more complex, and more positive interpretation of the role of NIMBY conflict in political life.

NIMBY in the Social Science Literature

The term "NIMBY" has appeared in a great variety of academic fields and contexts. By the early 1980s, NIMBY had become a common acronym in the American social science literature, employed to discuss the wide range of community protest activities that emerged in response to local environmental threats (Portney 1984; Matheny and Williams 1985). It was most often used to describe community protests against government-sponsored polluting facilities such as power plants and hazardous waste dumps. NIMBY was eventually joined by other formulations, including LULU (Locally Unwanted Land Use), NIABY (Not In Anybody's Backyard), NOPE (Not On Planet Earth), and even BANANA (Build Absolutely Nothing Anywhere Near Anything [or Anyone]).[1]

Local protests against certain types of facilities, most notably hazardous waste disposal sites and nuclear power plants, often resulted in a failure to site the facilities at all (McAvoy 1999). As the acronyms make clear, these local movements were often derided in the press as uninformed, purely obstructionist, and detrimental to economic and social progress. Social scientists, too, commonly described NIMBY in terms of illness, as a "syndrome" in need of a cure (Dear 1992; Mazmanian and Morell 1994; Inhaber 1998). Underlying many of these critiques was a largely unexamined conception of NIMBY protest as a matter of particularistic versus general interests, parochial interests versus the public good.

Not all scholars have dismissed the NIMBY phenomenon as purely negative. Some early analyses, based primarily on hazardous waste siting, took a more differentiated view (Kraft and Clary 1991; Gerrard 1994; Rabe 1994). They sought to find ways to mitigate protest by understanding the positions of the various participants in the conflict. Studies focusing on the government/industry side showed how facility siting plans and processes often provoked a NIMBY reaction by essentially forcing polluting facilities on unwilling local populations. Barry Rabe, for example, characterized NIMBY as "a realistic local response to an immediate problem: national and subnational policies that were poorly designed and ham-handedly implemented" (1994: 3). In this view, NIMBY is not irrational or retrograde. Mitigation would involve restructuring local participation in the siting process. Such studies increasingly view the state or national government as a strategic actor that can broaden participation in policy decisions, either in order to avoid a NIMBY reaction in the first place (Lesbirel and Shaw 2005; Rogers et al. 2008; Haggett 2010), or in response to sustained local protest over its initial coercive strategies (Aldrich 2008).

Other studies focus on the affected communities, seeking to understand the motivations of the protesters in order to provoke a better response. Some of these examine factors such as psychological motivations, perceptions of risk, and attitudes toward government (Wildavsky and Dake 1990; Hunter and Leyden 1995; Snary 2004). Others examine demographic factors such as age, education, and income, as well as variations in support based on incentives offered by industry (Benford et al. 1993). The literature on social movements has challenged the notion that latent community characteristics are responsible for shaping community responses to unwanted projects. They draw attention instead to active framing processes that lead community members to mobilize outside the bounds of the official participation process (Snow et al. 1986; Snow and Benford 1992). Robert Futrell shows how the NIMBY frame emerges as a result of an "information haze" of conflicting information about the risks of a project (2003: 365). He points out that it is, however, just one of several frames that may be employed by communities over the course of a siting conflict.

In sum, many recent studies have challenged the initial, rather black-and-white interpretation of NIMBY protest. They have re-conceptualized conflict over siting in more strategic and contingent terms that treat all actors as rational and capable of learning. We have certain things in common with both of the above schools. Like Aldrich and others who focus on the government/industry side of NIMBY conflict, we assert that NIMBY actors are rational. But our emphasis is not on how NIMBY prompts government to dig deeper into its toolbox for new strategies. We find that NIMBY actors are much more engaged in devising solutions than this focus suggests. We show that, for our cases, local citizens are an active part of the innovation process. Like Snow, Futrell, and other social movement theorists who focus on the protest side of NIMBY, we share an interest in framing processes and strategic action; this literature, however, tends not to examine the influence of NIMBY beyond the bounds of the particular siting controversy, whereas we look for its sometimes more subtle but arguably more important broader societal impacts.

The central aim of most studies of NIMBY has always been to suggest ways to avoid or minimize the negative effects of local resistance. With this volume, we offer a more explicit challenge to the particularistic-general dichotomy that paints local resistance as contrary to the public good. We propose to view NIMBY mobilization not as regrettable intransigence, nor even as a legitimate response to a flawed policy process, but as a potentially *beneficial* component of participatory politics.

Taking a New Look at NIMBY Protest

The particularistic-general dichotomy is based upon four assumptions that our cases challenge directly. These include the ideas that conflict is undesirable, and a primary goal of analyzing NIMBY politics is to find a way to avoid or overcome it; that the projects around which the conflicts erupt can be improved, but their construction is in the interest of the broader public; that technical expertise resides in the state and industry; and that the NIMBY story ends with the construction or rejection of the controversial facility. We will examine each of these assumptions in turn.

The Desirability of Conflict

Conflict has long been viewed by political theorists and practitioners alike as evidence of a failed political process (Mazmanian and Morell 1994). This tendency has been strengthened in recent years by the move toward collaborative governance in many policy areas as well as in theories of the state (Hirst 2000; Fung and Wright 2001). For example, Mark Tewdwr-Jones and Philip Allmendinger write that, by the late 1990s, the commitment to collaboration had become "hegemonic" in the planning literature (1998; 1975). The shift in both theoretical emphasis and policy practice toward collaboration tends to reinforce the view of NIMBY conflict as a pathological response to a flawed policy process.

We, too, find that NIMBY activism arises from a flawed process, namely a blockage in the conventional channels for citizen participation. The blockage may be the result of technocratic design (Hager). Alternatively, it may have to do with the incentives of local officials (Gunter) or national officials (Kanatsu). Where we differ from the prevailing opinion is in our view of NIMBY more as a *corrective* to the flawed process than as a symptom of a deeper malaise. We find that NIMBY is not anti-industry, and it is not anti-government. It takes aim at particular facilities, institutions, and practices that shut out participation from those who must bear the consequences of the construction. It often draws attention to broader issues of environmental justice or challenges dominant political and economic paradigms. It sometimes forces a revision of the decision-making process toward greater inclusion, but at times the point is made through conflict alone.

Conflict, in other words, is not necessarily something to be avoided. It plays an important role in politics, a role that probably cannot and should not be usurped by collaborative arrangements. Furthermore, a collaborative decision process does not always fulfill its promise to give voice to the interests of all concerned citizens. Various authors have pointed out that disparities in power are often built into such processes and masked by their inclusive form (Tewdwr-Jones and Allmendinger 1998; Walker and Hurley 2004).

There is some support for this more positive view of conflict in the recent NIMBY literature; some authors argue for a more agonistic politics that acknowledges conflicting positions and tries to use them to achieve legitimate change (Barry and Ellis 2010; Devine-Wright 2010). As John Barry and Geraint Ellis explain, "an agonistic theory insists upon preserving democratic struggle as something both *inevitable* and indeed *intrinsically good* for the health of democracy and democratic citizenship" (2010: 35). Daniel Aldrich finds in his study of siting controversies in the United States, France, and Japan that sustained citizen protest is correlated with a healthy civil society (2008). Our case studies lend further support to this view. We find that grassroots conflict often brings positive results, from the protection of public health in China (Gunter) and culturally important landscapes in China and Russia (Plantan) to the accelerated implementation of emission control technologies in Japan (Kanatsu) to peaceful democratization in Korea and democratization in Taiwan (Haddad). Moreover, we find that, in general, the longer a conflict goes on, the more likely it is to result in political and social innovation (Poulos).

The Conception of the Public Good

A corollary of the view that NIMBY is particularistic and obstructionist is the assumption that the disputed facility serves a broader public good. This assumption is often couched in terms of diffuse benefits and concentrated costs of a project (Lesbirel and Shaw 2005). While the assumption is correct in some cases, in many others it is simply not supported by the facts. NIMBY protest often prevents the construction of projects that reveal themselves in the long run to have been ill-advised. In Gregory McAvoy's study, citizen protest prevented the siting of hazardous waste storage facilities in Minnesota. In response, the state shifted its strategy to waste prevention, with the result that no further storage facilities were needed (McAvoy 1999). Daniel Sherman records a similar result in this volume with the issue of low-level radioactive waste disposal siting in the United States. In the German case in this volume, cross-border protest mobilization prevented the construction of massive overcapacity in nuclear power (Hager). In Russia and China, industrial projects that would have destroyed World Heritage sites of great cultural value were prevented or relocated (Plantan). Our case studies show that it cannot simply be assumed that the disputed facility is in the public interest.

Our studies also suggest that public officials do not legitimately define the public good in isolation from the citizenry. There are competing conceptions of the public good, and those held by government officials are not necessarily more legitimate or more properly informed than those held by local citizens. We show how prevailing notions of the public good may be challenged and redefined in societally beneficial ways through NIMBY conflict.

The Value of Counter-Expertise

The particularistic-general dichotomy tends to promote the view that local resistance is motivated by selfishness rather than information. However, one of the primary challenges NIMBY poses to conventional politics is to question the legitimacy of excluding citizens from decision-making on grounds of a supposed lack of technical expertise (Fischer 1990; Dryzek et al. 2003). In our cases, NIMBY actors undermine technocratic decision-making in several ways. One is to challenge a project on technical or scientific grounds through the development of what we call "counter-expertise." Counter-expertise is knowledge generated in order to offer an alternative to an inaccurate or incomplete but popularly accepted scientific view. In Russia, NIMBY mobilization to save Lake Baikal from an oil pipeline provided an opening for dissenting scientific opinions to be aired (Plantan). In Germany, anti-nuclear protesters founded an institute that provided a home to scientists skeptical of nuclear power and eager to develop alternative sources of energy (Hager). NIMBY groups can build their own enduring networks of counter-expertise, resulting in a broader public discussion of alternatives.

Sometimes the challenge to technocratic decision-making is less direct, arising as a by-product of the conflict itself. Elite choices of particular technologies may be based upon debatable scientific, economic, and demographic assumptions that come to light in the course of the NIMBY conflict; the delays caused by ongoing protest force industrial and political elites to rethink the assumptions upon which the project was originally based. In the United States, citizens opposed to nuclear waste storage sites were able to paint officials as technically incompetent and politically motivated in their choices of technologies (Sherman). In so doing, they prompted changes that increased the technical soundness of the end result. In Japan, ongoing citizen pressure led government officials to adopt lower-emission automobile technologies years ahead of their previous timetable (Kanatsu). Both types of challenge—direct and indirect—serve to weaken the legitimacy of elites' claims to a monopoly on expertise. In so doing, they also weaken elites' claims to a monopoly on decision-making authority.

Finally, NIMBY actors may pose a more fundamental challenge to technocratic decision-making by questioning whether the decision to pursue a particular project is really of a technical nature at all or is more properly a matter for the broader society to decide (Hager 1995; Wolsink 2010). Many of our cases ended up posing such a challenge. In Germany and California, for example, NIMBY protest widened into a productive discussion about democratic participation in energy decisions (Schreurs and Ohlhorst). Recasting technological decisions as political ones can contribute to the democratization of decision processes and the empowerment of local citizens.

The Impact of NIMBY

The common analytical focus on the siting process means that the results of NIMBY protest beyond the particular siting controversy are seldom analyzed. This is true even of studies that focus on NIMBY groups as social movements. These may try to account for the expansion or transformation of movement goals during the course of a conflict (Shemtov 1999; Futrell 2003) or demonstrate how protest may expand geographically over time (Boudet 2011). But here, too, the analysis generally ends with the conclusion of the siting controversy. NIMBY is not generally credited with having any broader societal impact, perhaps in part because that change can be hard to see and harder to measure (Giugni 2007, 70–71).

Our cases show that NIMBY activity is not simply oppositional; it has important proactive components and significantly wider impact than commonly imagined. We focus on the sometimes subtle processes of political, technological, and social innovation set in motion by local protest. NIMBY can contribute to democratization of institutions or even regime change (Haddad), the formation of participatory networks and new political groupings (Hager, Schreurs and Ohlhorst), and improved technology or new technological initiatives (Sherman, Kanatsu). In cases in which a disputed project ultimately is built, it is often a "better" project in terms of environmental criteria (Plantan, Gunter).

Political Innovation

NIMBY protest can open new channels for citizen access. NIMBY engages and connects people who have not been politically active in the past. It involves building networks of support among diverse actors, including technical experts and government officials. Oppositional groups negotiate a variety of regulatory structures and levels of governance. In China, for example, opponents of a chemical plant were able to network with national and international-level groups after local officials blocked their participation (Gunter). NIMBY conflict sometimes brings inter-ministerial conflicts and overlapping policy responsibilities into sharp relief. Local groups can take advantage of political opportunities offered by these cracks in the institutional armor, sometimes to the point of changing the pattern of citizen participation, as environmental movements in Korea and Taiwan were able to do (Haddad).

NIMBY can also result in institutional change. Innovations in decision-making structures are often initiated by citizen groups. These include new, more democratic procedures. They can also include a new, differently structured political party as in the German case (Hager), or even a change in government as in the Korean case (Haddad). Other studies have pointed out that, even where institutions do not change much outwardly, they may function in a different way as a result of citizen activism (Haddad 2012). In our Japanese case, the national economic bureaucracy remained central after the NIMBY conflict, but participants had learned how to use lower levels of government to weaken its policy dominance (Kanatsu). Democratic process and function can be enhanced even in a context in which institutions do not change.

NIMBY can also result in substantive policy change, both locally and more broadly. In Japan, local activism not only forced enhanced local environmental regulations, but it also prompted government officials to negotiate new national emission standards with the "Big Four" automakers (Kanatsu). In Germany and California, NIMBY responses to renewable energy projects resulted in redesign aimed at taking account of societal goals such as nature protection and noise reduction (Schreurs and Ohlhorst). Schreurs and Ohlhorst also point out how YIMBY (Yes In My Backyard) movements in Germany fought to win cutting-edge renewables projects for their towns and helped devise creative forms of finance to promote citizen investment in projects that have been imitated across the country.

Technological Innovation

NIMBY conflict contributes far more to the development of new technological solutions than is commonly acknowledged. First, the development of counter-expertise helps to delegitimate technocratic policy making on the one hand and to legitimate alternative sources of technical expertise on the other. This can create a positive atmosphere for innovation, as we see in the German case (Hager). By calling into question the government's justification for nuclear build-out, anti-nuclear activists opened the door for the development of new energy forms.

Technological innovations that emerge from NIMBY protests are sometimes initiated under pressure from citizen groups. These include energy grid improvements (Schreurs and Olhorst) and new low-level radioactive waste treatment processes in the United States (Sherman). Sometimes the innovations are proposed by the groups themselves. In the German case, anti-nuclear activists wanted to do more than oppose; they wanted to develop alternatives to the nuclear energy technologies they rejected (Hager). They were some of the early innovators in solar-panel technology and solar architecture. They helped German businesses become global leaders in these new renewable energy industries, and they opened an important new source of employment.

Social Innovation

NIMBY politics often brings together people who would not see themselves as having much in common ordinarily, such as local vintners and dissenting scientists (Hager) or villagers and international environmental NGOs (Gunter). It helps forge new social networks and broaden civic competence generally, while referencing local culture and traditions (Plantan). It may activate formerly disenfranchised people or transform the nature of their participation, from that of victims seeking compensation for environmental harms to citizens actively shaping their own futures (Haddad).

NIMBY is Beautiful—Case Studies

The case studies yield a complex picture of citizen protest and provide a window into the societies in which NIMBY occurs. NIMBY is beautiful because local protests highlight critical issues and generate positive solutions that are relevant on a wide scale. Our analysis of NIMBY protest transcends the somewhat artificial distinction between local and supralocal, national and subnational political action by focusing attention on the long-term societal impacts of NIMBY.

The following chapters take a more detailed look at the process through which NIMBY leads to political, technological, and social innovation in a variety of contexts. In chapter 1, Helen Poulos offers a broad overview of the impacts of NIMBY through a multivariate quantitative analysis. Starting with an archive of newspaper accounts, Poulos develops classification trees to identify features of NIMBY protest associated with different forms of innovation. The remaining chapters are detailed case-study accounts of NIMBY conflicts in a variety of countries. They use process-tracing methodology (George and Bennett 2005) to identify the mechanisms through which NIMBY protest generates innovations.

The first three case-study chapters explore energy issues in advanced industrial democracies. Nowhere are the positive results of NIMBY clearer than in Germany, and this is why our substantive case studies proceed from the German case. In chapter 2, Carol Hager analyzes the Freiburg area's transition from the center of anti-nuclear protest to Germany's "solar region." Germany also demonstrates the evolving complexity of NIMBY politics; renewable energy projects themselves have become targets of NIMBY protest there. Miranda Schreurs and Dörte Ohlhorst address this issue in chapter 3. Their comparative study of Germany and California shows how NIMBY movements against renewables projects, along with YIMBY movements to attract such projects, help generate a positive debate about citizen participation in shaping Germany's and the United States's energy futures. In chapter 4, Daniel Sherman explores low-level radioactive waste disposal issues in the United States. He shows how NIMBY opposition resulted in changes in generation and on-site treatment of waste that reduced the hazard to host communities.

The next two chapters look at NIMBY mobilization around pollution and energy issues in the more authoritarian political settings of Russia and China. In chapter 5, Elizabeth Plantan shows how local environmental movements in China and Russia employed cultural heritage frames, counter-expertise, and international attention to protect threatened areas from development. Mike Gunter, Jr. explores how environmental groups achieved results against chemical pollution in China not by targeting the state, but by connecting with other domestic and international NGOs and local communities in chapter 6.

In chapter 7, we return to an advanced industrial democracy, but one in which civil society organizations are less well-established than in the United States and Germany. Takashi Kanatsu shows how NIMBY mobilization pressured the corporatist Japanese national government to rethink its automobile emission standards even in the absence of significant NGO activity in favor of environmental protection. Mary Alice Haddad explains in chapter 8 how local environmental activism in transitional societies Korea and Taiwan supported successful national-level democratizing movements. The conclusion sums up the case study findings in terms of the main themes of the book.

Notes

1. Some studies involving LULU: Schively 2007; Greenberg et al. 2012. Studies of NIABY: Lesbirel 1998; Boudet 2011. Schively 2007 also makes note of BANANA. Maize and McCaughey 1992 cite NIMBY, NOPE, LULU, and BANANA.

References

Aldrich, Daniel. 2008. *Site Fights: Divisive Facilities and Civil Society in Japan and the West.* Ithaca, NY: Cornell University Press.

Barry, John, and Geraint Ellis. 2010. "Beyond Consensus? Agonism, Republicanism and a Low Carbon Future." In *Renewable Energy and the Public: From NIMBY to Participation,* edited by Patrick Devine-Wright, 29–42. London: Earthscan.

Benford, Robert D., Helen A. Moore, and J. Allen Williams, Jr. 1993. "In Whose Backyard? Concern about Siting a Nuclear Waste Facility." *Sociological Inquiry* 63(1): 30–48.

Boudet, Hilary Schaffer. 2011. "From NIMBY to NIABY: Regional Mobilization against Liquefied Natural Gas in the United States." *Environmental Politics* 20(6): 786–806.

"Da geht es blind durcheinander." 1975. *Der Spiegel* 40: 96–104.

Dear, Michael. 1992. "Understanding and Overcoming the NIMBY Syndrome." *Journal of the American Planning Association* 583: 288–301.

Devine-Wright, Patrick, ed. 2010. *Renewable Energy and the Public: From NIMBY to Participation.* London: Earthscan.

Dryzek, John, David Downes, Christian Hunold, David Schlosberg, and Hans-Kristian Hernes. 2003. *Green States and Social Movements: Environmentalism in the United States, United Kingdom, Germany and Norway.* Oxford: Oxford University Press.

Fischer, Frank. 1990. *Technocracy and the Politics of Expertise.* Newbury Park, CA: Sage.

Fung, Archon, and Erik Olin Wright. 2001. "Deepening Democracy: Innovations in Empowered Participatory Governance." *Politics and Society* 29: 5–41.

Futrell, Robert. 2003. "Framing Processes, Cognitive Liberation, and NIMBY Protest in the U.S. Chemical-Weapons Disposal Conflict." *Sociological Inquiry* 73(3): 359–86.

George, Alexander L., and Andrew Bennett. 2005. *Case Studies and Theory Development in the Social Sciences.* Cambridge, MA: MIT Press.

Gerrard, Michael B. 1994. *Whose Backyard, Whose Risk: Fear and Fairness in Toxic and Nuclear Waste Siting.* Cambridge, MA: MIT Press.

Giugni, Marco. 2007. "Useless Protest? A Time-Series Analysis of the Policy Outcomes of Ecology, Antinuclear, and Peace Movements in the United States, 1977-1995." *Mobilization* 12(1): 53–77.

Greenberg, Michael R., Frank J. Popper, and Heather Barnes Truelove. 2012. "Are LULUs Still Enduringly Objectionable?" *Journal of Environmental Planning and Management* 55(6): 713–31.

Haddad, Mary Alice. 2012. *Building Democracy in Japan.* Cambridge: Cambridge University Press.

Hager, Carol. 1995. *Technological Democracy: Bureaucracy and Citizenry in the German Energy Debate.* Ann Arbor: University of Michigan Press.

Haggett, Claire. 2010. "'Planning and Persuasion': Public Engagement in Renewable Energy Decision-Making." In *Renewable Energy and the Public,* edited by Patrick Devine-Wright, 15–27. London: Earthscan.

Hirst, Paul. 2000. "Democracy and Governance." In *Debating Governance,* edited by J. Pierre, 13–35. Oxford: Oxford University Press.

Hunter, Susan, and Kevin M. Leyden. 1995. "Beyond NIMBY: Explaining Opposition to Hazardous Waste Facilities." *Policy Studies Journal* 23(4): 601–20.

Inhaber, Herbert. 1998. *Slaying the NIMBY Dragon.* New Brunswick, RI: Transaction.

Kraft, Michael, and Bruce Clary. 1991. "Citizen Participation and the NIMBY Syndrome: Public Response to Radioactive Waste Disposal." *Western Political Quarterly* 44(2): 299–328.

Lesbirel, S. Hayden. 1998. *NIMBY Politics in Japan: Energy Siting and the Management of Environmental Conflict.* Ithaca, NY: Cornell University Press.

Lesbirel, S. Hayden, and Diagee Shaw. 2005. *Managing Conflict in Facility Siting: An International Comparison.* Northampton, MA: Edward Elgar.

Maize, Kennedy P., and John McCaughey. 1992. "NIMBY, NOPE, LULU, and BANANA: A Warning to Independent Power." *Public Utilities Fortnightly* 130(3): 19–21.

Matheny, Albert R., and Bruce A. Williams. 1985. "Knowledge vs. NIMBY: Assessing Florida's Strategy for Siting Hazardous Waste Disposal Facilities." *Policy Studies Journal* 14: 70–80.

Mazmanian, Daniel, and David Morell. 1994. "The 'NIMBY' Syndrome: Facility Siting and the Failure of Democratic Discourse." In *Environmental Policy in the 1990s,* 2nd ed., edited by Norman J. Vig and Michael E. Kraft. Washington, DC: CQ Press.

McAvoy, Gregory E. 1999. *Controlling Technocracy: Citizen Rationality and the NIMBY Syndrome.* Washington, DC: Georgetown University Press.

Portney, Kent E. 1984. "Allaying the NIMBY Syndrome: The Potential for Compensation in Hazardous Waste Treatment Facility Siting." *Hazardous Waste* 1: 411–21.

Rabe, Barry. 1994. *Beyond NIMBY: Hazardous Waste Siting in Canada and the United States.* Washington, DC: Brookings.

Rogers, Jennifer C., Eunice A. Simmons, Ian Convery, and Andrew Weatherall. 2008. "Public Perceptions of Opportunities for Community-based Renewable Energy Projects." *Energy Policy* 36: 4217–226.

Schively, Carissa. 2007. "Understanding the NIMBY and LULU Phenomena: Reassessing our Knowledge Base and Informing Future Research." *Journal of Planning Literature* 21(3): 255–66.

Shemtov, Ronit. 1999. "Taking Ownership of Environmental Problems: How Local NIMBY Groups Expand Their Goals." *Mobilization* 4(1): 91–106.

Snary, Christopher. 2004. "Understanding Risk: The Planning Officers' Perspective." *Urban Studies* 41(1): 33–55.

Snow, David A., E. Burke Rochford, Jr., Steve Worden, and Robert D. Benford. 1986. "Frame Alignment Processes, Micromobilization, and Movement Participation." *American Sociological Review* 51: 464–81.

Snow, David A., and Robert D. Benford. 1992. "Master Frames and Cycles of Protest." In *Frontiers in Social Movement Theory,* edited by Aldon D. Morris and Carol McClurg Mueller, 133–55. New Haven, CT: Yale University Press.

Tewdwr-Jones, Mark, and Philip Allmendinger. 1998. "Deconstructing Communicative Rationality: A Critique of Habermasian Collaborative Planning." *Environment and Planning A* 30: 1975–989.

Walker, Peter, and Patrick Hurley. 2004. "Collaboration Derailed: The Politics of 'Community-based' Resource Management in Nevada County." *Society and Natural Resources* 17: 735–51.

Wildavsky, Aaron, and K. Dake. 1990. "Theories of Risk Perception: Who Fears What and Why?" *Daedalus* 119: 41–60.

Wolsink, Maarten. 2006. "Invalid Theory Impedes our Understanding: A Critique of the Persistence of the Language of NIMBY." *Transactions of the Institute of British Geographers* 31(1): 85–91.

———. 2010. "Near-Shore Wind Power—Protected Seascapes, Environmentalists' Attitudes, and the Technocratic Planning Perspective." *Land Use Policy* 27: 195–203.

CHAPTER 1

How do Grassroots Environmental Protests Incite Innovation?

Helen M. Poulos

Introduction

Although NIMBY protests are often characterized as promoting self-interest at the expense of the public good, local environmental activism can have long-lasting sociopolitical effects, and it can change the way people think about the environment and human health. This study examined how NIMBY mobilizations facilitate societal innovation. I used a multivariate analytical approach and a global database of sixty NIMBY cases to identify factors that differentiated protest cases into "innovation" and "no innovation" groups, using a classification tree approach. The database covered a global geographical scope and included a range of environmental protest topics, from chemical pollution to wind energy. The model revealed that the duration of the NIMBY protest, governmental action in favor of the activists, and the presence of external connections were the three key variables that differentiated cases resulting in no innovation from cases that stimulated innovation. Innovative NIMBY cases lasted longer than 1.5 years, and either resulted in governmental action in favor of the activists or had connections to other outside groups. Innovation outcomes included local NGO formation, solidification of social networks, empowerment of marginalized groups, and legal change. Short-duration protests lasting fewer than 1.5 years almost always resulted in no innovation. Longer-duration NIMBY mobilizations that lacked governmental action or external connections generally also did not result in innovation. The results of this study highlight the importance of NIMBY protests as agents of change in worldwide environmental policy and governance. Social capital appears to play a large role in NIMBY innovation, and the more visible and connected a grassroots group is, the more likely it is to have long-lasting impacts. Duration, government action, and connectedness were more important for generating innovative outcomes than the "success" of the particular NIMBY protest.

NIMBY protests have had success worldwide as a mechanism for mitigating the effects of anthropogenic environmental hazards on local populations. While NIMBY movements stem from grassroots collective action, over the years they have successfully blocked or modified the construction of numerous environmentally hazardous projects around the globe. The movements have forced polluting governments and private companies to strengthen environmental standards, remediate contaminated areas, and minimize the potential for future toxic disasters. While NIMBY protests are often characterized as promoting self-interest at the expense of the public good (Dear 1992; Hermansson 2007), local environmental activism can also have long-lasting sociopolitical effects, and it can change the way people think about the environment and human health (Freudenberg and Steinsapir 1991). Yes, most NIMBY cases tackle immediate problems faced by local residents, but the ramifications of the protests often extend beyond single issues to incite changes in social networks and political systems. Yet, the protest characteristics that lead to short-term outcomes versus long-lasting innovation remain poorly understood.

In the Introduction to this book, Hager provides in-depth characterization of the types of long-term innovation that can result from NIMBY protests, but here I summarize the three main types of innovation that can stem from grassroots environmental activism. Policy change is often the most visible of these. Both successful and unsuccessful protests can have an impact on political system structure by eliciting changes in governance (Kitschelt 1986), and insurgency is broadly and persistently influential in explaining policy spending and legal change (Evans 1995; Berry 1999; Jaynes 2002; Giugni 2004). Political changes can be non-governmental or governmental, and they can occur across a range of organizational levels, from local to international. The magnitude of their impacts depends upon many factors, including the visibility of the NIMBY case, the severity of the environmental and health hazards, and the strength and duration of NIMBY collective action. Some suggest that well-organized grassroots protests with extensive social networks are most successful in achieving negotiation and collective bargaining (Jenkins and Perrow 1977). However, the key factors that influence whether policy innovations occur in response to NIMBY activities remain largely unstudied.

NIMBY mobilizations can also elicit social change. Beyond the obvious effect of increasing citizen participation, NIMBYs often solidify social networks, empower formerly marginalized groups, and foster continued participant collaboration long after the culmination of the original NIMBY cause (Freudenberg and Steinsapir 1991). Internal social networks can be formed and solidified through NIMBY protest after initial citizen recruitment occurs (Shemtov 2003), and the organizational solidarity and social capital of NIMBY groups will often determine the protest outcome (Aldrich, 2008). The amplification of social networks through collective NIMBY action stimulates the generation of social capital[1] (Coleman 1988) that allows groups to defend themselves subsequently against other environmental hazards (Savage et al. 2005; Klyza et al. 2006). Moreover, leaders of local NIMBY movements may also go on to lead major environmental and social justice movements (Freudenberg 1984; McGurty 1997).

Technological innovation is the third long-lasting effect that can result from grassroots protest. Citizen activism can challenge environmental policy in ways that stimulate governmental shifts towards more environmentally sustainable technologies, especially in the power generation sector (Hager 1995; Hira et al. 2005). Participatory expertise can sway policy makers to shift priorities from traditional environmentally hazardous policies to publicly supported green technologies through counter-expertise[2] by grassroots activists (Fischer 1990). Technological innovations generated by counter-expertise not only have the capacity to stimulate shifts in environmental policy, they are also often responsible for enhancing civic representation and participation in the democratic process (Hager 1995; Macintosh et al. 2002).

Long-lasting innovations resulting from NIMBY activities can be local, or they can solidify sociopolitical networks in such a way that the local NIMBY cause translates into a larger NIABY movement (Collette 1989). NIABY can occur when a group of activists expands its geographical scope, increases the number of initial goals, or is used as a model for other subsequent NIMBY protests (Shemtov 2003). While not all NIMBY cases resulting in innovation end up tackling larger societal issues, the NIMBY-to-NIABY shift represents an important agent of larger societal change through local environmental activism (Hubbard 2006; Schively 2007; Boudet 2011).

A wide range of scholars has investigated the causes of (1) NIMBY success or failure (Walsh et al. 1993; Matejczyk 2001), (2) NIMBY participation (Lober 1995), and (3) the factors stimulating NIMBY opposition (Kraft and Clary 1991; Hunter and Leyden 1995, Johnson and Scicchitano 2012; Greenberg et al. 2012). While all of these elements are important for understanding NIMBY protest dynamics, none of them identifies the mechanisms underlying the generation of long-lasting NIMBY outcomes. This study strives for a deeper examination of the characteristics of NIMBY mobilizations that can lead to societal innovations by examining a suite of NIMBY cases to identify the factors that lead to either short-term, non-innovative outcomes or long-lasting innovations.

Much of the current NIMBY literature, including the other chapters in this volume, centers on case studies and qualitative research, which is essential for delving into the intricacies of the NIMBY innovation phenomenon. While case studies provide deep insights into how local citizen groups have elicited larger-scale shifts in policy and social networks, quantitative studies offer a way to answer questions about how NIMBY innovation happens. I use a multivariate analytical approach and a global database of sixty NIMBY cases to identify key protest characteristics leading to NIMBY innovation or no innovation. My goal is not to identify elements contributing to NIMBY success or failure, but rather to identify the key NIMBY characteristics that stimulate long-term changes in social structures and political systems.

Methodology

I compiled a global database of sixty NIMBY cases from a pool of 6,042 periodical sources using the Lexis-Nexis (http://www.lexisnexis.com) database to identify protest characteristics leading to longer-lasting NIMBY innovation[3] (see Appendix). Lexis-Nexis is an archive of popular articles from 1980 to the present and covers news from over 600 leading newspapers around the world. I chose Lexis-Nexis because newspapers are one of the most widely used sources of information for documenting protests (Almeida and Lichbach 2003). The relatively recent coverage of news by Lexis-Nexis (i.e. since 1980) may reflect a limitation of this database. The interpretation of the results of this study is thus limited to the last three decades of NIMBY protests. Nonetheless, newspapers are useful because they provide information about large numbers of events, and they document social movement dynamics (Almeida and Lichbach 2003). Cases were identified in Lexis-Nexis using searches involving the word "protest" in conjunction with the terms "nuclear," "pollution," "conservation," "environmental," "wildlife preserve," "toxic waste," and "wind energy." Articles that had no evidence of local activism or lacked sufficient qualitative information about protest characteristics and cases occurring in fewer than two media articles were excluded from the analysis. Evidence of local activism was determined from the newspaper articles, and cases that were not led either by local residents or community stakeholder groups were excluded from the dataset.

For each NIMBY case, newspaper articles were gleaned for information on potentially important attributes that could play roles in long-term NIMBY outcomes. For each case, I used the rubric in table 1.1[4] to code

Table 1.1. *Coding rubric for classification tree*

Variable	Values
Geographical Region of Interest	North America South America European Union Africa Asia Middle East
NIMBY success	Yes, no, partial, or can't tell yet
Transnational: issue affects more than one country	Yes or no
Duration of protest	Years
Parties present en masse against NIMBY?	Yes or no
Protest Outcome	Not yet sited On site to spec On site with modification Elsewhere to spec Elsewhere with modification Remediated Closed
Timing of protest in conjunction with other major events	Yes or no
Protest associated with a shift in political regime	Yes or no
Resident compensation	Yes, no, never reached residents
Did protesters have external backing from other, larger groups (i.e. Greenpeace, Sierra Club, Earth First!, etc.)?	Yes or no
International money involved	Yes or no
Invokes patriotism or local cultural sentiments	Yes or no
Different levels of government leveraged against one another	Yes or no
Connections to political parties	Yes or no
Governmental action taken on side of NIMBY activists	Yes or no
Documented hazards at location	Yes or no
Learning process occurred	Yes or no
Marginalized indigenous groups involved	Yes or no
Arrests	Yes or no
Violence	No, activist, against activist, bi-directional
Type of action	Pro-active or reactive
Used as a model for others	Yes or no
Counter-expertise involved	Yes or no

each case for a range of characteristics that could contribute to long-lasting effects from NIMBY protests. Information from the articles was then confirmed independently using secondary sources. Each case contained full attribute records for each potential predictor variable, which restricted the full dataset to sixty cases. The potential explanatory variables included in this study were chosen based on their prevalence in the newspaper articles and their prior identification as important predictors of environmental protest success by earlier researchers (Bernauer et al. 2012; Homer-Dixon 1994; Homer-Dixon 2010; Downey et al. 2010; Boyce 2009; Chenoweth 2013). I was entirely responsible for coding the database. I attempted to reduce coding biases by taking a random sample of twenty-five percent of the study cases and having an independent research assistant perform reciprocal recoding as a reliability test, which resulted in no significant changes to the database based on a general linear model analysis of the changes in variable frequency ($P > 0.001$).

Upon selection, cases were categorized based on whether or not the NIMBY protests resulted in innovation as defined by Hager in the introduction. Protests that stimulated innovation were those that resulted in any of the following outcomes: (1) social innovations in the form of solidified social networks, empowerment of formerly apolitical or marginalized groups, or continued collaboration after the NIMBY protest ended; (2) political innovations, including legal changes or the formation of new organizations (i.e., non-governmental organizations); (3) technological innovations as demonstrated in the development of new technology or scientific knowledge. Technological innovation was difficult to identify from newspaper articles, so this outcome was ultimately dropped from the study.[5] Innovation was initially identified in the articles, but it was also corroborated using secondary sources and grey literature. Many of the innovative NIMBY cases in this study resulted in both political and social innovation, so I chose to analyze the data using a binary case categorization scheme to classify cases as either innovative or non-innovative. Protests that lacked social or political innovations as a result of the NIMBY movement were categorized as resulting in "no innovation." This was determined via newspaper coverage of the NIMBY protests and through confirmation using secondary sources. In all of the "no innovation" cases, win or lose, I found no evidence of longer-lasting effects following the protest events themselves in either the newspaper articles or the secondary sources.

I used classification trees (Breiman et al. 1984) to identify protest characteristics that differentiated NIMBY cases having no effects beyond the scope of the individual protest from cases that stimulated social or political innovation. The NIMBY innovation model incorporated a total of twenty-three potential predictor variables to differentiate the NIMBY cases from Lexis-Nexis into two groups (innovation or no innovation).

While NIMBY success was included in the model as a predictor variable, the goal of the analysis was to identify factors influencing innovation as a result of NIMBY, not merely to differentiate factors affecting the success or failure of a protest.

Classification trees are useful for grouping or distinguishing two or more known classes of observations based on a suite of predictor variables (De'ath and Fabricius 2000). They work well with largely categorical datasets, their output is easy to interpret, and the decision rules created by the trees can be linked to large-scale sociopolitical phenomena. Classification trees are built using a recursive partitioning algorithm that iteratively subsets the data into successively more homogeneous groups through a series of binary splits (Venables and Ripley 2000). At each partition, the model computes an estimate of the within-partition heterogeneity or 'impurity' of the partitions. Classification trees are grown to overfit the model so that all the training data are correctly classified. A tenfold cross-validation procedure corrects this overfitting by evaluating each node of the initial decision tree in terms of the classification error rate on the training set using a cost-complexity function (Breiman et al. 1984). The classification tree is then pruned by selecting the optimal tree that is within one standard deviation of the minimum misclassification error.

The NIMBY model identified the key characteristics influencing whether or not socio-political innovation outcomes occurred through NIMBY protests. The fit of the NIMBY innovation model was built, pruned, and evaluated by examining the cost complexity parameter that measured how well the explanatory NIMBY characteristic variables separated the data into "innovation" and "no innovation" groups. All statistical analyses were completed in the R statistical language (R Development Core Team 2012).

Results

Fifty-six percent of the cases in this study stimulated innovations. The database covered a range of environmental protest topics, including chemical pollution (23), land conservation (9), hydroelectric power (10), nuclear power/energy (9), waste disposal (4), and wind energy (5). A large proportion of the protests was successful. Forty-three percent of the cases were successful in blocking the proposed action, 24 percent were partially successful (i.e. the project was only partially completed, or it was completed with modifications), 15 percent of the cases failed, and 18 percent were still under protest at the time the study was completed.

Governmental action and external connections were associated with roughly half of the NIMBY protests.[6] Half of the NIMBY protests involved arrests by police. Sixty percent of the cases were completely non-violent, 25 percent occurred with violence inflicted against the activists, and 15 percent of the cases involved violence either by the activists or by both sides.[7]

The classification tree model revealed that the duration of the NIMBY protest, governmental action in favor of the activists, and the presence of external connections were the three key variables that differentiated cases resulting in no innovation from cases that stimulated innovation (figure 1.1). Innovative NIMBY cases lasted longer than 1.5 years, and either resulted in governmental action or had connections to other outside groups. Longer NIMBY protests in which the government intervened or in which external connections were present stimulated a variety of types of innovations. Innovation outcomes included local NGO formation, solidification of social networks, empowerment of marginalized groups, and legal change. Short-duration protests lasting fewer than 1.5 years almost always resulted in no innovation.[8] Longer-duration NIMBY mobilizations that lacked governmental action or external connections also generally lacked innovation.

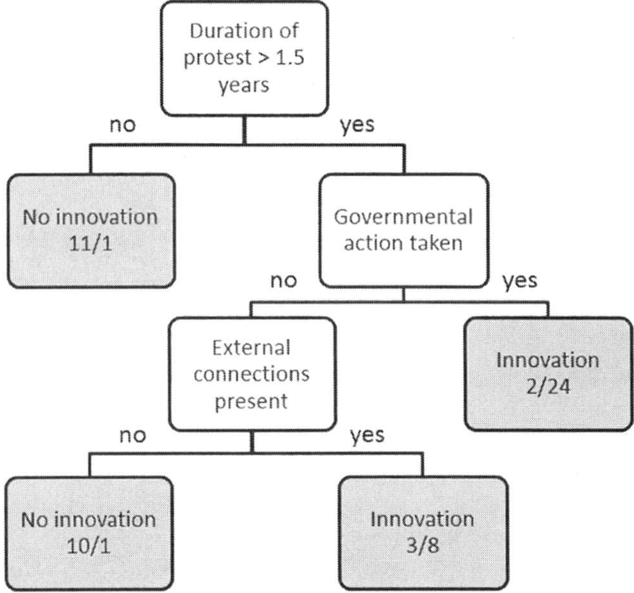

Figure 1.1. *Classification tree identifying how NIMBY case factors influence innovation or no innovation protest outcomes. The tree represents 60 NIMBY cases spanning the years 1980–2013. The numbers indicate terminal node purity where the number on the left of the ratio indicates the number of no innovation cases and the right number shows the number of cases stimulating innovations in each node. The shaded boxes are terminal nodes demonstrating how innovative or non-innovative outcomes occur.*

Discussion

The results of this study highlight the importance of NIMBY protests as agents of change in worldwide environmental policy and governance. My findings are quite straightforward; longer-duration NIMBY mobilizations that were able to sway governments or that had external connections had the highest probabilities of inciting sociopolitical innovations. Neither the outcome of the NIMBY protest (success or failure) nor the geographical scope of interest influenced whether innovation occurred. Longer-duration mobilizations were probably more likely to stimulate innovation because they provided more opportunities for building both internal and external social capital. Longer protests also had greater potential to generate media coverage and attract the attention of the government and outside parties that could facilitate changes in policy and social structures.

Others have demonstrated that longer-duration protests are likely to be repressed by local and national governments (Ash 2011), but little prior research has investigated how protest duration influences NIMBY outcomes. Kousis (1999) showed that grassroots environmental activists in southern Europe[9] who sustained protests for more than one year generated stronger social networks, and received more support from non-local environmental movement organizations. This suggests that the transformation of a NIMBY case from an isolated cause to a movement that stimulates larger social or political change takes time. Tilly (1993) defines social movements as complex forms of social interaction. Short-duration protests like the "no innovation" NIMBY cases in this study may have failed to spur innovation because they generally lacked complex social connections or governmental ties. Of the twelve short-duration protests, eleven were at least partially "successful" in their protests, with the government or corporation shutting down the offending factory or stopping or modifying a plan to build an objectionable facility. Although they were successful in achieving their NIMBY goals, their protests did not result in any measurable longer-term or broader social or political consequences.

Although Shemtov (2003) argued that external ties to other organizations such as Greenpeace and Earth First often impede NIMBY expansion, I contend that they often lead to innovation. Both cases that ended up strengthening local governance and those that became wider-scope movements that ultimately expanded into NIABY movements depended upon the existence of social capital that grew as social interactions solidified over the lifespan of the NIMBY protests. While Potapchuck et al. (1997) argue that NIMBY protests generally lack the social capital to incite major political change because communities are typically unable to act collectively across neighborhoods, my results demonstrate that interconnectedness is an important factor influencing NIMBY-based sociopolitical innovation.

However, interconnectedness had less effect on success. Of the eleven cases in which the NIMBY protest resulted in lasting social and political innovations because protesters were able to make connections to other groups outside their own locale, only two were successful in obtaining the goal of their NIMBY protest.

It is not surprising that NIMBY cases that either had external connections to outside parties or were able to stimulate governmental action were most likely to have long-lasting effects. Jaynes (2002) stated that successful movements have generally needed the support of power holders, political elites, or political insiders, and a great deal of prior research on social movements has demonstrated that links and bridges among actors strengthen information and resource flows (Obach 2004; McCammon and Van Dyke 2010). While my results did not indicate that diffusion (i.e., the subsequent use of the NIMBY case as a model for others) was an important factor influencing innovation, others have suggested that communication among movements can influence their salience, solidarity, and success (McAdam and Rucht 1993; Andrews and Biggs 2006; Givan et al. 2010; Wang and Soule 2012). Many of the grassroots protests included in my study were recent or ongoing through 2013.[10] Thus, while many of them may have had the potential to inform other subsequent environmental movements, they may have not occurred long enough ago for me to measure this impact.

The majority of the short-duration cases in this study failed to have any measurable long-lasting influences, likely because they were either immediately repressed by government or because the protesters were successful after only a few days or months of protest. However, innovation can sometimes occur as a result of short-duration protests. For example, the Dalian Chemical Plant protest highlighted by Gunter (chapter 6) provides an example of such a case. While the protesters were unable to close the Dalian chemical plant permanently, the NIMBY case was deemed a success because activists built a coalition through the use of technology and social media that allowed them to pit different levels of government against each other. Many of the short-duration cases in my study also took place in Asia, where brief, non-innovative cases are increasing exponentially both in number and magnitude (Gunter, chapter 6). Together, they represent a growing Asian environmental movement that could potentially lead to political innovation in the form of a democratic transition in China as it did in Taiwan and South Korea. These cases may also lead to social innovation through the solidification of environmental movements in Asia and elsewhere in the developing world.

NIMBY activism that occurs in the context of a growing environmental movement can also have long-lasting impacts. In many cases, local

NIMBY leaders have gone on to lead major environmental and social justice movements (Freudenberg 1984; McGurty 1997), and this study includes several examples of this type of innovation. For example, the NIMBY protest against the Giurgiu-Ruse Chemical Plant in the 1980s in Bulgaria was one such case in my analysis. The protest was led by local Ekoglasnost activists who subsequently led the Bulgarian environmental movement. Ekoglasnost ultimately expanded its scope to become a national environmental organization that ended up playing a major role on the wider post-Communist political stage in Bulgaria (Baker 1998). Other examples of cases in my study that demonstrate the importance of NIMBY as a stimulus for larger environmental movements include the Gordon River hydroelectric dam protests in the early 1980s in Australia and the two-decade protest against logging in Clayquot Sound in Canada. The Gordon River case spurred the contemporary Australian environmental movement (Hutchins and Lester 2006), and the Clayquot Sound protest represented the largest civil disobedience demonstration in Canadian history, which ultimately resulted in the formation of a UN Biosphere Reserve (Hoberg and Morawski 2008).

A secondary potential benefit of NIMBY serving as an entry point into activism is that it provides a venue in which activists can build counter-expertise, which can lead to governments asking them to inform subsequent legislation. For example, a grassroots NIMBY battle over a new incinerator in New Haven, Connecticut in the United States spurred the formation of a citywide municipal recycling program that the city hired protesters to lead (Von Stein and Savage 1994). The recycling program resulted in a long-term means of reducing waste generated by local residents, and it ultimately served as the foundation for the formation of the City of New Haven's Office of Sustainability. While counter-expertise was not considered a major predictor of NIMBY innovation in the classification tree model, this may have been due to the lack of information about the presence of counter-expertise in the media sources I accessed for this study. Counter-expertise has been hailed both in this volume and elsewhere (Van Benschoten 2000; Macintosh et al. 2002) as an important mechanism for inciting technological and social NIMBY innovation. For example, water pollution in Lake Baikal (chapter 5) was stopped by NIMBY activists largely through the involvement of scientific experts in the NIMBY protest. They ultimately influenced the debate about pipeline placement and challenged the neutrality of government/industry-supported experts. Thus, counter-expertise can influence the outcomes of local NIMBY causes and potentially mitigate or prevent future environmental hazards as activists later become incorporated into the political process.

Conclusion

This study demonstrates the power of grassroots NIMBY protests as mechanisms of enduring societal change. My results emphasize the importance of protest duration, swaying governments, and the need for external actor involvement in inciting NIMBY innovation. Social networks appear to play a large role in innovation, and the more visible and connected a grassroots group is, the more likely it is to have long-lasting impacts. Although this study did not explicitly look at NIMBY social network structure, an actor-network analysis of the NIMBY cases included in this study could provide insights into how the types and magnitudes of social interconnectedness could influence NIMBY innovation.

While the large-n analysis of the factors that can lead to NIMBY innovation presented in this chapter offers key insights into the general mechanisms underscoring long-lasting NIMBY outcomes, this approach can be limited by the way in which media cover grassroots environmental protest events. For example, the key predictor variables of protest duration, governmental action, and external connections were well-reported factors. Other variables may have also been important predictors of NIMBY innovation, but may have been of less interest to the media. The media's sometimes short-term interest in a conflict may also have resulted in limited coverage of some of the NIMBY protests in the dataset. Secondary sources were invaluable for determining the length of the protest events, as well as some of the broader impacts of the protests. Some of the cases in this chapter may have resulted in innovation, but the protests may have been too recent or too short to document NIMBY-related innovations. Studies with large sample sizes are useful because they present a method for understanding general trends in social phenomena. However, the case studies in the chapters that follow provide in-depth characterizations of how NIMBY protests can lead to long-term solutions to environmental problems.

Likewise, several key NIMBY characteristics, including counter-expertise and learning process,[11] were not well-examined through the decision-tree methodology. The multivariate statistical approach employed here was useful for elucidating the overarching mechanisms of grassroots NIMBY innovation. However, other approaches, such as case studies or interviews, are more useful for understanding the nuances of how activists interact with other parties to elicit change. The media coverage used to generate the database in this study often failed to include information about (1) when a set of government and/or corporate decision makers included representatives from the local community in their decision making processes, (2) whether activists developed expertise that challenged the conventional expertise offered by governments or businesses, and (3) whether a NIMBY case was subsequently used to fight other environmental hazards. The case studies in the following chapters of this volume offer in-depth characterizations of how activists use these tactics to incite change, and they represent other key elements outside the scope of this chapter about how grassroots protests can have major impact on social systems and governance.

Appendix. Sixty NIMBY Cases Used in Analysis Including Dispute Type and Country

NIMBY Protest	Issue	Country
Attica waste dump	waste disposal	Greece
Souselas industrial waste	waste disposal	Portugal
TAV protest in Val de Sousa	conservation	Italy
Messina Straights Bridge	conservation	Italy
Bakun hydroelectric dam	conservation	Thailand
Gulf Coast liquified natural gas terminal	chemical pollution	United States
Shintech PVC plant	chemical pollution	United States
Adams Lake Mine-Toronto waste	waste disposal	Canada
Cape Wind Project	wind energy	United States
Seabrook nuclear plant	nuclear power	United States
Chicomuselo Mining Mexico	conservation	Spain
Hanlon Creek Business Park	conservation	Canada
Gabcikovo dam	hydroelectric power	Slovakia-Hungary
Temelin power plant	nuclear power	Czech Republic
Orchid Island	nuclear waste	Taiwan
Gulup Island	nuclear waste	South Korea
Jaitapur nuclear plant	nuclear power	India
Kudankulam nuclear plant	nuclear power	India
Fukushima Accident	nuclear power	Japan
Giurgiu - Ruse chemical plant pollution	chemical pollution	Bulgaria-Romania
Brent Spar tanker disposal	chemical pollution	UK
Poolbeg incinerator	chemical pollution	Ireland
PT Inti Indorayon Utama Indonesian paper mill	chemical pollution	Indonesia

Kishon River	chemical pollution	Israel
Pengzhou petrochemical plant	chemical pollution	China
Buyun Incinerator	chemical pollution	China
Wugang manganese smelting plant	chemical pollution	China
Jinko Solar River pollution	chemical pollution	China
Qidong paper mill waste pipeline	chemical pollution	China
Ogoni Shell Oil	chemical pollution	Nigeria
Dalian chemical plant	chemical pollution	China
Goolengook Forest campaign	conservation	Australia
Jabiluka uranium mine	conservation	Australia
Ayrshire wind farm	conservation	Scotland
logging on crown owned land	conservation	New Zealand
logging by Ta Ann	conservation	Tasmania
Gordon river	hydroelectric power	Tasmania
Myitsone dam	hydroelectric power	Myanmar-China
HidroAysen dam project	hydroelectric power	Patagonia-Chile
Belo Monte dam	hydroelectric power	Brazil
Sardar Sarovar dam	hydroelectric power	India
Bhasha dam	hydroelectric power	Pakistan
Pubugou dam	hydroelectric power	China
Chixoy dam	hydroelectric power	Guatemala
Pak Mun dam	hydroelectric power	Thailand
Sichuan copper plant	chemical pollution	China
Xiamen xylene plant	chemical pollution	China
Petrobras oil	chemical pollution	Ecuador
Uruguay pulp mill	chemical pollution	Argentina-Uruguay
Clayoquot SoundlLogging	conservation	Canada
Kettleman City waste disposal site	chemical pollution	United States
Dutch toxic waste dumping	chemical pollution	Cote Ivoire
Tiega and Ouyen dump	chemical pollution	Australia
Dunbar toxic waste incineration	chemical pollution	Scotland
Crown Butte mines Yellowstone	conservation	United States
Corowa waste incinerator	chemical pollution	Australia
Montgomeryshire wind project	wind energy	UK
Nant y Moch wind farm	wind energy	UK
Fallago Rig windfarm	wind energy	UK
Project Hayes windfarm	wind energy	Australia

Notes

1. Coleman (1989) originally defined social capital as something that "inheres in the structure of relations between persons and among persons." The World Bank (2000) refined this definition to "the capability of individuals to secure benefits as a result of group membership."
2. Counter-expertise occurs when NGOs and other non-government, non-business persons or entities develop expertise that challenges the conventional expertise offered by government and business. See Hager (this volume) for an occasion on which NIMBY activists challenged the business and governmental expert assertion that nuclear power was safe based on their own expertise.
3. The compiled database had wide geospatial coverage, including 19 cases from Asia, 15 from the European Union, 9 from North America, 5 from Latin America, 8 from Australia, 2 from Africa, and 2 from The Middle East.
4. Predictor variables used in classification tree construction for predicting NIMBY cases that stimulated social or political innovations in Lexis-Nexis cited NIMBY cases spanning from 1980 to the present ($n = 60$). Variables of interest are reported in the left column, and all potential categories and values are reported in the right column.
5. It is likely that the lack of evidence of technological innovation leading from NIMBY cases was the result of relying on newspaper coverage that tended to focus more on social and political issues than on technological ones. It could also be that NIMBY influence on technological development tends to be subtle or indirect. More in-depth case study analysis is necessary to determine the extent of technological innovation owed to NIMBY protests.
6. The government took some form of action in 56 percent of the NIMBY cases. By governmental action, I mean that the government acted in favor of the NIMBY activists. This does not mean that the protest was repressed, nor does it mean that legislation was enacted in regard to the case. Exactly half of the cases had ties to external organizations such as Greenpeace, Earth First, Sierra Club, The Nature Conservancy, etc.
7. By this I mean that both activists and parties against the NIMBY cause carried out violent acts. The anti-NIMBY parties generally involved law enforcement or military personnel.
8. Eleven out of 12 short-duration cases lasting less than 1.5 years resulted in no innovation coming from the NIMBY case.
9. Greece, Spain, and Portugal
10. Over half of the NIMBY cases included in this study either ended in the last year or were ongoing, making it difficult to ascertain whether they were important models for future NIMBY mobilizations.
11. This learning process occurs when one or both sides of a conflict learn from their interaction, either through community involvement in the planning process or when NIMBY activists copy successful strategies from prior protests (also termed "diffusion" by McAdam and Rucht [1993], Andrews and Biggs [2006], Givan et al. [2010], and Wang and Soule [2012]).

References

Aldrich, Daniel P. 2008. *Site Fights: Divisive Facilities and Civil Society in Japan and the West.* Ithaca, NY: Cornell University Press.

Almeida, Paul, and Mark Lichbach. 2003. "To the Internet, From the Internet: Comparative Media Coverage of Transnational Protests." *Mobilization: An International Quarterly* 8(3): 249–72.

Andrews, Kenneth, and Michael Biggs. 2006. "The Dynamics of Protest Diffusion: Movement Organizations, Social Networks, and News Media in the 1960 Sit-ins." *American Sociological Review* 71(5): 752–77.

Ash, Konstantin 2011. "A Game-Theoretic Model for Protest in the Context of Post-Communism." *Communist and Post-Communist Studies* 44, 1–15.

Baker, Susan. 1998. *Dilemmas of Transition: The Environment, Democracy and Economic Reform in East Central Europe.* New York: Routledge.

Bernauer, Thomas, Tobias Böhmelt, and Vally Koubi. 2012. "Environmental Changes and Violent Conflict." *Environmental Research Letters* 7, 015601. Available at http://iopscience.iop.org/1748-9326/7/1/015601.

Berry, Jeffrey M. 1999. *The New Liberalism: The Rising Power of Citizen Groups.* Washington, DC: Brookings Institution.

Boudet, Hillary S. 2011. "From NIMBY to NIABY: Regional Mobilization against Liquefied Natural Gas in the United States." *Environmental Politics* 20(6): 786–806.

Boyce, James 2009. *Justice in the Air: Tracking Toxic Pollution from America's Industries and Companies to our States, Cities and Neighborhoods.* Amherst, MA: Political Economy Research Institute.

Breiman, Leo, Jerome Friedman, Richard Olshen, and Charles Stone. 1984. *Classification and Regression Trees.* New York: Chapman & Hall/CRC.

Chenoweth, Erica. 2013. "Terrorism and Democracy." *Annual Review of Political Science* 16: 355–78.

Coleman, James S. 1988. "Social Capital in the Creation of Human Capital." *American Journal of Sociology* 94: S95–S120. doi: 10.2307/2780243.

Collette, Christine. 1989. *For Labour and for Women: the Women's Labour League, 1906–1918.* Manchester: Manchester University Press.

De'ath, Glenn, and Katharina E. Fabricius. 2000. "Classification and Regression Trees: A Powerful yet Simple Technique for Ecological Data Analysis." *Ecology* 81(11): 3178–192.

Dear, Michael 1992. "Understanding and Overcoming the Nimby Syndrome." *Journal of the American Planning Association* 58(3): 288–300. doi: 10.1080/01944369208975808.

Downey, Liam, Eric Bonds, and Katherine Clark. 2010. "Natural Resource Extraction, Armed Violence, and Environmental Degradation." *Organization & Environment* 23: 417–45.

Evans, Peter B. 1995. *Embedded Autonomy: States and Industrial Transformation.* Princeton Paperbacks. Princeton, NJ: Princeton University Press.

Fischer, Frank. 1990. *Technocracy and the Politics of Expertise.* Newbury Park, CA: Sage.

Freudenberg, Nicholas. 1984. *Not in Our Backyards! Community Action for Health and the Environment.* New York: Monthly Review Press.

Freudenberg, Nicholas, and Carol Steinsapir. 1991. "Not in Our Backyards—the Grass-Roots Environmental Movement." *Society & Natural Resources* 4(3): 235–45.

Friedkin, Noah E. 1986. "A Formal Theory of Social Power." *Journal of Mathematical Sociology* 12(2): 103–26.

Giugni, Marco. 2004. *Social Protest and Policy Change : Ecology, Antinuclear, and Peace Movements in Comparative Perspective.* Lanham, MD: Rowman & Littlefield.

Givan, Rebecca K., Kenneth M. Roberts, and Sarah A. Soule. 2010. *The Diffusion of Social Movements: Actors, Mechanisms, and Political Effects.* Cambridge: Cambridge University Press.

Greenberg, Michael R., Frank J. Popper, and Heather Barnes Truelove. 2012. "Are LULUs still Enduringly Objectionable?" *Journal of Environmental Planning and Management* 55(6): 713–31.

Hager, Carol J. 1995. *Technological Democracy: Bureaucracy and Citizenry in the German Energy Debate.* Ann Arbor: University of Michigan Press.

Hermansson, Hélène. 2007. "The Ethics of NIMBY Conflicts." *Ethical Theory and Moral Practice* 10: 23–34.

Hira, Anil, David Huxtable, and Alexandre Leger. 2005. "Deregulation and Participation: An International Survey of Participation in Electricity Regulation." *Governance* 18(1): 53–88. doi: 10.1111/j.1468-0491.2004.00266.x.

Hoberg, George, and Edward Morawski. 2008. "Policy Change through Sector Intersection: Forest and Aboriginal Policy in Clayoquot Sound." *Canadian Public Administration* 40(3): 387–414.

Homer-Dixon, Thomas F. 1994. Environmental Scarcities and Violent Conflict: Evidence from Cases. *International Security* 19: 5–40.

———. 2010. *Environment, Scarcity, and Violence.* Princeton, NJ: Princeton University Press.

Hubbard, Phil 2006. "NIMBY by Another Name? A Reply to Wolsink." *Transactions of the Institute of British Geographers* 31(1): 92–94. doi: 10.2307/3804422.

Hunter, Susan, and Kevin M. Leyden. 1995. "Beyond NIMBY." *Policy Studies Journal* 23(4): 601–619.

Hutchins, Brett, and Libby Lester. 2006. "Environmental Protest and Tap-Dancing with the Media in the Information Age." *Media, Culture & Society* 28(3): 433–51.

Jaynes, Arthur. 2002. "Insurgency and Policy Outcomes: The Impact of Protests/Riots on Urban Spending." *Journal of Political and Military Sociology* 30(1): 90–112.

Jenkins, J. Craig, and Charles Perrow. 1977. "Insurgency of the Powerless: Farm Worker Movements (1946–1972)." *American Sociological Review* 42(2): 249–268.

Johnson, Renée J., and Michael J. Scicchitano. 2012. "Don't Call Me NIMBY: Public Attitudes Toward Solid Waste Facilities." *Environment and Behavior,* 0013916511435354.

Kitschelt, Herbert P. 1986. "Political Opportunity Structures and Political Protest: Anti-Nuclear Movements in Four Democracies." *British Journal of Political Science* 16: 57–85.

Klyza, Christopher, Andrew Savage, and Jonathan Isham. 2006. "Local Environmental Groups and the Creation of Social Capital: Evidence from Vermont." *Society and Natural Resources* 19(10): 905–19.

Kousis, Maria. 1999. "Sustaining Local Environmental Mobilisations: Groups, Actions and Claims in Southern Europe." *Environmental Politics* 8(1): 172–98. doi: 10.1080/09644019908414443.

Kraft, Michael E. and Bruce B. Clary. 1991. "Citizen Participation and the NIMBY Syndrome: Public Response to Radioactive Waste Disposal." *The Western Political Quarterly* 44(2): 299–328.

Lober, Douglas. 1995. "Why Protest? Public Behavioral and Attitudinal Response to Siting a Waste Disposal Facility." *Policy Studies Journal* 23(3): 499–518.

Macintosh, Ann, Elisabeth Davenport, Anna Malina, and Angus Whyte. 2002. "Technology to Support Participatory Democracy." *Electronic Government: Design, Applications, and Management.* Hershey, PA: Idea Group Publishing.

Matejczyk, Anthony P. 2001. "Why Not NIMBY? Reputation, Neighbourhood Organisations and Zoning Boards in a US Midwestern City." *Urban Studies* 38(3): 507–18.

McAdam, Doug, and Dieter Rucht. 1993. "The Cross-National Diffusion of Movement Ideas." *The Annals of the American Academy of Political and Social Science* 528(1): 56–74.

McCammon, Holly J., and Nella Van Dyke. 2010. "Applying Qualitative Comparative Analysis to Empirical Studies of Social Movement Coalition Formation." *Strategic Alliances: Coalition Building and Social Movements* 34: 292–315.

McGurty, Eileen Maura. 1997. "From NIMBY to Civil Rights: The Origins of the Environmental Justice Movement." *Environmental History* 2(3): 301–23. doi: 10.2307/3985352.

Obach, Brian K. 2004. *Labor and the Environmental Movement: The Quest for Common Ground.* Cambridge, MA: MIT Press.

Potapchuk, William R. 1997. "Building Community with Social Capital: Chits and Chums or Chats with Change." *National Civic Review* 86(2): 129.

R Development Core Team. 2012. *A Language and Environment for Statistical Computing.* Vienna, Austria: R Foundation for Statistical Computing.

Savage, Andrew, Jonathan Isham, and Christopher McGrory Klyza. 2005. "The Greening of Social Capital: An Examination of Land-Based Groups in Two Vermont Counties." *Rural Sociology* 70(1): 113–31. doi: 10.1526/0036011053294619.

Schively, Carissa. 2007. "Understanding the NIMBY and LULU Phenomena: Reassessing Our Knowledge Base and Informing Future Research." *Journal of Planning Literature* 21(3): 255–66. doi: 10.1177/0885412206295845.

Shemtov, Ronit. 2003. "Social Networks and Sustained Activism in Local NIMBY Campaigns." *Sociological Forum* 18(2): 215–44.

Tilly, Charles. 1993. "Social Movements as Historically Specific Clusters of Political Performances." *Berkeley Journal of Sociology* 38: 1–30. doi: 10.2307/41035464.

Van Benschoten, E. 2000. "Technology, Democracy, and the Creation of Community." *National Civic Review* 89(3): 185–92.

Venables, William N., and Brian D. Ripley. 2002. *Modern Applied Statistics with S,* 4th ed., Statistics and Computing. New York: Springer.

Von Stein, Edward, and George Savage. 1994. "Current Practices and Applications in Construction and Demolition Debris Recycling." *Resource Recycling* 13: 85–94.

Walsh, Edward, Rex Warland, and D. Clayton Smith. 1993. "Backyards, NIMBYs, and Incinerator Sitings: Implications for Social Movement Theory." *Social Problems* 40(1): 25–38.

Wang, Dan J., and Sarah A. Soule. 2012. "Social Movement Organizational Collaboration: Networks of Learning and the Diffusion of Protest Tactics, 1960-1995." *American Journal of Sociology* 117(6): 1674–722.

Yusuf, Shahid, and World Bank. 2000. "Entering the 21st Century: World Development Report, 1999/2000." New York: Published for the World Bank, Oxford University Press.

CHAPTER 2

From NIMBY to Networks

Protest and Innovation in German Energy Politics

Carol Hager

Germany is widely admired as a pioneer in renewable energy development. German scientists and entrepreneurs have made important advancements in solar, wind, and biofuel technologies. German local and regional governments have experimented broadly with new models for energy production and conservation. These innovations were aided by landmark federal legislation; the Electricity Feed-in Law of 1990 and the Renewable Energy Sources Act of 2000 facilitated a rapid expansion of the renewable energy sector. Figure 2.1 shows the growth trajectory of renewables in Germany between 1990 and 2012. By the end of 2012, renewables accounted for nearly 24 percent of total gross electricity consumption (BMU 2013), and the federal government is committed to reaching 80 percent by 2050 (BMU 2010). The renewable energy sector also accounts for close to 400,000 jobs (BMU 2012).

NIMBY politics has contributed to this result in unexpected ways. Renewable energy development was a bottom-up phenomenon in a country in which policy change normally comes from the top. Germany's policy-making style is generally characterized as corporatist. Policy is formulated by bureaucratic experts in cooperation with peak associations representing major industrial and societal interests. Elected officials are involved only after the policy details have been worked out behind the scenes (Rose-Ackerman 1995). This system puts a premium on technical expertise and tends to exclude non-economic interests (Dryzek et al. 2003: 40).

Energy planning involves closed-door collaboration between federal and state economics bureaucracies and large energy utilities.[1] In the case of renewable energy, the big players in government and industry dragged their feet. The innovation was sparked to a great degree by NIMBY protest against conventional energy sources, particularly nuclear power,

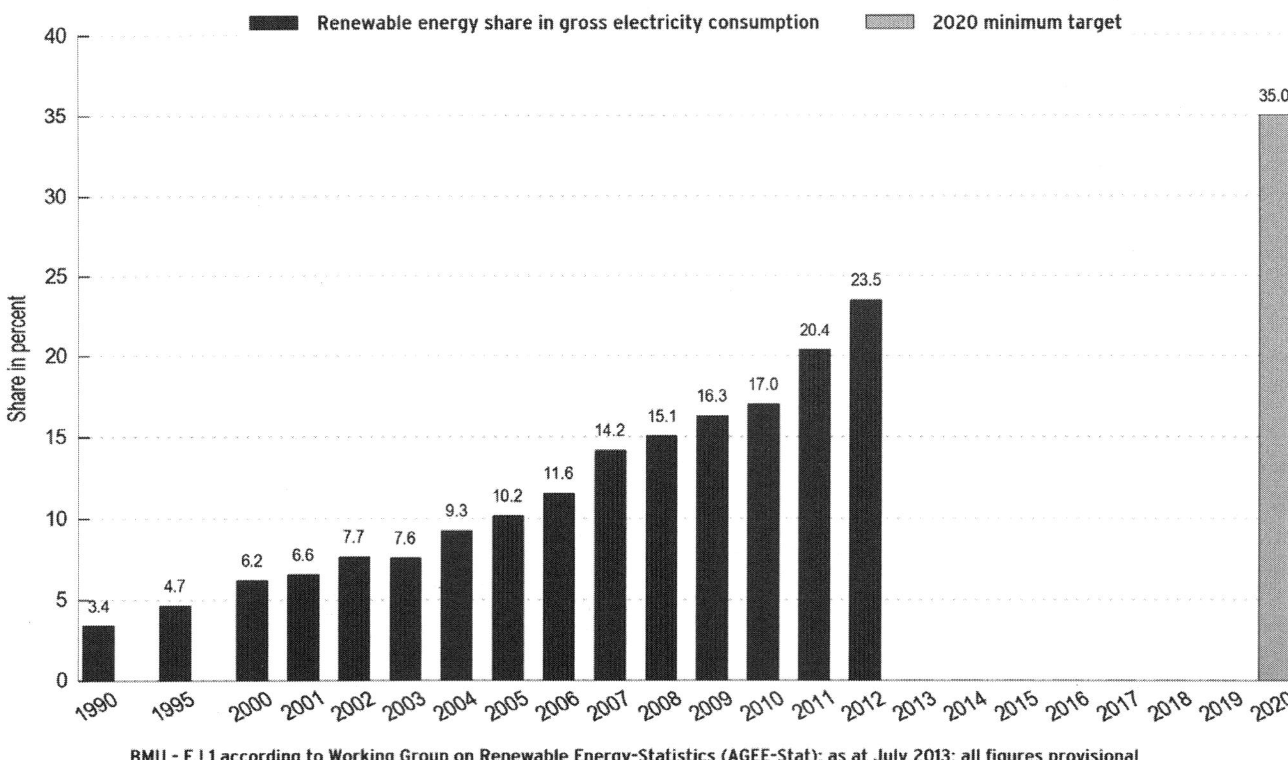

Figure 2.1. *Renewable energy sources as a share of gross electricity consumption in Germany. Source: Federal Ministry for Environment, Nature Conservation and Nuclear Safety. From Report Development of Renewable Energy Sources in Germany 2012, based on statistical data from the Working Group on Renewable Energy Statistics (AGEE-Stat).*

which came to symbolize the lack of citizen voice in policy making. Here, technological and political innovation went hand in hand. Coupled with the protest against particular power plants was a commitment to civic participation and the development of what came to be known as "counter-expertise". Activists argued that it was not enough to reject traditional energy sources or traditional politics. Almost from the beginning, they took it upon themselves to develop new energy sources and new forms of politics.

The evolution from NIMBY protest to networks of innovation is illustrated here by a case that has come to symbolize successful resistance against nuclear power—that of Wyhl, in the Freiburg/Breisgau region of Baden-Württemberg. The Wyhl resistance of the mid-1970s is widely known for popularizing new forms of citizen activism in Germany. What is less widely known is that it also provided the impetus for a solar energy boom that transformed the Freiburg/Breisgau region and ultimately helped revolutionize German energy policy.

"A Region of Tinkerers and Craftsmen"

The movement that would change Germany's energy future and reshape its political party system began in the early 1970s in a sparsely populated area along the Rhine in the southwestern corner of the Federal Republic where Germany, France, and Switzerland intersect. It is a region of farms, vineyards, and villages. Local residents are known for their self-sufficiency and resourcefulness. It is also known as the sunniest corner of Germany, receiving more hours of sunlight than any other German region.

Baden-Württemberg, a predominantly Catholic state, has been a stronghold of the Christian Democratic Union (CDU) throughout the postwar period. The CDU was a particularly vocal supporter of nuclear energy. In the 1970s, the state government planned an industrial buildout of the whole Upper Rhine region between the Swiss border and Mannheim (Engels 2003: 107). The French and Swiss governments were also eyeing this region for chemical and energy development. As part of the development, all three countries planned to construct multiple nuclear power plants. In the ninety-mile stretch from Gösgen (Switzerland) to Wyhl (Germany), there would be no fewer than eight nuclear parks with a total of up to seventeen reactors. The newspaper *Die Welt* called it "the most colossal energy concentration on earth" (*Der Spiegel* 40/1975: 102–3).

Local residents soon got wind of the plans. The proposed nuclear plant at Fessenheim in the Alsace region of France saw one of the first demonstrations in 1971. When information reached the public that Breisach, near Freiburg, had been chosen as the site for a nuclear plant on the

German side, local opponents began to mobilize. In July 1973, after numerous confrontations over the application, the Baden-Württemberg state Ministry of Economics announced that it had changed the site to Wyhl, a sleepy village along the Rhine twenty kilometers from Breisach.

Protest groups on all sides of the border took the form of "citizen initiatives." These had started in Germany in the late 1960s and early 1970s, mostly as self-help groups to provide community services like day care. In the course of the 1970s, they increasingly formed to protest large, state-sponsored industrial projects, especially power plants. People tended to choose this form of organizing because at that time the established political parties offered no support for their issues (Rucht 1980: 81). This organizational form took wing, and by the mid-1970s, more Germans identified themselves as members of grassroots citizen initiatives than of all political parties combined (Mez 1987: 264).

The fact that multiple nuclear and chemical industry projects were planned for the same border area was fortuitous for the local citizen initiatives. Opposition was mobilizing in Germany, France, and Switzerland. A successful site occupation in Alsatian Marckolsheim included many people who would later participate at Wyhl. As in many of the cases in this volume, the regional nature of the issue led local groups to broaden their focus and cooperate with groups based elsewhere. Their rhetoric, too, evolved from opposing potential harm in their own towns to questioning the safety and benefits of nuclear energy generally (Rucht 1980: 82).

The regionally active citizen initiatives of this area also contributed to the formation of nationwide umbrella organizations that would become major participants in the push for environmental policy in Germany: The Federal Association of Citizen Initiatives for Environmental Protection (*Bund Bürgerinitiativen Umweltschutz,* BBU) and the German Association for Environmental and Nature Protection (*Bund Umwelt- und Naturschutz Deutschland,* BUND).[2] These groups broke the mold of traditional environmental organizations. Axel Mayer of BUND explains that their founders tried to combine the traditional groups' focus on nature protection with the mass mobilization tactics of the citizen initiatives. The political activism would give them the voice in policy making that traditional groups lacked, and the more structured organization would give them the longevity that citizen initiatives lacked (interview with Axel Mayer 2012).

The center of the Wyhl protest organization was in the neighboring village of Weisweil, where a citizen initiative was founded immediately upon announcement of the new site. Other groups joined in to form the "International Committee of Badisch-Alsatian Citizen Initiatives" in 1974 (Engels 2003: 113). Energy protest in the Wyhl area, as in Germany as a whole, was embedded in a larger array of citizen movements concerned with the quality of life and critical of the economic growth mentality of government and industry. These included women's rights, civil rights, antiwar, student, and labor groups that had arisen in the 1960s as well as the peace movement. Disgruntled citizens began to question not only the substance of government decisions, but also the legitimacy of the corporatist form of decision-making that produced them (Guggenberger and Kempf 1984; Linse et al. 1988).

The close relationship between government and industry came under particular scrutiny in the Wyhl case. Key members of the state government, including the minister of economics and the governor himself, were on the supervisory board of the power company whose application they were judging. A referendum was held in Wyhl on the sale of the land. Fifty-five percent of voters approved the sale, amidst a war of information between the government and the local citizen initiatives. A number of carrots had been offered to the town—e.g., millions in financial incentives and promised tax income—as had a stick: a threat of taking the land by eminent domain if the referendum failed (Rucht 1980, 83–84; Karapin 2007: 130).

Events moved quickly after the sale. The utility began clearing the site for construction, despite pending legal objections. The next day, February 18, 1975, the Badisch-Alsatian citizen initiatives held a press conference to protest the project. Afterwards, several hundred protesters occupied the site and prevented work from taking place. Two tense days later, police cleared the occupation peacefully, and the site was secured with fencing and barbed wire. But the number of protesters grew into the thousands, and demonstrators began arriving from farther away. On February 23, the crowd broke through the barrier, and several thousand set up for a long stay (Rucht 1980: 85). After clashes with protesters, the police withdrew. The local police commissar had refused to take violent action against his own neighbors, and had pleaded successfully for local religious leaders to intervene with the state government.[3] The disciplined nonviolence at Wyhl, with the participation of local clergy, helped legitimate the protest movement with the wider German public.

The protest was broad-based and technically adept from the beginning. Among its early leaders was a group of mostly chemistry students from Freiburg University. They coalesced around several active and retired science professors who were raising questions about the appropriateness of nuclear energy for electricity generation (interview with Erhard Schulz 2012). After hearing a lecture by one of the professors, the Protestant pastor of Weisweil, Günter Richter, joined the activists of this group. There was a general feeling among the protesters that it was not enough to object to nuclear power; they had both to ground their objections in science and offer plausible alternatives (Schulz interview 2012). They also needed a way to keep people at the site in order to discourage the authorities from trying to retake it. Both of these goals were accomplished with the founding of a "Community College of the Wyhl Forest" in March 1975 at a makeshift "friendship house" on the construction site. The Community College idea was adopted from the earlier site occupation at Marckolsheim in France.

In addition to the more technical discussions, the Community College offered presentations on local customs, crafts, flora and fauna, and even travel. While the Baden-Württemberg state government denounced the protesters as left-wing radicals, in reality the movement was infused with technical experts and embedded in the traditional culture of the region. Left-leaning students stood side-by-side with conservative local vintners and farmers. The Community College was one way the movement maintained its breadth. Its programs, which at first took place almost daily, also kept a lively crowd at the site through the evening hours.

The protest at Wyhl caught both federal and state governments off guard. Nuclear power promised to be cheap and plentiful, and thus to aid the cause of rapid growth. Political and economic elites unquestioningly associated economic growth with the public good: "The blessing of nuclear energy seemed so clear and convincing that resistance was not anticipated or [they believed] could only arise from prejudices" (Engels 2003: 110). Officials dismissed the reservations of local citizens, answering the protest with arrogance, brute force, or dire warnings of a looming energy shortage. Their actions, however, seemed to affirm the meta-level concerns of the citizen initiative groups. The events in Wyhl, writes Dieter Rucht, had a "signal effect" on others. Site occupations multiplied, in Germany and abroad, as nuclear projects came to be seen as symptoms of a larger problem: "From about 1974 the protest against nuclear power plants developed beyond local impacts. It was no longer limited to the effects of nuclear facilities in the 'classical' sense of environmental pollution. The resistance against a concrete project became understood as resistance against the whole nuclear program. Questions of energy planning, of economic growth, of understanding of democracy entered the picture" (Rucht 1980: 86).

Citizen initiatives that had been concerned with other issues or with environmental protection generally began to target nuclear power as a symbol of a tainted political process resulting in decisions that benefited a few at the expense of the many. They blamed the behind-the-scenes collaboration between government and industry for policy decisions that seemed out of step with popular values. They aimed their critique increasingly at the established political parties, which in their view had failed to transmit new impulses from the citizenry to bureaucratic decision-makers. Figure 2.2 shows the most famous anti-Wyhl poster. Note that it gives a nod to the local dialect (*Nai hämmer gsait* is dialect for "No, we said") and also expresses frustration with a government/industry complex that refuses to listen to the public. It also demonstrates that the local groups had transcended a NIMBY formulation of the issue ("No atomic power plant in Wyhl or elsewhere").

Figure 2.2. *Wyhl protest slogan: No, we said! No atomic power plant in Wyhl and elsewhere. Source: BUND Südlicher Oberrhein.*

The site occupation at Wyhl lasted over eight months. After negotiations with the state government and the utility in late October 1975, facilitated by Pastor Richter of Weisweil, the citizen initiatives cleared their settlement of all but a few remaining "observers." All parties agreed to a temporary moratorium on construction and a commissioning of further scientific studies. The authorities also agreed to drop their legal actions against some of the protesters. This became known as the "Offenburg Agreement" (Engels 2003: 116). Now the conflict moved to the Freiburg Administrative Court. The plaintiffs were several neighboring municipalities as well as private citizens. The defendant was the State of Baden-Württemberg, whose economics ministry had issued the permit. On 14 March 1977, the administrative court vacated the construction permit, primarily out of concern about the safety of the containment structure in case of explosion (Rucht 1980: 87). The protesters had made their technical objections stick. The case continued to make its way through the appeals courts, but as one of the main negotiators put it, it was clear at this point that the project was politically infeasible, and the state government would no longer pursue it (interview with Günter Richter 2012).

This was not the only victory for the Badisch-Alsatian citizen initiatives. Regional, cross-border action helped defeat not only the proposed nuclear plants at Breisach and Wyhl in Germany, but also planned chemical and nuclear power plants in France and a nuclear plant in Switzerland. Wyhl's resonance in Germany was profound. The methods of mobilization and site occupation developed in these conflicts were copied nationwide as the nuclear fight expanded to recycling and storage facilities as well as other plant sites. And the cross-border network of citizen activists grew and strengthened over time. After the site occupation ended, the Community College rotated its presentations among the surrounding villages, continuing to host informational events for eight years. They often paired a scientific expert with a local farmer in order to relate to a broad spectrum of the population.[4]

From Protest to Innovation

The Wyhl protests set in motion a process of innovation that transformed the Freiburg region into a leader in solar energy development. The most important facets of this transformation are described below.

The Development and Legitimation of Counter-Expertise: The Eco-Institute Freiburg

NIMBY, in the case of Wyhl, was not simply about rejecting a site. Assembling accurate information for the public was also a high priority for the occupiers. The Community College was a way to inform and empower the anti-nuclear public in an era when virtually no critical dialogue with government or industry was occurring. Yet the administrative court proceedings—where the fate of the Wyhl plant and others would ultimately be decided—were a technical affair. They were not about airing concerns with the general direction of the federal energy program or challenging the economic growth paradigm of the industry/government alliance. They were about demonstrating that the facility was not permissible as proposed. Lay citizens were at a distinct disadvantage with this line of argument. In the "friendship house" at the site, critical experts who had taken up the cause answered residents' questions and familiarized them with the terms of the debate. "As a result," noted the German magazine *Der Spiegel,* "vintners and farmers with 300 hogs in the stall speak about radionuclides as expertly as they would about wine sugar levels and meat prices in the EC" (*Der Spiegel* 30/1975: 42).

Still, the disrespect with which the authorities treated their arguments left a deep impression on many of the participants. Twenty-seven community members decided to do something about it by founding the Institute for Applied Ecology ("Eco-Institute") in nearby Freiburg in November 1977. Their founding declaration made direct reference to the experiences at Wyhl: "Only when citizens made their demands together and demonstrated their collective will to stand up themselves for the preservation of their lives were they listened to" (Öko-Institut 1977). The courts had given them an opening, but those proceedings were also problematic:

> In court proceedings and hearings the critical citizen encounters a phalanx of experts who advise the bureaucracy and industry. More and more citizens recognize that science is not free of [special] interests. Only a few scientists have been prepared up to now to support the citizens. In the long run, however, the citizen initiatives will only succeed in achieving their demands in planning and in court if they themselves deliver the necessary scientific foundation.[5]

Two important lessons learned at Wyhl were thus, first, that science is not value-free, and second, that legal and technical expertise is essential in these conflicts. The anti-nuclear movement had seen that prevailing scientific opinion fell on the side of the utilities, and that mainstream scientists were largely dependent on the industry whose plans they were assigned to evaluate. From the beginning, part of the institute's purpose was to cultivate what its founders called "counter-expertise". They explicitly committed themselves to reevaluating scientific evidence and assessments that had been widely portrayed as truths. They chose the form of a registered voluntary association (*eingetragener Verein*), financed by donations and membership dues, in order to ensure their independence from government and industry.

Importantly, the Eco-Institute gave a voice to critical scientists, who worked for it mostly on a volunteer basis at the beginning. There was no real place at universities or established research institutions for experts who did not share the government and industry elite's enthusiasm for nuclear and fossil fuel energy (Roose 2002: 102). It was risky, says environmental expert Martin Jänicke, to work for an institution that was directly connected to oppositional citizen groups (quoted in Roose 2002: 92), which were often assumed to be bastions of left-wing radicalism. The Eco-Institute suffered withering critique from nuclear proponents in industry, government, and scientific institutes (*Öko-Mitteilungen* 1982). But as its findings were borne out with time, its reputation grew.

In addition to counter-expertise, the Eco-Institute's founders aimed to "promote ecologically sustainable progress by means of research and development of environmentally friendly techniques and means of action" (Krause 1982: 17). They wanted to demonstrate that a different future was possible. One of their first studies, which eventually appeared as a book entitled *Energy Turning Point*, made the then-revolutionary proposal that Germany withdraw completely from nuclear energy. Its authors also broke with convention and, instead of assuming steadily increasing energy demand, proposed flat demand as a preferable and technically feasible scenario (Roose 2002: 18–19). This was one of the first scientifically grounded shots across the bow of the growth paradigm.

Soon there were signs that the alternative scientific position was making headway in the federal government. Eco-Institute Board spokesman Günter Altner was appointed to a parliamentary commission entitled "Future Nuclear Energy Policy". The commission's report, issued in 1983, sketched a number of possible scenarios for development of energy supply and consumption. Although it had not yet achieved general acceptance, the Eco-Institute's energy study was incorporated as one of these scenarios (Roose 2002: 19).

The founding of the Eco-Institute, and the spread of scientific and legal counter-expertise it promoted, helped carry the whole ecological movement forward. Among the beneficiaries were alternative media, which began to take off at about the same time. Reiner Metzger, Deputy Editor-in-Chief of the newspaper *Die Tageszeitung* (TAZ), recounts, "After the founding of TAZ, the Eco-Institute was a virtual cornerstone of its reporting: finally there were experts whom the extensive eco-scene trusted" (Öko-Institut 2007). The Eco-Institute grew from a paid staff of two at its founding to 145 at three locations today, including some 100 scientists working on over 300 projects at the international, national, and subnational levels, and a turnover of €12.7 million (Öko-Institut 2013).

The Bottom-up Development of a Renewable Energy Industry

The founders of the Eco-Institute were not alone in wanting to move beyond a purely oppositional stance. During the site occupation, the feeling was widespread among the Badisch-Alsatian citizen initiatives that if they were going to reject nuclear power, they needed to offer an alternative. This feeling inspired many local activists to promote renewable energy in their later careers.

Solar Exhibitions

Together with members of the newly founded environmental organization BUND, some activists from the Badisch-Alsatian group put on what was perhaps the world's first exhibition for solar energy technology in the village of Sasbach, near Wyhl, in summer 1976. By today's standards, says Axel Mayer, who helped organize the first exhibition, the "Sasbach Sun Days" was tiny. There were only twelve exhibitors of solar devices. But this combination of technical exhibit/trade show and public festival attracted over 12,000 visitors (Mayer 2009). Everyone who wanted to make a statement against Wyhl turned up in Sasbach. Most importantly, the Sun Days showcased local innovations.

Werner Mildebrath, an electrician from Sasbach, was one of those "tinkerers and craftsmen" who participated in the Sun Days. He had helped the Wyhl protesters by installing sound equipment and lighting for events at the occupied site. He became fascinated by the potential for solar energy. In 1975 he built a solar system to heat water for his own house. After exhibiting his solar collectors, he founded a small solar energy firm that eventually won contracts as far away as Egypt (Janzing 2011: 43). His are estimated to have been some of the first functioning solar panels in Germany. He was eventually driven out of business by the arrival of mass producers, but many of the systems he installed locally are still in use.

It was no accident that renewables started small and found acceptance among ecologically minded citizens throughout Germany. Rüdiger Mautz explains that the ecology and alternative movements pushed for decentralized, environmentally friendly industry and participatory decision making, which for them went hand-in-hand (Mautz 2007: 115). Sustainable production using renewable resources was already a focus for the movements; small-scale solar energy fit well with the new environmental paradigm, and experiments with renewables became part of the movements' general attempt to practice what they preached locally. Thus, grassroots groups were key to embedding alternative technologies in society before there was a federal policy framework.

The Sasbach Sun Days outgrew their venue after three years and were replaced by a more broad-ranging annual Eco-Trade Fair in Freiburg, sponsored by BUND. These exhibitions lasted until 1998. By that time, the fair had grown to 540 exhibitors and 56,000 visitors.[6] In 2000, Freiburg became home to the Intersolar Exhibition, billed as the world's largest exhibition for the solar industry. The Intersolar outgrew its Freiburg site and was moved to Munich in 2008.

Renewable Energy-Related Businesses and Networks

The Wyhl experience continued to inspire participants long after the site occupation ended. Many found ways to promote alternatives to nuclear energy in their careers. Three local residents who trace their professional paths back to the Wyhl forest are Erhard Schulz, Astrid Späth, and Rolf Disch.[7] Their stories give a small sampling of the variety of ways in which the anti-nuclear movement became a force for societal change.

Erhard Schulz, BUND (Eco-Station) and Freiburg Innovation Academy

Erhard Schulz studied chemistry at Freiburg University during the early 1970s. He belonged to a group of about twenty professors and students who began to question the scientific claims made by the nuclear power industry.[8] This group was instrumental in organizing the Community College at the occupation site. Schulz, along with several of the others, gave presentations there outlining the hazards of nuclear power and raising the possibility of alternatives for power generation.

In 1975 Schulz helped form a regional BUND organization headquartered in Freiburg. He became the first managing director of the Baden-Württemberg organization, a position he held until 2000. His main task was to found local BUND groups throughout the state and to support their activities. Many volunteers helped with BUND's projects over the years, including forestry and chemistry department faculty from Freiburg University. Through his diverse contacts, Schulz was able to wed the expertise of the university group to the nature protection and anti-nuclear activities of BUND. This gave them what he calls "a good scientific backbone" (interview with Erhard Schulz 2012).

For Schulz, as for many of his contemporaries, making headway against nuclear power was only one side of the coin; the other was bringing alternative energy technologies to fruition. Under Schulz's leadership, BUND sponsored the Sasbach Sun Days and later the Eco-Trade Fairs. Of all his projects, Schulz is proudest of the Eco-Station in Freiburg, which was erected as part of the State Garden Show in 1986. Maintained by the

City of Freiburg and run by BUND, it serves as an environmental education center and demonstration project in ecological living (Havlik and Schulz 1987). It includes a "nature house" that showcases natural, traditional construction techniques and state-of-the-art solar and cogeneration technologies. It is surrounded by organic gardens that illustrate various ecotopes. Built to inspire ideas about living in harmony with nature, the Eco-Station hosts educational events for the general public and for schoolchildren, including a summer camp.

As part of his work promoting the Eco-Fairs, Schulz drove the press to different ecologically innovative area businesses, some of whose owners had also been at Wyhl. After his departure from BUND, he and a partner expanded this work by founding the nonprofit Innovation Academy Freiburg, which showcases renewable energy projects to diverse international audiences, from local school classes to Japanese scientists. The idea, Schulz says, is to introduce visitors not only to the many technological innovations in the region, but also to the people behind the innovations. He believes that meeting people who have invested in renewable energies will inspire others to make the leap themselves. Schulz spends much of his time scouting new tour destinations for the Academy. The organization, which is funded by customer fees, member dues, and donations, now offers about 150 destinations in the region, and in 2012 it led customized tours for some 6,000 visitors from all over the world. With seven full-time employees, it participates in the Green City Freiburg Cluster, a regional network of firms and institutions that promotes the environmental and solar economy (Green City 2013). Through this network, members share information among themselves and with the broader public regarding developments in local renewable energy.

Astrid Späth, Victoria Hotel

One of the destinations of the Innovation Academy's tours is the Victoria Hotel in Freiburg. This 66-room "green hotel" employs renewable energies and energy-saving technologies large and small. These range from LED lights and superior insulation to wood-pellet combustion heating with a flue gas-cleaning system to solar roof panels and mini-wind turbines. Many of these initiatives came from Astrid Späth, who owns the hotel with her husband Bertram.

Astrid Späth was introduced to the Wyhl resistance through the Protestant church. She joined a group of young people Pastor Richter was taking regularly to the construction site. As a young teenager, she was fascinated by the cultural programs and the music. She was deeply affected by the fact that "with such a joyful resistance they really succeeded in stopping [the plant]". She wanted to spread the message, she says, that "with determination you can change the world" (Interview with Astrid Späth 2012).

In 1985 Späth and her husband, another Wyhl veteran, took over the hotel, which had been in his family for two generations. She began looking for small ways to help the environment in her new business. She eliminated plastic packaging in the breakfast bar and began to buy from local organic farmers. She initiated a switch to a less-harsh detergent for hotel laundry. Through these measures, she developed an awareness of the overall imprint that one's purchases and activities have on the environment and on the local economy. This would be a way to foster change.

The Späths eventually took on the larger issue of energy use, with the goal of becoming a carbon-neutral hotel. They upgraded the insulation, installed solar roof panels, and began looking for an ecologically sound alternative to their oil heating system. They chose wood pellets and developed a flue gas-treatment system that would allow them to install such heating within city limits. They also innovated in cooling, forgoing energy-intensive air conditioning for a heat-transfer piped water system that recycles pumped groundwater (Hotel-Victoria 2013). Each of these improvements, Späth says, met with resistance locally, but each ultimately became a model for others and a calling card for the hotel.

It was the wife of prominent local architect Rolf Disch who convinced Späth to begin advertising as a green hotel in the 1990s. Since then, the Victoria has received numerous environmental awards and designations. Späth now considers it part of her job to educate others about ecological hotel management and support of local sustainable suppliers. She is a member of the Freiburg Sustainability Board. The Victoria is a founding member of the Green City Freiburg Cluster and of Sleep Green Hotels, a group of especially environmentally engaged European hotels.

Rolf Disch, Rolf Disch Solar Architecture

On the website of Rolf Disch's renowned solar architecture firm is a photo of a young Disch at the Wyhl site, with the caption, "And so it all began—in Wyhl". By the time of the protests, Disch had already completed his studies and founded a solar architecture firm. He was impressed that so many people, from a broad cross-section of the population, kept gathering at the site. What began for him at Wyhl, he says, was the idea that the public could be inspired, not just to oppose, but also to make a positive change in the society (interview with Rolf Disch 2012).

Disch's main focus in the 1980s was solar-powered automobiles. He displayed one of his vehicles at the State Garden Show in Freiburg in 1986 (where Schulz's BUND Eco-Station was also unveiled) and developed a vehicle capable of traversing 3,000 miles to win the World Solar

Challenge race in Australia. Afterwards, pondering how best to promote solar energy, he decided to rededicate himself to architecture. He initiated a community-funded solar installation on the roof of Freiburg's soccer stadium. In 1994 he completed the Heliotrope, described as the first house in the world with a positive energy balance (Rolf Disch 2012). It serves as a demonstration project and also his family residence.

More than once, Disch had to sell his possessions in order to finance a project. Nevertheless, his projects grew more ambitious. He wanted to develop housing that would change the way people interacted with their environment. In an effort to overcome the reservations of large investors and potential buyers, his firm held an open house in 2000. They were "overrun," he says, mainly by people who just wanted to see what he was up to. When the sponsorship raveled and the state lending institutions withdrew their support, Disch found new sponsors. They completed a scaled-down settlement of fifty-nine positive-energy houses in 2004. Two years later, they opened a solar-powered commercial addition, known as the "Sun Ship," which now houses not only Disch's firm but also the Eco-Institute and several other environmentally related businesses.

One of the lessons he learned at Wyhl, says Disch, is that, when it comes to finding support for innovative ideas, "it works best with people one knows." The acquaintances from the Wyhl forest maintained contact through a growing network of mutual support that was critical at several points when more conventionally minded investors balked or public officials declined to promote a new idea. When some of the local solar pioneers decided they needed an energy agency to promote their products, they cooperated in founding FESA (interview with Josef Pesch 2012). FESA (Association for the Promotion of Energy and Solar [in the] Freiburg Region) and other organizations like it enabled area residents to invest in renewables projects and navigate the permitting and construction processes. Together, renewable energy entrepreneurs began to overcome the power of traditional utilities and the reservations of politicians, bureaucrats, and the public.

The Development of Renewable Energy R&D: The Fraunhofer Institute for Solar Energy Systems

The third facet of the regional transition from protest to innovation was the establishment of an R&D institute devoted to solar energy. Neither the German federal government nor the traditional utilities showed much interest in this. The government's contribution to the early phase of renewable energy development mostly took the form of funding through the Ministry of Research. It enabled universities, institutes, and firms to experiment with renewables, provided that these remain in a pre-market phase (Jacobsson and Lauber 2006: 263). But the scientific prejudices against this line of research were formidable, as was the skepticism of the big utilities; few believed there would be much of a market for renewable energy technologies.

The pioneer in solar energy systems was Professor Adolf Goetzberger. At the time of the Wyhl protests, he was an esteemed physicist who had worked in the United States with the pioneers of semiconductor technology. He had been wooed back to Germany in 1968 to serve as head of the Fraunhofer Institute for Solid State Physics in Freiburg (Fraunhofer ISE 2008: 2). The Fraunhofer Society is a nonprofit organization that "occupies a mediating position between the fundamental research of universities and industrial practice" (Fraunhofer ISE 2012: 10). It runs a prestigious chain of R&D institutes, each of which is required to back up its commitment to applied research by winning a proportion of its funding through contracts with industry. One of Goetzberger's departments worked on display technologies, and they had started to develop a display that worked without energy input. It did not get far in the marketplace, says Goetzberger, but it got him thinking that this would be a way to collect solar energy (interview with Adolf Goetzberger 2012). At the same time, he became aware of the Club of Rome's report *The Limits to Growth* (Club of Rome 1972). Putting the two together, he decided it would be worthwhile to start research on solar energy.

Goetzberger founded a solar energy group at his institute, but the theme found little resonance there. He began to develop a vision for a separate institute devoted solely to this new line of research. It was important to him to stay within the Fraunhofer Society in order to win funding for the work. Based upon his sterling reputation, he was finally able to convince the president of the Fraunhofer Society to approve the project.

Goetzberger continued to run the Solid State Physics Institute while launching the new Fraunhofer Institute for Solar Energy Systems (Fraunhofer ISE), and about twenty colleagues from the former worked with him in the latter. But he eventually decided to devote the rest of his career to the solar institute. This was a big risk. At a scientific meeting, he recalls, a colleague took Goetzberger's wife aside to ask whether her husband was still "right in the head," as he was giving up an established position to work on something as "hopeless" as solar energy. Nevertheless, the institute opened its doors in 1981.

Goetzberger was encouraged by Freiburg's favorable atmosphere toward renewable energies. Although he had not been involved in the anti-nuclear movement, he says he realized the local enthusiasm for renewables was related to that experience. What he and the veterans of Wyhl had in common was a desire to create something positive for the environment. He met and encouraged solar architecture pioneer Rolf Disch. He was aware of local citizens like Werner Mildebrath who were building solar collectors in their garages. These people ignored the experts who warned them against investing in solar energy. The reason the early solar market took off, he says, is that people invested in solar technologies as a hobby, and their customers cared more about developing the new energy source than they did about cost.

Fraunhofer developed solar cell technology and eventually thermal conversion, smart grids, and storage technologies. One of Goetzberger's pet projects was a self-sufficient solar house, which opened in 1992 and is still used in research. The institute had several "cliffhangers", where the Fraunhofer Society and the federal government threatened to shut it down due to the technology's failure to find large private investors in Germany (Fraunhofer ISE 2008: 1). But Goetzberger was involved in a growing international solar research network, and he had the support of the Freiburg mayor, who saw this field as a possible selling point for the region. He also had the ear of rising political elites in the Social Democratic and Green parties. Goetzberger further notes that the institute's work was aided at key points by public outcry after catastrophic events, especially the Chernobyl nuclear accident, and growing scientific awareness of the greenhouse effect. The latter had not been a factor in the initial arguments for solar research, but it soon overtook the others in immediacy.

In addition to supporting local experiments with solar technologies, Goetzberger helped draw the International Solar Energy Society to Freiburg in the late 1980s. His successors built strong ties with Freiburg University in the 1990s and beyond. Today, the Fraunhofer Institute for Solar Energy Systems is the largest solar energy research institution in Europe, with some 1,200 employees and an operating budget of €66.8 million. It educates hundreds of students for careers in solar energy (Fraunhofer ISE 2013).

Political Innovation: The Founding of the Greens

The fourth aspect of the transition from protest to innovation was the development of new forms of political participation. NIMBY protest, much of it around energy projects, had already led to innovations in citizen participation. BUND was a new kind of group that combined political mobilization with nature protection. Site occupation and civic education tactics evolved as movements learned from each other. The grassroots activism around energy projects also contributed to the founding of green and alternative voting lists throughout West Germany and, eventually, the national-level Greens in 1980. The original members conceived of the

Greens not as a conventional political party, but as the parliamentary arm of the citizen initiative movement (Kleinert 1992). One of its founders famously called it the "anti-party party" (Kelly 1984).

There was a direct connection between the mobilization against nuclear power in the Freiburg region and the founding of the Greens there. The original protest group against the Breisach plant was closely allied with a citizen initiative that played an important role in pushing for a green voting list.[9] Although Freiburg was a fairly liberal city, the surrounding winegrowing region was politically quite conservative. While anti-nuclear activists and renewables advocates were found across the party spectrum, the party organizations had been slow to take up the cause. Veterans of the Wyhl protest felt ill-served by the existing party constellation, particularly the CDU. They decided to try for direct representation by running one of their members for the state legislature. Although he ran under the auspices of one of the smaller political parties, none of his campaign materials mentioned any affiliation. Instead, he used the label "Citizen Initiative." His convincing win signaled to the group that they could gain local office with candidates connected directly to the anti-nuclear movement. This was one impetus for the founding of the local Greens.[10]

The Greens cleared the five percent hurdle for representation in the national parliament, the Bundestag, in the 1982 elections. They earned their best result nationwide in the region around Freiburg, with 12.3 percent (Engels: 120, ftnt. 50). In the Bundestag, they worked to bring the concerns of the citizen initiatives to government. One of their early actions was to force the formation of two special parliamentary commissions on energy issues.

Renewable Energy Networks Go National

In the Wyhl Forest were the first stirrings of an advocacy network that eventually reached the federal level. From the Freiburg region came research institutions such as the Eco-Institute and the Fraunhofer Institute for Solar Energy Systems, whose leaders began to penetrate federal bureaucratic and parliamentary commissions; small businesses and emerging business networks for renewables; environmental citizen initiatives and their umbrella networks, for which grassroots mobilization continued to be an effective tool; political advocates, especially in the Greens and the SPD, at all levels of government; and a rising alternative press. They demanded a withdrawal from nuclear power and lobbied for federal support for a transition to renewable energy.

Anti-nuclear protests delayed or halted construction of a number of plants nationwide, gradually souring the German public on nuclear power

(Rucht 1980; Linse et al. 1988). The Chernobyl accident in 1986 reinforced dramatically the concerns of the protesters, turning public opinion strongly and permanently against nuclear power (Kolb 2007: 211, Jahn 1992: 396–97). Since nuclear energy had been considered the main alternative to carbon-based energy, and since this industry had been particularly hostile to the participatory concerns of environmentalists and to the introduction of alternative energies (Toke and Lauber 2007: 683), this development would prove crucial to the emergence of renewables. After Chernobyl, the Eco-Institute found itself rather suddenly in the position of go-to source for information on a nuclear-free future, and the Fraunhofer Solar Institute saw its fortunes rise. What had once seemed utopian ideas were now taken seriously as alternatives to fossil fuels and nuclear energy.

Dramatic cases of forest die-off (*Waldsterben*) in the 1970s and 1980s raised public concern over the negative impacts of coal-fired power plants as well. Grassroots groups mobilized against acid rain and global warming. Their position was strengthened by several widely publicized scientific reports warning of impending climate disaster (Weingart 1998: 877). By the end of the 1980s, all the major political parties had declared climate change one of their priorities (Quaschning 2010: xi). When the Bundestag formed a special commission on climate change in 1989, Eco-Institute board member Peter Hennicke was one of its members.

These developments augured well for the expansion of renewables, but it was clear that the government would have to step in to help make them marketable in this early phase. The major utilities, which enjoyed territorial monopolies on energy supply, were slow to innovate and to accept new participants. The Ministry of Economics showed little interest in developing a "strategic framework" for expanding the renewables sector (Lipp 2007: 5488). The Research and Environment ministries were more supportive but much less powerful. The concept of a feed-in tariff, which has roots in Denmark, was developed into a policy proposal in Germany not by these established players, but rather in the "counter-expert" institutes that had arisen from the energy protest of the previous decades (Vasi 2009: 328). The 1990 Feed-in Law granted access to the grid to small energy producers at a guaranteed price, lowering the perceived risk to investors (Toke 2011). Pressured by public unrest and by organized advocates and their allies in the Bundestag, the government "more or less reluctantly" adopted the measures to promote renewable energy production (Jacobsson and Lauber 2006: 264). The established utilities, distracted by German reunification and the takeover of East German utilities, devoted little energy to stopping the Feed-in Law (Laird and Stefes 2009: 2628) and, by some accounts, underestimated its potential impact (Pesch interview 2012; Toke and Lauber 2007: 683).

The Feed-in Law facilitated a boom in capacity, and the cost of wind power in particular began to drop. It was not smooth sailing, though. The big utilities challenged the law both politically and in the courts. The federal government, too, was reluctant to increase support for renewables. The new technologies still lacked significant industry buy-in, and their advocates had to stay mobilized in order to keep the support framework intact. The Fraunhofer ISE, having failed to win adequate investment contracts from industry, was on the verge of being shut down by the German government in the early 1990s. Only after Goetzberger wrote to all the political party organizations and went to Berlin to plead his case to the Bundestag directly was the funding approved, over the objections, he recounts, of the Ministry of Research (interview with Adolf Goetzberger 2012). In 1997, the government proposed reducing the feed-in tariff. The German Wind Energy Association mobilized a large and diverse demonstration in its favor, and the proposal to reduce the tariff was eventually dropped (Vasi 2009: 328).

When support for renewables flagged at the national level, committed local investors kept the ball rolling. After the Chernobyl accident, for example, several families in the South Baden village of Schönau came together to take local action against nuclear power. They decided to try to buy the local grid and produce hydropower themselves in order not to have to buy from a utility that owned nuclear plants (Janzing 2008). The "Schönau Electricity Rebels" weathered a determined campaign by the utility and eventually won the right to form their own company. The new federal law enabled them to sell clean energy nationwide. The residents of Freiamt, a village near Freiburg, also took energy production into their own hands. They became a "plus energy village" with solar, wind, and biomass. In 2012, Freiamt produced 160 percent more energy than its residents consumed (Erneuerbare Energien 2013).

The research network in the Freiburg region was growing as well. The university founded a Center for Renewable Energies (ZEE) in the 1990s, which was affiliated with, among others, the Fraunhofer ISE and the Eco-Institute (ZEE 2013). Solar panel manufacturing took off with the founding of the Solar Factory, which opened the world's first zero-emissions plant in Freiburg in 2000 (Solar Factory 2013).

In 1998, the Kohl government gave way to a coalition of the Social Democratic Party and the Greens, some of whose members had entered politics through participation in the citizen movements of earlier decades. This was a turning point for renewable energies nationwide. The new "Red-Green" government committed itself to finding markets for renewables. Prominent nuclear skeptics/renewables advocates such as Hermann Scheer (SPD Baden-Württemberg) saw their proposals become policy. The coalition pressured the economics ministry into forming a "100,000

Roof Program" to promote solar power and passed the Renewable Energy Sources Act (2000), which expanded support for renewable energy. The new law established generous guaranteed feed-in prices over a 20-year period for solar energy, facilitating a further boom in the industry (Jones 2010; Jacobsson and Lauber 2006: 267).

The Red/Green government also made changes to the federal bureaucracy. As a result of Green gains in the 2002 elections, renewable energy was moved from the Ministry of Economics to the Ministry of the Environment (Laird and Stefes 2009: 2626). The latter viewed renewables as a matter of environmental urgency, rather than as potential competitors to major industrial interests. Importantly, nuclear skeptics now penetrated federal agencies. Michael Sailer, head of the Eco-Institute's Nuclear Engineering and Facility Safety Division, was appointed to the Environment Ministry's Reactor Safety Commission in 1999 and was tapped to lead the commission in 2002. The government replaced nearly the entire membership of this commission as a "corrective", said Sailer, better to reflect the diversity of technical viewpoints regarding nuclear energy (Schuh 2002). Stephan Kohler, who had joined the Eco-Institute in 1981 and had headed its energy division, was appointed Managing Director of the newly created German Energy Agency (DENA) in 2000. DENA is described as the "center of expertise for energy efficiency, renewable energy sources, and intelligent energy systems" (DENA 2013).

The Red/Green government left office in 2005. The subsequent, CDU-led coalitions were not as friendly to renewables. But when Chancellor Angela Merkel's government tried to backtrack on the energy policies of its predecessor, the grass roots responded with new mobilization. Things came to a head in spring 2011, when the chancellor announced that the government would delay Germany's transition from nuclear power. A wave of demonstrations followed. Soon thereafter, the Fukushima nuclear disaster in Japan confirmed the public's worst fears. Support for the Greens' hard line against nuclear power shot up, along with anger at the government's reversal. Merkel's subsequent reversal of her reversal seemed only to inflame public sentiment, resulting in the CDU's loss of two state elections and the selection of the first-ever Green governor in conservative stronghold Baden-Württemberg.[11] The Merkel government was compelled to commit to a complete withdrawal from nuclear energy by 2022 and a faster transition to renewable energy sources.

Meanwhile, constant advancements in solar technologies are making this form of energy cheap enough that many believe it will soon be able to compete even without the enticement of the feed-in tariff. In the Freiburg region, the bottom-up model of energy investment and innovation is now firmly anchored in the population. A 2012 survey showed that respondents from this region support the energy transition more strongly than elsewhere in Germany and even elsewhere in Baden-Württemberg. They also express more willingness to invest personally in renewable technologies.[12] Freiburg has been recognized nationally and internationally for its environmental orientation. The "solar region" designation has become a marketing factor for the whole region and a professional advantage for those who have trained there (interview with Bernward Janzing 2012).

Conclusion

This case study of the Freiburg region has shown how Germany's renewable energy sector emerged from NIMBY protest. The grassroots opposition to nuclear power, and the desire to find alternatives to it, help explain how renewable energy developed from the bottom up in a country where top-down policy making is the norm and in a region whose political leadership was tied particularly strongly to the nuclear energy industry. Wyhl was the inspiration for technological, political, and social innovations that have parallels in other chapters in this volume.

Counter to the NIMBY stereotype, the Wyhl protest was scientifically and technologically forward-looking. Its participants helped to debunk the myth of neutral expertise and to expose the economic and political interests behind the pro-nuclear coalition. They also developed their own sources of expertise and their own scientific institutions, which gave a home to experts critical of nuclear power. Wyhl was also the catalyst for local development of solar technologies and sustainable business practices. These dovetailed with the larger-scale solar pioneering efforts of the Fraunhofer Institute and connected Freiburg innovators with like-minded people and organizations at the national and international levels.

The anti-nuclear protests also fostered political innovation. Citizen initiatives learned from one protest to the next to broaden their appeal, develop alternative proposals, and navigate the legal system. Organizations like BUND (now part of Friends of the Earth International) combined the strengths of traditional nature-protection organizations and citizen initiatives. The Greens arose as the parliamentary arm of the citizen initiative movement and learned to flourish in the party system while retaining a connection to the grass roots. This two-pronged pattern of influence has helped propel Germany's energy transition despite resistance from state and industry elites. The corporatist partnership has not changed much in Germany, but new powerful networks have arisen to challenge it.

Finally, NIMBY protests at Wyhl and other sites fostered social innovation. The anti-nuclear movement supported a new societal model based on decentralized, small-scale, ecologically sustainable production and community-based democratic decision making. This model poses a direct challenge to the centralized corporatist one. Corresponding energy paradigms have developed in German society, which are now reflected in national party politics as well as the energy industry itself (Reiche 2004; Mautz 2007: 126–27). The major advocates of the traditional energy paradigm, the coal and nuclear industries, have continued to try to overturn the Renewable Energy Sources Act (Toke 2011: 74), or at least to reshape it to their advantage. On the other side, advocates of the ecological energy paradigm have the ear of some government officials and business investors, and public opinion has turned strongly their way.

A memorial stone was dedicated in 2002 at the site of the Wyhl protests. It bears the inscription *Nai hämmer gsait!* (No, we said!), made famous through the site occupation. It stands before an unspoiled forest that would have given way to a nuclear power plant had the occupation failed. The road back to the village winds through a profusion of solar-paneled roofs, bearing testimony to the popular rejection of one vision for Germany's future and the enthusiastic embrace of another.

Notes

1. The latter are nominally privately owned but enjoy substantial subsidies and, until 1998, enjoyed territorial monopolies (Toke and Lauber 2007, 683).
2. "Rhine Valley Action" was the nucleus of the BBU, which was founded in early summer 1972 (Rucht 1980, 241n24).
3. Letter from Pastor Günter Richter to Dr. Erhard Eppler, September 29, 2001.
4. Interview with Hans-Dieter Stürmer 2012. This pairing can be seen in the Community College programs ("Vierwochenprogramme der Badisch-Elsässischen Bürgerinitiativen").
5. This passage is excerpted from the "Founding Declaration of the Eco-Institute Freiburg," delivered at Wiedenfelsen on November 5, 1977 (my translation).
6. BUND statistics are from BUND Eco-Trade Fair information brochure.
7. Quotes and opinions attributed to the people profiled in this section, and to Prof. Adolf Goetzberger in the following section, were drawn from the author's interviews with them and were translated by the author.
8. These included Professor Brauer in the Chemistry Department and his teaching assistant, Ulrich Roeter. Schulz and Pastor Richter were also influenced by a retired professor of nuclear physics, Hans Klump, who lived in Schulz's hometown of Emmendingen and who began publicly to criticize the use of nuclear energy for electricity generation (Schulz and Stürmer interviews 2012).
9. According to Jens Ivo Engels, the "Freiburg Action Association against Environmental Endangerment through Nuclear Power Plants in Breisach and Fessenheim," the original protest group founded in 1971, was closely allied with the "Action Association of Independent Germans," which played an important role in the founding of the Greens (2003, 108n19).

10. Hans Erich Schütt, a pharmacist from Emmendingen, ran as a member of the Free Democratic Party (FDP), which had not been too tainted in the eyes of the oppositional public by the Wyhl conflict (Axel Mayer interview 2012).
11. In Baden-Württemberg, the Greens' 2011 electoral victory was aided by ongoing protest surrounding a huge project to enlarge and revamp the Stuttgart train station. "Stuttgart 21" became for many a symbol of corporatism run amok, a self-interested behind-the-scenes alliance among subnational politicians, German Railroad personnel, and railroad-affiliated technical experts. Opposition to Stuttgart 21 followed the two-pronged pattern of activism described here for energy protest, with citizen initiative groups mobilizing the grass roots and the Greens fighting the project in state and local parliaments, aided by counterproposals prepared by independent experts. The activists succeeded in forcing a referendum on the project, in which their position ultimately lost (*The Local* 2011).
12. The survey was carried out by the organization Upper Rhine Climate Partner (*Klimapartner Oberrhein*). Approximately 500 people were surveyed in each of three areas: Germany as a whole, the state of Baden-Württemberg, and the Upper Rhine region (around Freiburg) (*Badische Zeitung* 2012).

References

"Am Oberrhein soll ein Energie-Wende-Index entstehen." 2012. *Badische Zeitung,* November 23. Accessed November 25, 2012. http://www.badische-zeitung.de/am-oberrhein-soll-ein-energiewende-index-entstehen.

"Bid to Halt Stuttgart 21 Rail Project Fails." 2011. *The Local,* November 11. Accessed February 20, 2012. http://www.thelocal.de/20111127/39151.html.

Bundesministerium für Umwelt, Naturschutz, und Reaktorsicherheit (BMU) and Bundesministerium für Wirtschaft und Technologie (BMWT). September 2010. *Energy Concept for an Environmentally Sound, Reliable and Affordable Energy Supply.* Berlin: Federal Ministry of Economics and Technology.

BMU. August 2012. *Renewably Employed: Short and Long-Term Impacts of the Expansion of Renewable Energy on the German Labour Market.* Berlin: Federal Ministry of Environment, Nature Conservation, and Nuclear Safety.

BMU. July 2013. *Development of Renewable Energy Sources in Germany 2012.* Berlin: Federal Ministry of Environment, Nature Conservation, and Nuclear Safety.

Club of Rome. 1972. *The Limits to Growth: A Report for the Club of Rome's Project on the Predicament of Mankind.* New York: Universe Books.

"Da geht es blind durcheinander." 1975. *Der Spiegel* 40: 96–104.

Deutsche Energie-Agentur (DENA). Accessed April 4, 2013. http://www.dena.de.

Dryzek, John S. et al. 2003. *Green States and Social Movements: Environmentalism in the United States, United Kingdom, Germany, and Norway.* Oxford: Oxford University Press.

Engels, Jens Ivo. 2003. "Geschichte und Heimat: Der Widerstand gegen das Kernkraftwerk Wyhl." In *Wahrnehmung, Bewusstsein, Identifikation: Umweltprobleme und Umweltschutz als Triebfedern regionaler Entwicklung,* edited by Kerstin Kretschmer, 103–30. Freiberg: Technische Universität Bergakademie.

Erneuerbare Energien in Freiamt. Accessed December 28, 2013. http://www.freiamt.de/erneuerbare_energien.php.

Fraunhofer Institut für Solare Energiesysteme. 2008. "Ein Platz in der Sonne: Der Wegbereiter der Solarenergie Adolf Goetzberger ist 80 Jahre alt." December 1. Presseinformation 34/08. Accessed October 4, 2012. http://www.ise.fraunhofer.de/de/presse-und-medien/pdfs-zu-presseinfos/bis-2008/presseinformation-ein-platz-fuer-die-sonne-der-wegbereiter-der-solarenergie-adolf-goetzberger-ist-80-jahre-alt.pdf.

———. 2012. *2011 Annual Report.* Freiburg, Germany. Accessed December 9, 2014. http://www.ise.fraunhofer.de/en/publications/veroeffentlichungen-pdf-dateien-en/infomaterial/annual-reports/fraunhofer-ise-annual-report-2011.pdf.

———. 2013. Accessed December 30, 2013. http://www.ise.fraunhofer.de.

Green City Freiburg Regional Cluster. Accessed March 30, 2013. http://www.greencity-cluster.de.

Guggenberger, Bernd, and Udo Kempf, eds. 1984. *Bürgerinitativen und repräsentatives System,* revised ed. Opladen: Westdeutscher Verlag.

Havlik, Renate, and Erhard Schulz. 1987. *Ökostation: Leben mit sanfter Technologie.* Cologne: Edition Fricke im Rudolf Müller Verlag.

Hotel-Victoria Freiburg. Accessed April 12, 2013. http://www.hotel-victoria.de/seiten/umweltschutz-im-hotel-energiegewinnung.html.

Interview with Rolf Disch, architect, November 15, 2012.

Interview with Dr. Adolf Goetzberger, Founding Director, Fraunhofer Institute for Solar Energy Systems, November 13, 2012.

Interview with Bernward Janzing, freelance journalist, November 14, 2012.

Interview with Axel Mayer, Managing Director, BUND South Upper Rhine Regional Organization, November 14, 2012.

Interview with Dr. Josef Pesch, Managing Director FESA gmbH, November 16, 2012.

Interview with Günter Richter, retired Protestant pastor (Weisweil), November 16, 2012.

Interviews with Erhard Schulz, former Managing Director, BUND Baden-Württemberg, and co-founder, Innovation Academy Freiburg, November 12 and 15, 2012.

Interview with Astrid Späth, co-owner, Victoria Hotel Freiburg, November 14, 2012.

Interview with Hans-Dieter Stürmer, Director, Freiburg Institute for Environmental Chemistry, November 15, 2012.

Jacobsson, Staffan, and Volkmar Lauber. 2006. "The Politics and Policy of Energy System Transformation—Explaining the German Diffusion of Renewable Energy Technology." *Energy Policy* 34: 256–76.

Jahn, Detlef. 1992. "Nuclear Power, Energy Policy and New Politics in Sweden and Germany." *Environmental Politics* 1(3): 383–417.

Janzing, Bernward. 2008. *Störfall mit Charme: Die Schönauer Stromrebellen im Widerstand gegen die Atomkraft.* Vöhrenbach: Doldverlag.

———. 2011. *Solare Zeiten: Die Karriere der Sonnenenergie.* Freiburg: Picea Verlag.

Jones, Jackie. 2010. "Solar Hero Dr. Hermann Scheer Dies." *Renewable Energy World,* October 15. Accessed October 22, 2013. http://www.renewableenergyworld.com.

Karapin, Roger. 2007. *Protest Politics in Germany.* University Park, PA: Penn State University Press.

Kelly, Petra.1984. *Fighting for Hope.* Boston, MA: South End Press.

Kleinert, Hubert. 1992. *Aufstieg und Fall der Grünen: Analyse einer alternativen Partei.* Bonn: Dietz.

Kolb, Felix. 2007. *Protest and Opportunities: A Theory of Social Movements and Political Change.* New York: Campus.

Krause, F. 1982. *Energieversorgung der Bundesrepublik ohne Kernenergie und Erdöl,* abridged version. Freiburg: Öko-Institut.

Laird, Frank, and Christoph Stefes. 2009. "The Diverging Paths of German and United States Policies for Renewable Energy: Sources of Difference." *Energy Policy* 37: 2619–629.

Linse, Ulrich, Dieter Rucht, Winfried Kretschmer, and Reinhard Falter. 1988. *Von der Bittschrift zur Platzbesetzung: Konflikte um technische Großprojekte.* Berlin: Dietz.

Lipp, Judith. 2007. "Lessons for Effective Renewable Electricity Policy from Denmark, Germany and the United Kingdom." *Energy Policy* 35: 5481–495.

Mautz, Rüdiger. 2007. "The Expansion of Renewable Energies in Germany between Niche Dynamics and System Integration—Opportunities and Restraints. *Science, Technology and Innovation Studies* 3(2): 113–31.

Mayer, Axel. 2009. "Sasbach Sonnentage: Sonnenenergie, Windkraft und Energiesparen—bundesweit erste Ausstellung am Kaiserstuhl." *BUND* Website. Accessed September 29, 2012.. http://vorort.bund.net/suedlicher-oberrhein/print.php?id=240.

Mez, Lutz. 1987. "Von den Bürgerinitiativen zu den Grünen." In *Neue soziale Bewegungen in der Bundesrepublik Deutschland,* edited by Roland Roth and Dieter Rucht, 263–76. Frankfurt: Campus.

Öko-Institut Freiburg. 1977. "Erklärung zur Gründung des Instituts." Wiedenfelsen, press release, November 5.

———. 1982. "Angriffe gegen das Institut." *Öko-Mitteilungen,* 5/82. Accessed October 14, 2012. http://www.energiewende.de/fileadmin/user_upload/pdf/015_OEM.pdf

———. 2007. "30 Jahre Öko-Institut: Grußworte." Accessed November 21, 2012. http://www.oeko.de/aktuelles/30-jahre-oeko.institut/grussworte/dok/538.php.

———. 2013. *Thinking and Researching in Networks. Annual Report 2012.* Berlin: Öko-Institut.

Quaschning, Volker. 2010. *Renewable Energy and Climate Change.* Chichester: Wiley.

Reiche, Danyel. 2004. *Rahmenbedingungen für erneuerbare Energien in Deutschland. Möglichkeiten und Grenzen einer Vorreiterpolitik.* Frankfurt: Peter Lang.

Rolf Disch Solar Architecture. Accessed April 12, 2013. http://www.rolfdisch.de/index.php?p=home&pid=78&L=O&host=2#a287.

Roose, Jochen. 2002. *Made by Öko-Institut: Wissenschaft in einer bewegten Umwelt.* Freiburg: Öko-Institut.

Rose-Ackerman, Susan. 1995. *Controlling Environmental Policy: The Limits of Public Law in Germany and the United States.* New Haven, CT: Yale University Press.

Rucht, Dieter. 1980. *Von Wyhl nach Gorleben: Bürger gegen Atomprogramm und nukleare Entsorgung.* Munich: C. H. Beck.

Schuh, Hans. 2002. "Zwischen allen Neutronen". *Die Zeit Online,* July 4. Accessed October 2, 2012. http://www.zeit.de/2002/28/Zwischen_allen_Neutronen.

Solar Factory. Accessed March 30, 2013. http://www.solar-fabrik.de.
Toke, David. 2011. "Ecological Modernisation, Social Movements and Renewable Energy." *Environmental Politics* 20(1): 60–77.
Toke, David, and Volkmar Lauber. 2007. "Anglo-Saxon and German Approaches to Neoliberalism and Environmental Policy: The Case of Financing Renewable Energy." *Geoforum* 38: 677–87.
Vasi, Ion Bogdan. 2009. "Social Movements and Industry Development: The Environmental Movement's Impact on the Wind Energy Industry." *Mobilization* 14(3): 315–36.
Weingart, Peter. 1998. "Science and the Media." *Research Policy* 27: 869–79.
"Waldeslust und Widerstand." 1975. *Der Spiegel* 30: 41–43.
Zentrum für Erneuerbare Energien an der Albert-Ludwigs-Universität Freiburg (ZEE). Accessed March 30, 2013. http://www.zee-uni-freiburg.de/index.php?id=17&L=1.

CHAPTER 3

NIMBY and YIMBY

Movements For and Against Renewable Energy in Germany and the United States

Miranda Schreurs and Dörte Ohlhorst

"Doubts as springboards rather than quagmires."
—Christopher J. Newfield

After years of slow growth, renewable energy is booming. In 2011, renewables accounted for close to half of all new electricity capacity added and produced an estimated 19 percent of global electricity. Renewable energy growth rates have been particularly strong in Europe, where 71 percent of total electricity capacity growth was due to renewables. In Germany, renewables accounted for less than 12 percent of electricity consumption in 2006. At the end of 2013, they accounted for 25 percent, a fantastic expansion in just a few years' time. In the United States too, there has been considerable growth in renewable energy capacity (39 percent of electricity capacity additions in 2011). Nine states generated more than 10 percent of their electricity from non-hydro renewables in 2011 (REN 21 2012: 14). Concerns about climate change, a recognition that fossil fuel supplies are limited, a desire to reduce energy import dependency, demands from environmentalists, and the diffusion of interest and know-how are some of the factors behind this growth.

Support for renewable energy is quite high in many parts of the world. Opposition to renewable energy projects, however, is also becoming a reality that policy makers and the renewable energy industry must address. To understand both support for and opposition to renewable energy projects, the cases of Germany and California—two leaders in renewable energy development with publics that are strongly environmentally-minded—are examined. Both have plans for large-scale and rapid development of renewable energy infrastructure but are facing protests to specific renewable energy projects. In some cases, these protests are leading to delays or even cancellations of projects, while in others they are resulting in project redesign, the rethinking of goals and assumptions, and more inclusive decision-making processes.

The chapter explores how local protest in Germany and California has contributed to meeting environmental protection goals, spurring innovation in technology and project design, alterations in planning procedures, societal learning, and the democratization of governance processes. It shows that local protests and conflicts are important because they often lead to greater scrutiny of public and private energy concepts. Such scrutiny can serve the public good by forcing adjustments to large-scale renewable energy plans, enhancing environmental protection measures, or altering the distribution of the costs and benefits of energy development. Whereas governments and energy firms tend to favor energy production that is dominated by centralized large firms, bureaucratic processes and corporatist relationships, local activists often point to the possibilities provided by more bottom-up and decentralized paths of energy production.

Germany's *Energiewende*

In many ways, Germany is at the forefront of international efforts to launch a new energy path towards a low-carbon, non-nuclear energy future (Weidner and Mez 2008). Germany plans to transition from an energy supply system that was primarily based on fossil fuels and nuclear energy to one that cuts out nuclear energy altogether, drastically cuts back use of fossil fuels, and relies predominantly on renewable energy not only for electricity, but also for heating and transportation (Bundesministerium für Wirtschaft und Energie 2014). This transformation is known as the *Energiewende* (Bundesministerium für Umwelt, Naturschutz und Reaktorsicherheit and Bundesministerium für Wirtschaft und Technologie 2011; Schreurs 2013).

Although primary energy consumption is dominated by fossil fuels (about 80 percent in 2011) and some nuclear energy (9 percent in 2011), Germany has a goal to obtain 60 percent of its total energy (final energy consumption) and 80 percent of electricity generation from renewables by 2050. The *Energiewende* is more than just a reaction to the Fukushima nuclear accident. It grew out of decades of protest against nuclear energy that began in the 1970s and concerns about climate change (chapter 2, this volume). The subsequent rise of the anti-nuclear Green Party gave protesters direct access to parliamentary debates, and the Chernobyl nuclear accident led to a virtual moratorium on new construction. These movements contributed to the opening up of decision-making structures to greater citizen input, the pluralization of political party debate, and reforms in planning processes and procedures.

A cross-party consensus on the *Energiewende* has now been reached. Hildegard Müller, Chief Executive of the Federal Association of Energy and Water Industries, acknowledged that "the energy transition is no longer a question of if, but how it is implemented" (Eder 2012). The phasing out of nuclear energy is being accompanied by a phasing out of reliance on fossil fuels. The government has set goals for decarbonizing the economy: reducing greenhouse gas emissions by 40 percent of 1990 levels by 2020 and 80 to 95 percent by 2050. This means doing away with the majority of the country's coal-fired power plants and reducing reliance on oil. Natural gas is seen as a bridging technology, but eventually it, too, will need to be largely scaled back.

This planned transformation can be likened to a low-carbon energy revolution. It will require large-scale improvements in energy efficiency and the development of much new renewable energy infrastructure, including on- and offshore wind parks; rooftop as well as large-scale photovoltaic installations; biomass and biogas plants, and geothermal facilities. It will also be necessary to increase electricity storage capacity and extend and reinforce the electricity grid (Sachverständigenrat für Umweltfragen 2011).

The idea of going renewable is broadly supported by the German public. There are even many YIMBY movements, such as the local regions striving to become energy independent or low carbon and to benefit from the jobs and economic stimulus that renewable energy projects can bring with them. Wind parks, solar installations, and biogas plants are often positively embraced by communities.

At the same time, however, NIMBY protests against wind parks, mega solar projects, grid infrastructure, and rising prices are also spreading. Some wonder whether NIMBY protests against renewable energy infrastructure or against rising energy prices have the potential to put the brakes on the *Energiewende,* much as they did with nuclear energy. Having a wind park go up in the backyard does not, however, necessarily result in NIMBY activities. It is thus important to ask why in some cases renewable energy facilities are accepted or even invited into communities (YIMBY) while in others they are opposed by various groups.

Public Support for the Energiewende

There is a high degree of social acceptance of renewable energy in Germany. Public opinion polls and interviews suggest the majority of society agrees with the country's ambitious environment and climate protection goals as well as the nuclear phase out (Kuckartz, Rheingans-Heintze, and Rädiker 2007; forsa 2009; Agentur für Erneuerbare Energien 2012a; Gradmann and Vohrer 2010; Gullberg, Schreurs, and Ohlhorst 2014). Renewables are viewed positively due to their contribution to mitigating climate change, their more limited environmental impact compared to more polluting fuels like coal, oil, or natural gas, and the role they play in enhancing energy security (Gullberg, Schreurs, and Ohlhorst 2014).

A public opinion survey of 4,060 people conducted by TNS Infratest on behalf of the German Renewable Energy Agency in 2012 found a 93 percent approval rate for a stronger development of renewable energy. Seventy-five percent supported the building of renewable facilities in their immediate neighborhood, even in states in which there are already many wind and solar parks. The acceptance for renewable energy facilities is significantly higher than for fossil or nuclear power plants. Acceptance levels were higher for those with, than for those without, renewable energy facilities in their neighborhood.

There are signs, however, of growing concern about the costs of the feed-in-tariff. Over three-quarters of respondents found the 2011 feed-in-tariff support level of 3.5 Euro cents per kilowatt hour reasonable or even too low, but slightly over half found a level of five Euro cents per kilowatt hour too high. Still, a remarkably large 46 percent accepted this level of increase in their electricity bills (Agentur für Erneuerbare Energien 2012b).[1] Whether the support for renewables can be sustained if costs continue to increase as projected remains to be seen. The cost of the renewables surcharge is set to rise to 6.2 Euro cents per kilowatt hour in 2014. There are signs of growing resistance to the rapid rise in support costs.

Another key component of the *Energiewende* is enhancing the electricity grid's capacity for the fluctuating electricity produced by wind and solar. A majority of Germans support the need for grid expansion, but no one is eager to see overhead power cables in their communities. Thus, a large majority wants to have the power cables put underground (Agentur für Erneuerbare Energie 2012a), although it is not clear that they realize that this would cost two to ten times as much as overhead lines.

Roland Menges, an economist at the Technical University of Clausthal, found that the public disapproves of the design of the German feed-in-tariff, which exempts large industries (the biggest electricity consumers) from having to pay the renewable energy surcharge. He found that higher costs are better accepted when there is a sense that there has been a fair and inclusive distribution of those costs (Agentur für Erneuerbare Energie 2012b).

Opposition to Renewable Energy Infrastructure

Despite the generally high degree of support for the *Energiewende*, it is important to understand why there is resistance to specific renewable energy projects. Research has found that technology conflicts are often tied to competing values, equity concerns, political views, and the diverging societal and aesthetic preferences of various societal actors (Bruns and Ohlhorst 2012). The German energy transformation is strongly supported, but it is nevertheless confronted by real and important societal controversies regarding how burdens and benefits should be shared across society, and how conflicts regarding values should be solved.

In a densely populated country like Germany, the introduction of new overhead transmission lines, wind parks, and mega-photovoltaic facilities is prone to conflict. Opposition comes mainly from local conservation organizations, local citizen initiatives and municipalities (Bruns et al. 2011). As a result, the government, industry, and renewable energy promoters are becoming increasingly sensitive to the need to enhance public debate and address public concerns. Failing to do so could jeopardize not only specific energy projects but the *Energiewende* itself.

Although the term NIMBY implies that people protest simply to prevent construction of renewable facilities in their own backyards, some protests are stimulated by serious criticisms of planning and implementation processes or by sound and informed doubts about the scale, location, or need for a specific project. There are often real or perceived threats to human health, the environment, residential surroundings, or the economic well-being of a community from specific projects.

NIMBY Protests in Germany

Renewable energy projects were begun in Germany in the 1980s. In the 1990s, after a law was passed requiring grid operators to purchase electricity from renewable energy producers, interest in renewable energy began to expand and larger wind parks began to be built, including along the country's coast (Ohlhorst 2009; Bruns et al. 2011). In those early days of wind turbine technology and policy planning knowhow, many problems emerged.

The first wind parks met with considerable opposition. Wind park opponents were concerned about health risks due to noise, infrasound (low-frequency sound), the shadows cast by turbines, and icy blades. They were also worried about damage to their communities' aesthetic appearance, the loss of land for agriculture and other purposes, and a reduction in the value of their real estate (Rehfeldt, Gerdes, and Schreiber 2001: 38; Ohlhorst and Schön 2010). In this early period, wind turbines were often sited very close to residential areas. Conflicts erupted between communities selected for renewable energy development and outside investors, who were often viewed with distrust.

In the early years of renewable energy development, planners did not take citizens' concerns sufficiently into consideration. This triggered protests and lawsuits, and developers were faced by court orders to dismantle some facilities (Rehfeldt, Gerdes, and Schreiber 2001: 38). Learning from these conflicts, state (Länder) building codes were modified, and minimum distance requirements between wind turbines and homes and other facilities were established. The minimum mandatory distances differed by state, but were generally around 700 to 1000 meters (about 765 to 1110 yards) (Bund-Länder-Initiative Windenergie 2012). Smaller minimum distances were set for single buildings, commercial and industrial areas, and nature and landscape protection areas.

The growing number of renewable energy facilities and their ever-increasing dimensions were criticized by citizens' groups as a technical reshaping of the land. Conservation organizations campaigned to protect landscapes and wildlife species, especially birds and bats. As a result of their efforts, developers are now obliged to file separate reports on the potential impact of projects on the landscape and wildlife (especially birds). Since the mid-1990s, wind power decrees have been developed in many states with the aim of reducing local approval conflicts. Nature conservation categories and building restriction criteria have been included in state ordinances; this has limited the areas available for renewable energy development. In sum, protest activities have resulted in the development and inclusion of a number of planning principles that have improved planning processes, thereby helping to minimize future conflicts (Bruns et al. 2008, 55f).

Still, various citizens' groups against renewable energy projects remain active. For example, in the Vogelsberg region near the Hoher Vogelsberg Nature Park that lies in the center of Germany, a group has formed to protest the building of wind parks. At an informational meeting that gathered 100 visitors, the organizers explained: "We are not opposed to wind energy. At issue is the protection of people and animals and making sure that enough distance is secured." The group was arguing against a siting decision, but also against the industrialization of a natural area: "The Vogelsberg is being threatened with becoming a wind industry park" (Zimmermann 2013). The opposition movements appear to have had some impact in planning processes and in assuring that the siting of wind farms does not encircle communities. Quoted in the local newspaper, Dr. Norbert Herr, member of the Working Group on Energy of the Regional Assembly of North Hesse, stated: "The first disclosure in the search for priority areas for wind energy in the administrative district of Kassel is nearly completed … The second disclosure is prepared, and I can say we will not do in the second round, as we did in the first. There will be significant benefits for the citizens, especially in the district of Fulda" (*Fuldaer Zeitung* 2013).

Another opposition group emerged to express its concern with the threatened loss of a particularly picturesque landscape. The group developed a video of the region that uses computer imaging to show people what it might look like were the planned wind turbines installed. The group's initiatives had some success. Their challenges led to changes in the regional plan for wind parks and a removal of the Wurzacher Becken from the list of areas for renewable energy expansion. They caution, however, that in other areas, such as the beautiful Mennisweiler, wind turbines are still being planned (Landschaftsschuetzer n.d.). Yet another group is working against the building of more wind parks in their region, arguing the landscape is already full of wind turbines. A cartoon in the local newspaper with a picture of two lovers under a forest of wind turbines is described: "A walk in the Diepholz region in 2011: The region produces 500 Megawatts of electricity from wind turbines, double as much as is used here. But, as the cartoonist, Lothar Liesmann puts it: 'Romantic used to be more exciting'" (*Sulinger Kreiszeitung* 2010).

Compared with the early years of wind energy, the technology has progressed tremendously. In the mid-1980s, wind turbines had an average production capacity of about 30 kW and rotor diameters of less than 15 meters (16 yards). By the early 2010s, wind turbines had production capacities of 7 MW, rotor diameters of 120 meters (131 yards), and heights of 130 meters (142 yards). A single early wind turbine could produce enough electricity to meet the annual needs of about three households. In comparison, a single 7 MW wind turbine can power several thousand houses for an entire year. Since the larger wind turbines are as tall as large cathedral towers, it is understandable that people are concerned about their views and property values.

Opposition movements are not confined to wind parks; they also target mega solar parks. One example is a group along the A60 country highway near the town of Fliessem. A community petition was organized to oppose an eight-hectare (about 20 acres) photovoltaic park planned along the roadway. Opponents explained: "We are not against photovoltaic, but against the location" (Hentschel 2012). It is likely that they felt the land could be better used in other ways. In another region, near Mindelheim, a movement emerged against plans for a solar park. The opponents say they do not mind photovoltaics on rooftops, but they do not want them on their fields (TV Allgäu Nachrichten 2011).

Germany's largest pumped hydro storage project, Atdorf, was also under threat from opposition groups (Hustedt 2011). Pumped hydro storage is a means for storing electricity produced from renewable energy. Wind or other renewable energy is used to pump water into the dam for storage until a time when extra electricity is needed (for example, on a low wind day). That electricity can then be produced by allowing the water out of the dam and through a hydro power facility. The project, however, "is opposed by environmental organizations and a local initiative fearing a loss of tourists. However, the respective municipalities agreed to the project in exchange for a new drinking water supply system" (Steffen 2011, 6).

There have also been protests related to the grid infrastructure that is critical to the energy transition. Without more high voltage grid infrastructure, it will be impossible to transport renewable electricity from major production areas, which are primarily in the regions with much onshore and offshore wind in the north, to industrial demand centers, which are largely in the south. Additional grid infrastructure will also be necessary to enhance the inter-regional stability of the entire system.

In the counties of Peine and Hildesheim in Lower Saxony, farmers protested against the low level of compensation they were offered for electricity masts that were to be built on their farms. For the overhead grid, masts have to be erected every 300 to 450 meters (about 330 to 500 yards). The farmers negatively compared the one-time compensation of 3,000 to 4,000 Euros they were offered per mast with the annual profits of up to 45,000 Euros that they could receive if they agreed to put a wind turbine in a field. The initiative in Hildesheim collected 40,000 signatures on a petition calling for the cables to be put underground (Göres 2012).

Due to public opposition and delays in approvals, more than 50 percent of grid expansion projects are as much as five years behind the original construction schedule. To accelerate the grid implementation, the planning authority for high-voltage transmission lines has been shifted from the Länder (state) to the federal level. This move has met with considerable resistance from the Länder, citizens' initiatives and nature protection organizations, which worry that more centralized planning will mean less influence in decision making at the regional level.

Renewable Energy in the United States

There is no real parallel to the *Energiewende* in the United States. On the contrary, there are strong pressures for the further expansion of the use of fossil fuels—coal, oil, conventional natural gas, and, most recently, shale gas. Still, there have been some measures taken to promote renewable energy at the federal level.

The 1978 Public Utility Regulatory Act (PURPA), which was introduced to promote renewable energy production and required grid operators to purchase renewable electricity, helped launch the renewable industry. The 1992 introduction of a wind production tax credit (which was 1.5 cents per kWh for 10 years when it was introduced and 2.3 cents per kWh in 2013) was a major impetus for the wind-power industry, even though there has been great uncertainty about the tax credit's future each time it has come up for renewal in Congress. These federal incentives plus state-level priorities helped make the United States more generally, and California more specifically, early global leaders in renewable energy production, representing close to 100 percent of global wind energy generation between 1980 and 1987. Indeed, from 1987 to 1995, California produced almost all of the wind energy generated in the United States. As Matt Hopkins (2013, 4) put it, "California in a sense *was* the world market for wind energy for a long time, as it was the location of almost all wind capacity in the United States." Since then other states, including Iowa, Minnesota, and Washington, have become relatively large producers, and Texas is now the giant of wind energy production, with close to three times the installed capacity of California (Hopkins 2013).

Due to the withdrawal of federal policy support in the mid-1980s, a situation that lasted into the early 1990s, the United States temporarily lost its leadership position to Europe, and especially to Germany and, later, China. Since the mid-2000s, with many more global players in the wind energy field, the United States once again began to invest more heavily in wind power, with net capacity additions exceeding those of Germany starting in 2005 (but behind those of China since 2009) (Hopkins 2013).

The Energy Policy Act of 2005 set a goal of achieving 10,000 MW of electricity from non-hydro renewable energy sources within a decade (Public Law 109-58, Section 211). This has been supported by a renewable energy production incentive. Support was also provided for renewable energy development under the American Recovery and Reinvestment Act, which was put in place to help stimulate the economy at the height of the global financial recession. In October 2012, the Obama administration finalized a program for solar energy development on public lands in six western states. Additional zones could be added in the future under the Programmatic Environmental Impact Statement, which established seventeen Solar Energy Zones, covering 285,000 acres of public lands. The initial program foresees the production of 23,700 megawatts of solar energy (Department of Energy 2012). Similarly, onshore wind and geothermal projects are being pursued on federal lands, and sites have been designated for offshore wind along the coasts of New Jersey, Delaware, Maryland and Virginia (Wade 2011). As of March 2013, the Obama administration had approved thirty-seven renewable energy projects, including twenty solar facilities, eight wind parks, and nine geothermal installations as well as accompanying transmission corridors to connect to power grids (Reuters, March 14, 2013).

State-Level Initiatives

Although there is no federal renewable energy portfolio standard, there are numerous states with specific goals and targets for renewable and alternative energy sources. In the United States, climate change policy is being led by individual states; it is a transition that is being led by bottom-up initiatives (Betsill and Rabe 2009; Schreurs 2008). As of March 2013, twenty-six states had mandatory renewable energy portfolio standards, and six had voluntary renewable energy portfolio goals (C2ES, Center for Climate and Energy Solutions 2013). Some of these states have energy plans that look similar to those of Germany. Particularly significant are California's plans, given the state's large population, economy, and history as an environmental trendsetter in the United States.

California: An Environmental Trailblazer

California is a leader in climate-change mitigation (Rabe 2009; Mazmanian, Mazmanian et al., 2008; Mazmanian et al., 2013). California is dependent on energy imports from other states to meet about one-third of its electricity demands. In 2012, the electricity consumed was approximately 43 percent natural gas, 9 percent nuclear, 8 percent large hydro, 8 percent coal, 16 percent renewables, and 17 percent unspecified. Of the renewables, geothermal and wind held the largest share (California Energy Commission Energy Almanac 2013). As in Germany, the system is still heavily dependent on fossil fuels and nuclear energy, but a low-carbon energy transition is underway.

California has had a de facto moratorium on nuclear power development since 1976. In mid-2012, it had only one operating nuclear power plant, Diablo Canyon, located on the coast near San Luis Obispo about halfway between San Francisco and Los Angeles. It is contracted to operate through 2024. As with Germany, there is a long and active history of anti-nuclear protest in California. Anti-nuclear activists have thwarted plans for new plants and forced the closing of others. In 1976, the state legislature passed legislation placing a moratorium on the construction of new nuclear plants until a solution to radioactive waste was found. Efforts to remove the moratorium by supporters of nuclear energy have failed.

Because of California's growing population, rising energy demand, and environmentally-minded and nuclear skeptical public, as in Germany, the state has plans for large-scale expansion of renewable energy in the coming decades. California introduced a Renewable Energy Portfolio Standard in 2002. The program was accelerated in 2006, requiring that 20 percent of electricity retail sales be derived from renewable energy sources by 2010. In November of 2008, Governor Arnold Schwarzenegger called for the setting of a new target of 33 percent by 2020. This goal was codified and signed into law by his successor, Governor Edmund G. "Jerry" Brown, Jr., in April 2011. The program requires investor-owned utilities, electric service providers and community choice aggregators to procure 33 percent of their electricity from renewable energy sources, with interim goals of 20 percent of retail sales by 2013 and 25 percent by 2016 (California Energy Commission 2013).

As part of an implementation strategy, the 2007 California Solar Initiative established a goal of 1,940 MW of newly installed photovoltaics by 2016. In addition, a New Solar Homes Partnership and various solar programs offered through publicly owned utilities were introduced. Collectively known as Go Solar California, a combined campaign target of 3,000 MW by 2016 was set for these initiatives (California Public Utilities Commission 2013).

The state's renewable energy goals are bolstered by California's Global Warming Act (2006), which set a state target for the reduction of greenhouse gas emissions by 80 percent by 2050. The climate and renewable energy goals are quite comparable to Germany's plans to expand the use of renewables while reducing reliance on nuclear energy and fossil fuels.

During his electoral campaign, Governor Brown called on California to achieve 20,000MW of renewable energy by 2020 as part of his Clean Energy Program. He called for 8,000 MW of this to come from utility-sized renewable energy projects. The remaining 12,000 MW he proposed should be generated at the more local level, in distributed energy systems. In July 2011 Governor Brown's office organized a Conference on Local Renewable Energy Resources, arguing that this was a critical element of the state's plan to go low-carbon and create green energy jobs. The conference argued that "achieving this goal calls for new approaches and coalitions between [*sic*] consumers, community leaders, utilities and power providers" (Office of Governor, Edmund G. Brown, Jr., 2011).

There are numerous communities that are taking a more decentralized approach to renewable energy development. The Sierra Club California Clean Energy Committee and the Local Clean Energy Alliance argue that it is possible for a decentralized or distributed renewable energy strategy to fulfill California's energy needs if major energy efficiency improvements are made (Weinrub 2010).

As in Germany, there are generally high levels of support for renewable energy in California. In the November 2012 California state elections, a referendum proposing $500 million a year in support for efficiency and clean energy projects passed despite the opposition of many large and powerful businesses (Proposition 39, Clean Energy Jobs Act) (SustainableBusiness.com News 2012). Still, as in Germany, protests against renewable energy projects—especially large-scale projects—are emerging.

NIMBY Protests in California

Dozens of large-scale renewable energy projects (wind, solar, and geothermal) have been planned for construction on public lands, including in California. While there is strong interest in going low-carbon, some specific renewable energy projects are being challenged. Environmental groups, Native American tribes, and local residents have questioned, protested, and even sued the government to stop plans for specific renewable energy projects on public lands.

Writing for the Daily Climate, environmental journalist Rae Tyson notes: "So-called 'NIMBY' activism, once reserved for projects like landfills, prisons and big box stores, has started to impact proposed renewable energy projects throughout the nation. Last year, not-in-my-backyard opposition delayed or cancelled a wide range of proposals involving wind and solar power and biofuels production nationwide" (Tyson 2012). The opposition included California's powerful and progressive Senator Dianne Feinstein—an advocate of climate change and renewable energy policies. She joined local conservation groups to stop a concentrated solar power project planned for the Mojave Desert in an area she wanted to transform into a national monument (Roberts 2009).

There are several projects targeted for the deserts of the southwestern United States, which cover a large part of southeastern California and extend into Nevada, Arizona, and Utah. One of these projects is the Calico Solar Project. The Defenders of Wildlife, Natural Resources Defense Council (NRDC) and the Sierra Club jointly filed a lawsuit against the U.S. Department of the Interior to oppose the Calico Solar Project. Stated Sierra Club representative Barbara Boyle: "We need to build renewable energy, but we can find much better places that don't harm important wildlife and habitat." NRDC's senior attorney is recorded as saying: "My colleagues and I tried very hard to avoid litigation and filed this suit as the last resort. We have focused instead on consensus building to improve as many large-scale solar projects as possible to transition our nation to clean energy sources while protecting wild lands and wildlife. The Calico project, however, is an example of a solar project done wrong from the start" (Quotes in Natural Resources Defense Council 2012). The company behind the project reacted to the protests with proposals to reduce the project's size, not build in some of the most sensitive ecological areas, and add a wildlife migration corridor through the project (California Energy Commission n.d.).

Protesters have also opposed wind parks, such as the Ocotillo facility, planned on a stretch of land 80 miles to the east of San Diego. Native American tribes and local conservationists have teamed up to protest the installation, which is to be built on land sacred to Native Americans and in an area in which the groups say local ecology could be threatened. Various criticisms have been launched against these mega renewable energy projects. The desert conservation group Basin & Range Watch, "a group of naturalists, artists, and writers who are drawn to the beauty and richness of the desert," runs a website that tracks large renewable energy projects. They track these projects with an air of skepticism and concern: "Already a dead Golden eagle was found ... at a wind turbine generator in the Spring Valley, a place with a dense population of eagles. Those who knew the area had predicted eagle mortality was likely, but no one thought it would be so soon after the project was completed" (Basin & Range Watch 2013).

Professor Emeritus G. Sidney Silliman of California State Polytechnic University, Pomona has also questioned the mega-renewable energy projects:

> Behind this transformation of desert lands is a model of energy production by large power plants situated great distances from urban centers rather than a model of local, small-scale energy production in the built environment—decentralized or distributed generation. Fossil fuel, nuclear, and hydropower generation favor large-scale power plants and transmission-distribution infrastructure appropriate to a central-station generating system, and this model is reflected in each of the renewable energy projects approved for or requesting approval for siting on public lands. It is a model that, applied to desert lands, transforms ecosystems into industrial zones linked to urban centers by miles of buzzing power lines. (Silliman 2012)

The State of California responded to nature conservation concerns tied to the development of large-scale renewables with a Desert Renewable Energy Conservation Plan (DRECP). The DRECP is intended to provide protection and conservation of desert ecosystems while allowing for the development of "compatible" renewable energy projects. It includes a Natural Community Conservation Plan, a Habitat Conservation Plan, and an Environmental Impact Report. An independent science panel in 2012, however, raised serious concerns about the scientific quality of the DRECP and its processes. Echoing the concerns of protestors, the scientific panel complained that the majority of their 2010 recommendations "have been handled inadequately or ignored." The report states: "Simply obtaining or mapping a particular data set or discussing an issue in a Biological Baseline Report is not equivalent to *actively applying this information toward achieving plan goals.*" Various specific failures were singled out, and the panel called for enhancing scientific expertise and senior science leadership in the planning process and during implementation (Desert Renewable Energy Conservation Plan Independent Science Panel 2012). Such harsh critique will certainly place pressure on the state to make improvements to the DRECP.

Comparing California and Germany

A comparison of California and Germany in terms of their responses to renewable energy development finds that in both, opposition to renewable energy development is often a call for more open and democratic decision making structures and an appeal for more decentralized approaches to energy development. Protests have often led in the long run to improved project designs and new approaches to thinking about energy development. There are, however, also important differences between the two areas, suggesting that there is room for mutual learning.

Germany and California: Cultures of Angst?

Could Germany and California be labeled cultures of *Angst* ("fear") in which opposition emerges to just about any kind of project regardless of its merits (Scott 2000)? It is true that Germans and Californians have protested many types of projects. They have opposed carbon capture and storage facilities, airport expansions (e.g. in Los Angeles, Berlin, and Frankfurt), fracking for shale gas, genetically modified organisms, high-speed rail facilities (e.g. the Stuttgart 21 project in Baden-Württemberg and plans for high-speed rail in the Central Valley of California), and the disposal of radioactive waste. There have also been many protests against various renewable energy facilities, including solar and wind parks, biomass facilities, and geothermal installations.

This characterization of cultures of *Angst* is far too simplistic. While there certainly are many who are generally opposed to large industrial projects, the protests usually have to do with very legitimate concerns—disruptions to personal lifestyles, damage to ecosystems, cost factors, aesthetics, the design or scale or location of a project, or more basically, a project's necessity. While in some cases citizens may be ideologically against renewable energy facilities on cost, aesthetic, or other grounds, in other cases they may simply want a reconsideration of a project's design, location, or scale (Dietz and Stern 2008).

The protests against nuclear energy in California and Germany are far more than just NIMBY protests against an energy technology; they are protests against decision-making structures that are viewed as closed and not transparent, beholden to powerful economic interests, and insufficiently attentive to the public's health and safety or environmental concerns. The protests against mega-solar and wind-park projects in the deserts of California and the southwestern United States have challenged how siting decisions are made and questioned the adequacy of environmental impact assessments. Protests against new transmission lines, wind parks, and pumped hydro storage need to be considered in this context.

The protests against renewable energy projects are widening into a debate about more democratic participation. In Germany, 71 percent of the population perceives that they are not sufficiently included in decision making in relation to major construction projects (Institut für Demoskopie Allensbach 2011). In California, the demand for more direct citizen input has led to growing use of public referenda to promote, oppose, and redesign major projects (Igarashi 2012).

Citizen participation and community activism have had many positive impacts in Germany. A German study showed that citizens acquired new knowledge and skills and that learning processes were set in motion as a result of participatory procedures. Participants developed more informed and differentiated opinions through their engagement in planning processes and protests. Such activities also triggered greater media attention to development plans, raising public awareness. Conflicts over the development of new renewables or grid infrastucture also at times triggered debates about whether alternatives could be explored, such as making improvements in current energy efficiency.

Protests and other forms of participation in renewable energy planning decisions have helped communities obtain compensation for disruptions caused by the implementation of renewable energy projects. In some regions, win-win solutions have been developed—for example, local energy costs have been reduced for communities hosting wind farms (Hübner 2011), and older power lines have been removed as compensation for acceptance of new ones. In many cases, adjustments were made to a facility's siting or to the route of an overhead power line; sometimes, but rarely, projects have been completely abandoned in response to opposition.[2]

Plan N in Germany is a catalogue of over eighty policy recommendations for the renovation and expansion of electricity networks developed in 2010 by the Grid Integration of Renewable Energies Forum of the German NGO Deutsche Umwelthilfe. The forum brings together different stakeholders and citizens affected by grid development. An analysis conducted in 2012 of what has become of the recommendations showed that, on balance, some citizens' demands were met, but many remain only partially addressed, or have not been addressed at all. The greatest progress has been made in terms of meeting demands for early citizen access to information, rights to participation, and transparency in planning processes. Planning data are now regularly made available for examination and public consultation in federal network planning. The assessment found that Plan N's recommendation that new power lines be buried underground when the additional cost factor is within 2.75 times the cost of an overhead line appears to have been partially implemented (Forum Netzintegration Erneuerbare Energien 2012).

The protests in California have also led to efforts to find alternative solutions. Senator Feinstein, for example, introduced a bill in Congress to protect the Mojave Desert and to seek support from competing environmental and economic interests. Although the bill failed to become law, she has another one in the works. Senator Feinstein has sought to bring together various "stakeholders, environmental groups, local and state government officials, off-highway recreation enthusiasts, hunters, cattle ranchers, mining interests, the Department of Defense, wind and solar energy companies, California's public utility companies, the Department of the Interior, and many others." The goal with this consultative process has been to find alternative approaches that would help meet climate change goals, but not at the expense of desert conservation. Their proposal is for a policy that "carefully balances conservation, recreation, and renewable energy development" (Feinstein 2011). The compromise solution includes proposals for land trades between the federal and state levels. The biggest obstacle to this solution will be getting the necessary votes in the U.S. Congress.

YIMBY Movements in California and Germany

Energy is a critical element of any economy. Energy installations can provide jobs to a community and stabilize energy supply. Increasingly, many individuals and communities wish to have more say over what kind of energy they consume and what kind of energy infrastructure is being built in their backyards. One of the more remarkable shifts in this area is the large number of communities that are choosing to take the energy revolution into their own hands. Civil society actors have played a major role in the diffusion of wind energy and photovoltaics.

About half of all capacity-investment in renewable energy in Germany has been made by farmers (11 percent) and other private individuals (40 percent). Partly supported by a fixed feed-in tariff that is guaranteed for twenty years under the Renewable Energy Act, photovoltaic capacity has seen huge growth since the Fukushima crisis of 2011. In 2012, Germany produced about 5 percent of its electricity from photovoltaics (compared with only 1 percent a few years earlier). Wind turbines and wind parks are also common parts of the landscape. Many rural towns are eager to introduce renewable energy facilities, as they bring investment into their regions and create jobs for young people (Happenbrock and Fischer 2012).

As of 2014, there are more than 140 districts, municipalities, cities and regions in Germany pursuing a 100 percent renewable energy goal, and some have already achieved it. Of these, seventy-nine regions are already getting 100 percent of their energy from renewable source, or have set themselves goals to achieve a 100 percent renewable supply in the short- to medium-term. These areas have substantial policies in place to achieve their objectives. In addition, there are fifty-eight starter regions that are building on the positive experience of the pioneer regions and have developed initial implementation concepts (Institut dezentrale Energietechnologien n.d.). The initiators include politicians, administrators, citizens' initiatives, and energy utilities.

The small village of Feldheim, just outside of Berlin, is one of the first to become a 100 percent renewable electricity community. The village has combined a wind park, solar photovoltaics, and a biomass facility to achieve its energy independence. The small city of Dardesheim and the surrounding region, with a combined population of 80,000, are working to become 100 percent renewable not only for environmental reasons, but also to create new jobs and businesses, as the investment in renewables is money that stays in the community rather than being used to pay for energy imports. There are also ideological dimensions to the town's interest in renewable energy. Farmers who are profiting from the support they get for putting wind turbines in their fields share those profits with neighboring communities and invest in community facilities. There is greater support for renewable energy when the entire region profits from it. Moreover, the town's renewable energy information center is located at the site of a former Russian anti-ballistic missile radar station. By supporting renewables, the community is promoting the value of peace, as reliance on fossil fuels is seen as a major contributing factor to international conflict.

Interestingly, the concept appears to be spreading. San Francisco, California hosted the first 100 percent renewable energy conference in April 2013 (Renewables 100 Policy Institute 2013). The internet company Google, with its headquarters in Mountain View, California, has committed to a 100 percent renewable energy supply for its global operations. Lancaster, CA wants to be "net zero power by 2020." San Jose aims to obtain 100 percent of its electricity on balance from renewables by 2022, and Santa Barbara by 2033 (GO 100 percent Renewable Electricity n.d.). San Jose's plan, launched in 2007, aims to achieve this through major improvements in energy efficiency and investment in renewable energy sources, especially photovoltaics. The plan is extremely ambitious, given that in 2011 only 21 percent of electricity was being generated from renewables, but the goal illustrates the desire of the community to go green and clean. San Jose's plan is a larger sustainability plan that also involves planting 100,000 trees, an alternative-fuel-based fleet of public vehicles, diverting all waste from landfills and converting waste to energy, recycling 100 percent of wastewater, greening buildings, and creating more hiking trails. Behind these ambitious goals is a vision of a city of the future with 25,000 clean tech jobs that will operate as a world center of clean tech innovation (San Jose n.d.).

Communities pursuing 100 percent renewable energy are combining environmental, economic, and democratic goals. They are acting as test sites for technology and system innovation. By increasing citizen involvement in how energy decisions are made, they are also enhancing their sense of community and democratic decision making. These initiatives can be considered YIMBY movements; they are remarkable symbols of the "people energy" behind the energy revolutions upon which California and Germany are embarking.

Publicly Owned and Operated Renewable Energy Facilities

Cooperatively owned and operated wind parks, photovoltaic systems, and biomass facilities are some of the most important innovations seen in Germany in the past two decades. In comparison, the idea of citizen-owned renewable energy utilities has yet really to take off in California, where there is apparently still only one solar company wholly owned by its customers, Cooperative Community Energy (www.cenergy.com). In Germany, there are over 650 local cooperatives that have formed to invest in renewable energy. They bring together not only individuals with an interest in supporting renewable energy, but bundle finances, roof space, legal and technical know-how, and investment and insurance risk. At times, the cooperatives are formed by individuals within a community. At other times, they may bring numerous villages together. Through such local cooperation, projects can be realized on a larger scale or go beyond the financial means of just a few people. Importantly, the cooperatives retain the profits, ownership, and a sense of pride in the community (DGRV Die Genossenschaften and Agentur für Erneuerbare Energien n.d.). They also play a critical role in stimulating technological innovation and heightening public acceptance of renewable energy systems (Mautz and Byzio 2005; Byzio, Heine, and Mautz 2002).

In Germany, there are now efforts to allow the public to share in profits associated with the new grid infrastructure that will be needed as renewable energy expands. This could expand the willingness of the public to accept this essential component of a renewable energy infrastructure. Former German Minister for the Environment Peter Altmaier proposed to let the public share profits from the operation of new power lines. Under his proposal, the public could become involved in grid ownership with shares starting at 500 Euros and an interest rate of 5 percent (*Handelsblatt* 2012).

In response to multiple protests from citizens and municipalities against new high-voltage power lines along the coastline of Schleswig-Holstein in northern Germany as part of a plan to connect wind rich regions of the north with energy-intensive industrial areas in the south, a new experiment in public ownership of the power grid has been launched (http://www.arge-netz.de/buergernetze.html). Residents of the region who are already familiar with wind and solar park cooperatives and private renewable energy infrastructure ownership are being offered the chance to purchase a share of the grid, and in return gain a share of the returns from the grid's operation. At present, a model is being developed by the network operator Tennet together with the state government, a bank, and the Federal Network Agency (Grundmann 2012). Also in some big cities like Hamburg, Berlin, and Dresden, citizens' movements have tried to gain enough public support to buy back the grid, albeit with mixed success; the goal is greater public ownership of this important electricity infrastructure.

The concept of "citizens' power lines" is based on the model of citizens' wind farms and solar installations. These innovative financial shareholding models were developed as a means of strengthening public acceptance by allowing people to share in the profits of the infrastructure with which they must live in their backyards. A survey has found that about half of all Germans can imagine making a financial contribution to the expansion of electricity networks when doing so is linked to old-age pensions, as long as their investments are hedged by the government (Morgenstern 2012).

Deepening Democracy through Public Participation

As Thomas C. Beierle and Jerry Cayford (2002, 1) put it, "A broad array of processes that emphasize face-to-face deliberation, problem-solving, and consensus building have joined traditional public hearings and public comment procedures. Policy dialogues, stakeholder advisory committees, citizen juries, facilitated mediations, and various other processes are now familiar components of the public participation mix." Public participation is important for enhancing the quality of assessments and decisions, as it can help identify the views, interests, and concerns of stakeholders, widen the range of options to be considered, improve the understanding of possible effects and uncertainties, and enhance available information. Moreover, it can contribute to the legitimacy of decisions—a particularly important matter when hard decisions must be reached—and can help educate regulators and the community (Deitz and Stern 2008).

In many ways, both NIMBY and YIMBY movements are symbols of active citizen engagement in energy policy decisions. Citizens' fights for more participation rights show their desire to be a part of decision-making processes and to have an influence on the shape of policy. Experience shows that social movements—whether opposition movements or support movements—can contribute to positive changes in existing societal structures and policy processes.

In a democracy, citizens expect to have the ability to influence decisions. Public participation related to energy infrastructure and planning can take place at many different levels—in debates about the future of the energy supply system and its social impacts, in the development of energy supply scenarios, in making decisions about where to lay new power lines, or in the design or siting of a wind park. The positive effects of participation do not, however, come about automatically. Local resistance mainly occurs when the population is insufficiently involved in the planning and design of projects or when no modifications to project plans are possible (Schweizer and Renn 2013). The German and Californian energy revolutions can only succeed if the people in the communities and regions are involved as active process partners.

Policy makers and industries pursuing development projects often underestimate the power and will of opponents. When protestors are not taken seriously, battle lines can harden. Especially in cases in which conflict could easily erupt, participatory processes are necessary to appreciate competing views and find ways to minimize potential conflicts.

Clean energy economies can be achieved either with more centralized or more decentralized models of infrastructure distribution, and with more bureaucratic and corporatist versus more democratic and participatory decision-making processes. Local protests have the potential to point us towards more democratic paths to a clean-energy future. The more that various local interest groups and individuals are involved in planning and implementation processes, the more open discussions are; the more responsibility local actors are given in the search for solutions and the balancing of alternatives, the more likely it is that they will perceive decision-making processes as fair (Krause and Pannke 2013: 4). Participatory processes are likely to help stakeholders identify with the process and its results. The result is a kind of "collaborative democracy," in which participation processes are likely to be considered effective and innovative if they go beyond merely providing information and consultation, and involve a genuinely deliberative and collaborative participatory process. Not only formal but also informal dialogue and participatory processes are democratic innovations that can result in successful solutions to concrete conflicts and further the development of democracy (Reidinger 2013: 2 ff.).

Conclusion

Transformation of the energy supply system to a low-carbon structure can only succeed if users can see an advantage in doing so. While some advantages of the *Energiewende* taking place in California and Germany are easily understandable (e.g. cleaner air, less nuclear waste), other aspects are highly complex and difficult to explain. Many benefits will only be visible in the long term. This is why developing broad public support for energy transitions is important. This means clearly communicating overarching objectives.

The public has good reason to be skeptical and unaccepting of concepts or projects that benefit only a few, or in instances in which the reasons for major changes as well as the scale and direction of change and are not sufficiently debated. The likelihood of winning acceptance for electricity-generating facilities, networks, and storage systems is closely associated with transparency, openness, and attention to ecological and human health, as well as natural aesthetics in the newly developing system design.

Responding to public demands, both California and Germany are struggling with ways to promote transparency in decision-making processes, to open decision-making processes to greater citizen input, and to address public concerns. They have both made some positive progress, but there are still many debates about how energy transitions should be implemented.

There are many questions that need to be considered: What kind of electricity system will best meet low-carbon goals? Are more centralized systems more cost-effective, or are more decentralized systems that are close to demand centers the better approach? Given the fluctuating nature of many renewable energy sources (wind and sun are not available at all times), how much conventional power is necessary to assure the stability of the electricity supply? Is gaining greater low-carbon energy inputs worth it at all costs? How much renewable energy infrastructure is acceptable, and how are conflicts with biodiversity conservation and the protection of the living environment to be addressed?

These kinds of questions are behind some of the citizen challenges to renewable energy development goals and decisions in both California and Germany. Those challenging renewable energy projects in desert regions in California and other southern states argue that they will threaten the sensitive local ecology, and require too much transmission grid, as demand centers are hundreds of miles away. Those opposing plans for thousands of new kilometers of high-voltage grid in Germany are pushing for more local renewable energy development. More local production could bring more jobs to their regions, focus investment in their communities, and reduce the amount of grid infrastructure needed. Critics of too much decentralized electricity development argue that it will be too inefficient and costly, and could require more land in total than larger-scale centralized projects.

Although participatory decision making under such high degrees of uncertainty and in relation to such big and complex questions is challenging, it is a necessary part of democratic debate. Furthermore, flexible planning procedures are particularly important to allow new knowledge, technologies, and values to influence policy direction over the long term. Once electricity grids are established, a path dependency is determined, and the infrastructure will remain for decades to come. Renewable energy infrastructure decisions must be made in a comprehensive, comprehensible, and transparent manner given the strong intervention in nature, landscape and the living environment required (Forum Netzintegration 2012). At the same time, the costs of inaction, of staying with the existing fossil-fuel dominated electricity structure that is also very damaging to natural environments and human health, must be taken seriously. NIMBY and YIMBY movements are invaluable contributors to technological, social, and political innovation in response to the challenges of energy transformation.

Acknowledgments

The authors would like to express thanks to Pam Doughman, Daniel Mazmanian, Carol Hager, and Mary Alice Haddad, as well as to the anonymous reviewers recruited by Berghahn Books who provided valuable comments on drafts of this chapter.

Notes

1. The German Renewable Energy Law of 2001 has been crucial to the growth of renewable energy. Producers of renewable energy have guaranteed access to the electricity grid. Grid operators are required by law to purchase the renewable power they produce. Producers of renewable energy are guaranteed fixed feed-in tariffs for 20 years, with different support rates for different renewable energies. The difference between the wholesale prices and the feed-in-tariff is the cost that is passed on to the consumer, and is known as the feed-in-tariff surcharge. Due to a compromise that was made with large industry when the Renewable Energy Law was introduced, intensively energy-consuming industries are exempt from paying the surcharge. Since peak electricity prices have dropped due to the renewable electricity in the system, wholesale prices have dropped. Industry pays less for electricity than it would without the feed-in-tariff. The costs of electricity for households, however, increased by an average of nearly 2.4 percent in 2012 and about 2.5 percent in 2013. The surcharge is not the sole cause of rising electricity prices; indeed, it accounts for only a small fraction of the electricity price. Still, it is slowly eating into the high levels of support for the renewable energy transition.
2. http://www.bfn.de/fileadmin/MDB/documents/ina/vortraege/2012/2012-Energielandschaft-Becker.pdf.

References

Agentur für Erneuerbare Energien. 2012a. Bürger stehen weiterhin hinter dem Ausbau der Erneuerbaren Energien. Repräsentative Umfrage des Meinungsforschungsinstituts TNS Infratest im Auftrag der Agentur für Erneuerbare Energien von August bis Oktober 2012. Accessed December 7, 2014. http://www.unendlich-viel-energie.de/themen/akzeptanz2/buerger-stehen-weiterhin-hinter-dem-ausbau-der-erneuerbaren-energien.

———. 2012b. Unterstützung für Erneuerbare Energien von der Küste bis zu den Alpen ungebrochen. Accessed December 7, 2014. http://www.foederal-erneuerbar.de/landesinfo/bundesland/D/kategorie/top+10.

"Altmaier will Bürger am Netzausbau verdienen lassen." 2012. *Handelsblatt,* September 30. Accessed December 7, 2014. http://www.handelsblatt.com/politik/deutschland/-buergerdividende-altmaier-will-buerger-am-netzausbau-verdienen-lassen/7199264.html.

Beierle, T. C., and J. Cayford. 2002. *Democracy in Practice: Public Participation in Environmental Decisions.* Washington, DC: Resources for the Future.

Betsill, M. M., and Barry G. Rabe. 2009. "Climate Change and Multilevel Governance: The Evolving State and Local Roles." In *Toward Sustainable Communities: Transitions and Transformations in Environmental Policy,* 2nd ed, edited by D. A. Mazmanian and M. E. Kraft, 201–25. Cambridge, MA: MIT Press.

Bruns, E., J. Köppel, D. Ohlhorst, and S. Schön. 2008. *Die Innovationsbiographie der Windenergie. Absichten und Wirkungen von Steuerungsimpulsen.* Münster: LIT Verlag.

Bruns, E., M. Futterlieb, D. Ohlhorst, and B. Wenzel with F. Sailer and T. Müller. 2012. *Netze als Rückgrat der Energiewende—Hemmnisse für die Integration erneuerbarer Energien in die Strom-, Gas- und Wärmenetze.* Berlin: Universitätsverlag der TU Berlin.

Bruns, E., and D. Ohlhorst. 2012. "Innovationsbiographien erneuerbarer Energien im Stromsektor: Impulse durch StrEG und EEG im Wechselspiel mit heterogenen treibenden Kräften." In *20 Jahre Recht der Erneuerbaren Energien,* edited by T. Müller, 158–89. Baden-Baden: Nomos Verlag.

Bruns, E., D. Ohlhorst, B. Wenzel, and J. Köppel. 2011. *Renewable Energies in Germany's Electricity Market. A Biography of the Innovation Process.* Dordrecht, Heidelberg, London, New York: Springer.

Bund-Länder-Initiative Windenergie. 2012. *Überblick zu den landesplanerischen Abstandsempfehlungen für die Regionalplanung zur Ausweisung von Windenergiegebieten.* Accessed December 7, 2014. http://www.windland.ch/doku_wind/abstand/abstandempfehlungen_bf.pdf.

Bundesministerium für Umwelt, Naturschutz und Reaktorsicherheit; Bundesministerium für Wirtschaft und Technologie. 2011. *Energiekonzept. Für eine umweltschonende, zuverlässige und bezahlbare Energieversorgung.* Berlin. Accessed December 7, 2014. http://www.bundesregierung.de/ContentArchiv/DE/Archiv17/_Anlagen/2012/02/energiekonzept-final.pdf?__blob=publicationFile&v=5.

Bundesministerium für Wirtschaft und Energie. 2014. *Zeitreihen zur Entwicklung der erneuerbaren Energien in Deutschland. Unter Verwendung von Daten der Arbeitsgruppe Erneuerbare Energien-Statistik (AGEE).* Accessed December 7, 2014. http://www.erneuerbare-energien.de/EE/Redaktion/DE/Downloads/zeitreihen-zur-entwicklung-der-erneuerbaren-energien-in-deutschland-1990-2013.pdf?__blob=publicationFile&v=13.

Byzio, A., H. Heine, and R. Mautz with W. Rosenbaum. 2002. *Zwischen Solidarhandeln und Marktorientierung. Ökologische Innovation in selbstorganisierten Pro-*

jekten—autofreies Wohnen, Car Sharing und Windenergienutzung. Göttingen: Soziologisches Forschungsinstitut an der Georg-August-Universität (SOFI).

California Energy Commission. n.d. "Calico Solar Project." Accessed January 15, 2014. http://www.energy.ca.gov/sitingcases/calicosolar/.

"California Referendum Passes: $500 Million a Year for Efficiency, Clean Energy Projects." 2012. *SustainableBusiness.com,* November 8. Accessed January 15, 2014. http://www.sustainablebusiness.com/index.cfm/go/news.display/id/24259.

California Energy Commission. 2013. "California Renewable Energy Overview and Programs." Accessed January 15, 2014. http://www.energy.ca.gov/renewables/.

California Energy Commission Energy Almanac. 2013. "Total Electricity System Power." http://energyalmanac.ca.gov/electricity/total_system_power.html.

California Public Utilities Commission. 2013. "About the California Solar Initiative." Accessed January 15, 2014. http://www.cpuc.ca.gov/puc/energy/solar/aboutsolar.htm.

Center for Climate and Energy Solutions (C2ES). 2013. "Renewable and Alternative Energy Portfolio Standards." Accessed January 15, 2014. http://www.c2es.org/us-states-regions/policy-maps/renewable-energy-standards.

"Das Erreichte." 2010. *Sulinger Kreiszeitung*, December 31. Accessed January 15, 2014. http://wkaweg.jimdo.com.

Department of Energy. 2012. "Obama Administration Approves Roadmap for Utility-Scale Solar Energy Development on Public Lands." October 12. Accessed January 15, 2014. http://www.doi.gov/news/pressreleases/Obama-Administration-Approves-Roadmap-for-Utility-Scale-Solar-Energy-Development-on-Public-Lands.cfm.

Desert Renewable Energy Conservation Plan (DRECP) Independent Science Panel. 2012. *Initial Recommendations of the DRECP Independent Science Panel Based on Review of Draft DRECP Materials.* Accessed January 15, 2014. http://www.drecp.org/documents/docs/Independent_Science_Panel_2012_Initial_Recommendations.pdf.

DGRV die Genossenschaften and Agentur für Erneuerbare Energien. n.d. "Energiegenossenschaften: Bürger, Kommunen und lokale Wirtschaft in guter Gesellschaft." Accessed December 7, 2014. http://www.kommunal-erneuerbar.de/fileadmin/content/PDF/Energiegenossenschaften_web_normal.pdf.

Dietz, T., and P. C. Stern, eds. 2008. *Public Participation in Environmental Assessment and Decision Making.* Washington, DC: National Academies Press.

Eder, S. W. 2012. "Strombranche beklagt Hindernisse bei der Energiewende." *INGENIEUR.de,* April 27. Accessed January 15, 2014. http://www.ingenieur.de/Politik-Wirtschaft/Energie-Umweltpolitik/Strombranche-beklagt-Hindernisse-Energiewende.

Feinstein, D. "The California Desert Protection Act of 2011." Accessed January 15, 2014. http://www.feinstein.senate.gov/public/index.cfm/files/serve/?File_id=2ab86bf7-eb36-4335-914c-de6aa7ddf3d7.

forsa—Gesellschaft für Sozialforschung und statistische Analysen. 2009. *Umfrage zum Thema "Erneuerbare Energien" 2009.* Berlin. Accessed January 15, 2014. http://www.unendlich-viel-energie.de/uploads/media/Ergebnisse_forsa09.pdf.

Forum Netzintegration Erneuerbare Energien. 2012. *PlanN 2010—Handlungsempfehlungen an die Politik. Bilanz April 2012.* Accessed January 15, 2014. http://www.forum-netzintegration.de/uploads/media/Bilanz_Plan_N_2012_01.pdf.

GO 100 percent Renewable Electricity. n.d. Accessed January 15, 2014. http://www.go100percent.org/cms/index.php?id=77&tx_ttnews%5Btt_news%5D=238&cHash=253a48367b472ab0cf41ede6ff0e1dd5.

"Golden Eagle Killed by Spring Valley Wind Project." 2013. *Basin & Range Watch,* March 8. December 7, 2014. http://www.basinandrangewatch.org/SpringValleyUpdates.html.

Göres, J. 2012. "Sie brauchen eine lange Leitung." *Süddeutsche Zeitung,* December 5. Beilage Energie, V2/2.

Gradmann, H. and P. Vohrer. 2010. *Akzeptanz der Erneuerbaren Energien in der deutschen Bevölkerung. Ergebnisse einer repräsentativen Umfrage in Deutschland 2009/2010.*

Grundmann, M. 2012. *Netzausbau und Bürgernetze. Bürgerbeteiligung und Akzeptanz beim Netzausbau.* Breklum. Accessed December 7, 2014. https://www.arge-netz.de/fileadmin/template/uploads/dokumente/12-15-11_Studie_Netzausbau_und_B%C3%BCrgernetze.pdf.

Gullberg, A.T., M.A. Schreurs, and D. Ohlhorst. 2014. "Towards a Low Carbon Energy Future—Renewable Energy Cooperation between Germany and Norway." *Renewable Energy,* forthcoming.

Happenbrock, C., and B. Fischer, 2012. "Was ist eine 100ee-Region und wer darf sich so nennen? Informationen zur Aufnahme und Bewertung." Kassel: IdE Institut dezentrale Energietechnologien. Accessed December 7, 2014. http://www.100-ee.de/downloads/schriftenreihe/?eID=dam_frontend_push&docID=1137.

Hentschel, U. 2012. "Bürger wehren sich gegen Solarpark." *Volksfreund.de,* August 19. Accessed January 15, 2014. http://www.volksfreund.de/nachrichten/region/bitburg/aktuell/Heute-in-der-Bitburger-Zeitung-Buerger-wehren-sich-gegen-Solarpark;art752,3255223.

"Herr: Bei Windkraft-Vorranggebieten auf dem richtigen Weg." 2013. *Fuldaer Zeitung,* November 27. Accessed January 15, 2014. http://www.fuldaerzeitung.de/artikelansicht/artikel/1305451/herr-bei-windkraft-vorranggebieten-auf-dem.

Hopkins, M. 2013. "The Makings of a Champion or, Wind Energy for Sale: The Wind Industry in the United States, 1980-2011," Air Working Paper Series, #13-08/02. Cambridge, Massachusetts, Academic-Industry Research Network. Accessed January 15, 2014. http://www.theairnet.org/files/research/WorkingPapers/Hopkins_MakingChampions_AIR-WP13.0801.pdf.

Hübner, G. 2011. "Nicht ohne lokale Expertise." *Politische Ökologie* 29: 69–74.

Hustedt, M. 2011. Abschlussbericht zum Runden Tisch Pumpspeicherwerk Atdorf. November 11. Accessed January 15, 2014. http://runder-tisch-atdorf.de/documents/Abschlussbericht_Stand_2011-11-21.pdf.

Igarashi, A. 2012. "A Comparison of Environmental Policy-Making by Referenda in Germany, Japan, and the United States." *Rikkyo Hogaku St. Paul's Review of Law and Politics* 86: 1–27.

Institut für Demoskopie Allensbach (2011). Akzeptanzprobleme großer Infrastrukturprojekte. Ergebnisse einer bundesweiten Repräsentativumfrage. Accessed December 7, 2014. http://www.baustoffindustrie.de/root/img/pool/downloads_2011/130911/text_handout_koecher.pdf.

Institut dezentrale Energietechnologien. 100ee-Regionen. Accessed January 15, 2014. http://100ee.deenet.org/.

Krause, J., and Pannke, D. 2013. „Bürgerbeteiligung ist kein Instrument der Akzeptanzbeschaffung! Fünf Thesen aus dem Pilotprojekt ‚Energiewende und Demokratie'". eNewsletter Netzwerk Bürgerbeteiligung 03/2013 vom 22.10.2013.

Kuckartz, U., A. Rheingans-Heintze, and S. Rädiker, 2007. "Klimawandel aus der Sicht der deutschen Bevölkerung." *Umweltbewusstsein in Deutschland,* Philipps-Universität Marburg, Klimawandel im Bewusstsein 2/07.

Landschaftsschuetzer. n.d. Landschaftsbild Wurzacher Becken durch Windräder in Gefahr. Accessed January 15, 2014. http://www.landschaftsschuetzer.de.

Mautz, R., and A. Byzio. 2005. *Die soziale Dynamik der regenerativen Energien—am Beispiel der Fotovoltaik, der Biogasverstromung und der Windenergie.* Zwischenbericht. Göttingen.

Mazmanian, D., H. Nelson, and J. Jurewitz. 2013. "Climate Change Policy: A Race to the Top." In *Governing California: Politics, Government and Public Policy in the Golden State,* 3rd ed, edited by E. Rarick, 405–28. Berkeley: Berkeley Public Policy Press, University of California.

Mazmanian, D., J. Jurewitz, and H. Nelson. 2008. "When a Sub-National State Actor Confronts a Global Challenge: California Setting the Pace and Tone of U.S. Climate Change Policy." *Journal of Environment and Development.* Special Issue. 17, no. 4: 401–23.

Morgenstern, K., 2012. "Die Rente aus dem Netz." *DIA Quarterly,* no. 1 (Deutsches Institut für Altersvorsorge). Accessed December 7, 2014. http://www.dia-vorsorge.de/quarterly-ausgaben/dia-quarterly-1-2012/fokussiert.html.

Natural Resources Defense Council. 2012. "Right Idea, Wrong Place: Groups Sue Solar Project to Protect Imperiled Wildlife and Wild Lands." Press Release, March 26. Accessed January 15, 2014. http://www.nrdc.org/media/2012/120326a.asp.

"Nein zum Sonnenstrom: Mindelheimer Bürgerinitiative wehrt sich gegen Solarpark." 2011. *all-in.de,* December 10. Accessed January 15, 2014. http://www.all-in.de/nachrichten/lokales/Nein-zum-Sonnenstrom-Mindelheimer-Buergerinitiative-wehrt-sich-gegen-Solarpark;art16873,1027414.

Office of Governor Edmund G. Brown, Jr. 2011. "The Governor's Conference on Local Renewable Energy Resources: California's Path Towards the Future." Accessed January 15, 2014. http://gov.ca.gov/s_energyconference.php.

Ohlhorst, D. 2009. *Windenergie in Deutschland. Konstellationen, Dynamiken und Regulierungspotenziale im Innovationsprozess.* Wiesbaden: VS-Verlag, Reihe Energiepolitik und Klimaschutz.

Ohlhorst, D. and Schön, S. 2010. "Windenergienutzung in Deutschland im dynamischen Wandel von Konfliktkonstellationen und Konflikttypen." In *Umwelt- und Technikkonflikte,* edited by T. Saretzki and P. Feindt. Wiesbaden: VS Verlag für Sozialwissenschaften. 198–218.

Rabe, B. 2009. "Governing the Climate from Sacramento." In *Unlocking the Power of Networks: Keys to High-Performance Government,* edited by S. Goldsmith and D. F. Kettl, 34–61. Washington, DC: Brookings Institution.

Rehfeldt, K., G. Gerdes, and M. Schreiber. 2001. Weiterer Ausbau der Windenergienutzung im Hinblick auf den Klimaschutz—Teil 1, F&E-Vorhaben 999 46 101 im Auftrag des Bundesministerium für Umwelt, Naturschutz und Reaktorsicherheit; 3. Zwischenbericht (April). Berlin.

Reidinger, F. 2013. "Direkte Demokratie und Bürgerbeteiligung: Zwei Seiten einer Medaille." eNewsletter Netzwerk Bürgerbeteiligung 02/2013 vom 09.07.2013.

REN 21. 2012. "Renewables 2012: Global Status Report." Paris: REN21 Secretariat.

Renewables 100 Policy Institute. 2013. "Pathways to 100 percent Renewable Energy." April 16. Accessed January 15, 2014. http://www.renewables100.org/pathways-to-100/.

Reuters. 2013. "U.S. Approves 3 Major Renewable Energy Projects." *Financial Post,* March 14. Accessed January 15, 2014. http://business.financialpost.com/2013/03/14/u-s-approves-3-major-renewable-energy-projects/?__lsa=7dc2-7cf4.

Roberts, J. 2009. "Solar Power on Public Lands Faces More Opposition." Solarenergy.net, September 30. Accessed January 15, 2014. http://www.solarenergy.net/News/9300901-solar-energy-on-public-lands-faces-more-opposition.aspx.

Sachverständigenrat für Umweltfragen. 2011. *Wege zur 100 percent erneuerbaren Stromversorgung.* Berlin.

San Jose. "Goal 3: Receive 100 percent of Our Electrical Power from Clean, Renewable Sources." Accessed January 15, 2014. http://www.sanjoseca.gov/index.aspx?NID=2948.

Schreurs, M. A. 2008. "From the Bottom Up: Local and Subnational Climate Change Politics." *Journal of Environment and Development.* Special Issue. 17, no. 4: 343–55.

———. 2013. "Orchestrating a Low Carbon Energy Future without Nuclear: Germany's Response to the Fukushima Nuclear Crisis." *Theoretical Inquiries in Law* 14: 67–92.

Schweizer, P. J., and O. Renn. 2013. "Partizipation in Technikkontroversen: Panakeia für die Energiewende?" *Technikfolgenabschätzung—Theorie und Praxis* (TATuP), Nr. 2, Jg. 22, 42–47. Accessed January 15, 2014. http://www.tatup-journal.de/tatup132_scre13a.php.

Scott, A. 2000. "Risk Society or Angst Society? Two Views of Risk, Consciousness and Community." In *The Risk Society and Beyond,* edited by B. Adam, U. Beck, and J. Van Loon, 33–45. London: Sage.

Silliman, S. G. 2012. "The Politics of Renewable Energy in the Deserts of California." Basin and Range Watch. Accessed January 15, 2014. http://www.basinandrangewatch.org/Guest-Silliman.html.

Steffen, B. 2011. "Prospects for Pumped-Hydro Storage in Germany." EWL Working Paper No. 7, Universität Duisburg-Essen. Accessed January 15, 2014. http://www.wiwi.uni-due.de/fileadmin/fileupload/BWL-ENERGIE/Arbeitspapiere/RePEc/pdf/wp1107_ProspectsForPumpedHydroStorageInGermany.pdf.

Tyson, R. 2012. "The New Look of NIMBYism." *Daily Climate,* January 4. Accessed January 15, 2014. http://wwwp.dailyclimate.org/tdc-newsroom/2012/01/green-nimbyism.

Wade, W. 2011. "U.S. Selects Zones in Four States to Accelerate Offshore Wind Energy." *Bloomberg,* February 7. Accessed January 15, 2014. http://www.bloomberg.com/news/2011-02-07/u-s-selects-zones-in-four-states-to-accelerate-offshore-wind-energy.html.

Weidner, H., and L. Mez. 2008. "German Climate Change Policy: A Success Story with Some Flaws." *The Journal of Environment and Development.* Special Issue. 17, no. 4: 356–78.

Weinrub, A. 2010. *Community Power: Decentralized Renewable Energy in California. Oakland, California.* Accessed January 15, 2014. http://www.localcleanenergy.org/files/CommunityPowerPublication_12-3-10.pdf.

Zimmermann, H. 2013. "Kritik an Windkraft-Standorten: BI hatte ins Bürgerhaus Jossa eingeladen/100 Besucher," *Fuldaer Zeitung,* March 4. Accessed January 15, 2014. http://www.gegenwind-vogelsberg.de/gegenwind-in-jossa/.

CHAPTER 4

Hell No, We Won't Glow!

How Targeted Communities Deployed an Injustice Frame to Shed the NIMBY Label and Defeat Low-Level Radioactive Waste Facilities in the United States

Daniel J. Sherman

A 1979 film called *The China Syndrome* depicted a United States nuclear industry and government bureaucracy with an arrogant disregard for public safety. In this fictionalized account, an industry whistleblower warned of a core meltdown at a nuclear reactor that would hit groundwater and explode back through the ground as radioactive steam and "render an area the size of Pennsylvania permanently uninhabitable." Two weeks after the film was released, a jammed pressure indicator at the Three Mile Island (TMI) nuclear plant near Harrisburg, Pennsylvania gave erroneous readings and set off a series of events resulting in a partial meltdown and the evacuation of thousands of area residents. The contaminated materials from this accident were considered "low-level radioactive waste" (LLRW). They were destined for disposal in Barnwell, South Carolina, which hosted one of three LLRW landfills in the nation. Despite its name, LLRW is not necessarily characterized by a low-level radioactivity or a low risk to human health (Parker 1988: 92–93). Instead, it is defined as any radioactive "by-product" material that is not spent nuclear fuel, materials from weapons production, or uranium mill tailings. This broad category includes materials that can be combustible or stable, with half-lives ranging from fifteen to 100,000 years. Some LLRW materials are benign enough to handle, while others, such as the irradiated metal parts from a nuclear reactor, could be instantly fatal to an unshielded human.

As the shipments of LLRW from the accident made their way to the South Carolina State border, they were intercepted and turned back by the State Secretary of Health and Environmental Control, who proclaimed:

"We take a lot of waste down here, but we don't want to take all of it for the whole country" (O'Toole and Peterson 1979: A1). Soon, the governors of Washington and Nevada, the other two states hosting LLRW sites, also turned back the shipments. The resulting LLRW embargo revealed tensions over equity and authority in the U.S. federal system of government.

The U.S. Congress responded to this crisis by devolving responsibility for the disposal of LLRW to state governments under the Low-level Radioactive Waste Policy Act of 1980 (LLRWPA). This law and subsequent amendments sought to create as many as two dozen disposal sites more equitably distributed across the country, administered by states acting alone or with shared responsibility in regional compacts. Between 1986 and 1993, individual states and regional compacts identified candidate disposal sites in twenty-one counties (Sherman 2011a: 45).

The LLRWPA assumes that states have the financial resources, organizational infrastructure, and technical expertise to select and build the disposal facilities, as well as the legal authority to impose them on local communities. Under a nineteenth-century doctrine known as "Dillon's rule," U.S. constitutional law holds that states can create, destroy, abridge, and control local units of government. By law, the states certainly seemed to hold Dahl's classic "intuitive" notion of power over local communities—the ability to get someone to do something he or she would not otherwise do (1969: 2).

The simple conception of state government power reflected in the LLRWPA left this law (and the states) ill-equipped to deal with the more complicated dimensions of power exercised between states and local communities and among the states themselves. By the mid-1980s, when the LLRW siting efforts began, the power of local opposition against undesirable land uses had been realized and framed as NIMBY. State siting authorities, wary of this phenomenon, augmented technical site selection criteria with demographic profiles designed to identify acquiescent host communities; however, these efforts to avoid local opposition failed. The local opponents to LLRW sites deftly juxtaposed the technical criteria established to guide site selection with the socioeconomic and political aspects of the siting processes employed by siting authorities—creating a sophisticated injustice frame that attacked the technical competence and democratic legitimacy of the siting agencies and contractors. This frame effectively countered the NIMBY label put forth by siting authorities and motivated significant active opposition in the candidate counties. The opponents organized more than 900 collective events of public opposition across twenty-one counties, ranging from petition drives to clashes with state troopers by masked protesters on horseback (Sherman 2011a: 2). An examination of the site selection and implementation process reveals the power of local government and citizen opposition to thwart national policy objectives. Early and intense local opposition in some states altered the implementation calculus nationwide as state governments sensitive to local pressure took strategic actions to avoid hosting sites. None of the twenty-one candidate counties ended up hosting an LLRW waste site. The local movements that thwarted these sites contributed to both technological and political innovations in radioactive waste management. By constraining the number of available waste sites, the LLRW opposition inspired innovative waste reduction strategies on the part of waste producers. By demonstrating the power of local resistance, these communities also contributed to new consent-based guidelines for the federal government's most recent efforts to locate a national facility for spent nuclear fuel.

The Creation of the NIMBY Frame

At the time Congress passed the LLRWPA, local opposition to everything from halfway houses to hazardous waste was widely recognized as a potent political force. In 1979 the U.S. Environmental Protection Agency (EPA) recognized the challenge of local public opposition in a national report on hazardous waste facility siting. The agency recommended a "low-profile" approach to reduce the "potential for opposition," noting that "when the public is unaware of a siting attempt, they are unlikely to oppose it" (1979: 18).

Hazardous waste became one of the most prominent news stories of the decade with the revelation that a small working-class neighborhood in Niagara Falls, New York, was sitting on top of a hazardous waste site called Love Canal. There was at least one national television news story a week on Love Canal or hazardous waste for two full years (1978–1980), often accompanied by images of citizens struggling against government and industry (Szasz 1994).

In 1981, by identifying "locally undesirable land uses," such as hazardous waste sites, as LULUs, Frank Popper (1981) was just the first of many observers to pen clever and increasingly pejorative acronyms for local opposition. These included NOOS (not on our street), NOPE (not on Planet Earth), CAVE (citizens against virtually everything), and the still-popular NIMBY (Dear 1992). This last acronym became the most pervasive. As described in the Introduction, academics studying waste policy picked up on the term and enriched it with telling metaphors, presenting NIMBY as a syndrome to cure (Portney 1991), a new feudalism to overcome (Dear 1992), a dragon to slay (Inhaber 1998), or an obstruction to remove (O'Hare and Sanderson 1993).

In 1988, *New York Times* reporter William Glaberson traced the usage of NIMBY to business executives employing a "mocking nickname" for local opponents of new developments, whom they believed "could push the country toward an unprecedented economic paralysis." He reported that industry had been busy in the 1980s devising ways to defeat the "NIMBY commandos." Glaberson published the results of a 1984 report prepared by Cerrell Associates for the California Waste Management Board, predicting the demographic groups least and most likely to be resistant to a waste facility. The report revealed that for state agencies and private industry charged with siting developments like LLRW facilities, local public opposition had become part of the problem definition, and schemes to avoid this opposition were programmed into the implementation of site selection. Cerrell advised its state client that "constructing a demographic profile" would "assist in selecting a site that offers the least potential of generating public opposition" (1984: 29–30). Among other characteristics, the least-resistant community profile, according to Cerrell, was a small rural population with stable residency, a relatively low median household income, a majority of residents having no more than a high school diploma, and a voting record that was Republican and conservative.

The Selection of Candidate Counties

The selection of candidate counties that began in 1986 revealed that state siting authorities recognized and even feared the potential power of local opposition. Interestingly, the candidate counties for LLRW facilities chosen between 1986 and 1992 seem to match closely the Cerrell profile of least-resistant communities. The average proportion of the population that lived in rural areas in these counties was 65.9 percent, more than forty percent greater than the national average. At $25,979, the 1990 median household income across these counties was over $4,000 less than that of the country as a whole. With 61.8 percent of the population holding a high school diploma or less, they were less educated than the rest of the country (the national average was 69.8 percent). The candidate counties tended to support Republicans in U.S. House of Representatives elections, averaging a 56.3 percent Republican vote in elections preceding the siting processes.

When the demographics of each county are compared with those of its home state, the same pattern seems to follow. U.S. Census data from 1990 show that more than two-thirds of the candidate counties had smaller populations than the county average in their states; eighteen of the twenty-one counties were more than 50 percent rural; eighteen of the counties had a higher percentage of people with no more than a high-school diploma compared to their home states as a whole; all but two counties had more stable residencies than their states overall, with a greater percentage of people occupying the same houses for the past five years; and all but two counties had lower median household incomes than their states' averages. Political ideologies across these regions are difficult to draw during this era, but voting records reveal that two-thirds of the counties cast a higher percentage of ballots for conservative Republican presidential candidate Ronald Reagan in 1984 than was the average across their home states.

The idea of demographic profiling puts a sociopolitical twist on what had been understood as a technical approach. Scholars have characterized this approach as technocratic (Dahl 1989; McAvoy 1999) or managerial (Williams and Matheny 1995), whereby technical experts implement policy according to criteria that are perceived to be objective. For example, New York's siting authority was required to identify "technically suitable" sites and "demonstrate that no obviously superior alternatives can be identified" (National Research Council 1996: 35–36). To identify technically suitable sites, the authority was set up to map, model, and score each region of the state according to "natural site features" such as geology, groundwater hydrology, meteorology, climatology, and ecology (NYSLLRWSC 1989: 1). Siting agencies in other states emphasized the technical nature of site selection. In North Carolina, a siting representative explained that site selection was based on "an examination of technical information by technical professionals using technical criteria" (Rosenberg 1991).

However, fear of local opposition inspired a different sort of process or a different understanding of technical expertise. Siting authorities turned to people like Robert E. Leak to conduct demographic profiles. In an interview in 2003, Leak told me he was an "industry hunter," working "to recruit new industries and businesses" to communities across his home state of North Carolina. Leak assessed the likelihood of opposition to an LLRW facility in counties based on "general socioeconomic and demographic information" and "political profiles" (Epley 1989: I000997). Leak said that he and others took part in "windshield" surveys of the state, where they traveled by car looking for places that were unlikely to oppose construction of an LLRW disposal facility. Notes from these surveys were later released during court proceedings challenging the site selection. One consultant wrote comments about certain sites visited during the windshield survey such as "trailers everywhere," "distressed county," or "very depressed area," then found undesirable physical characteristics such as sandy soil or marshy wetlands, and still summed up the site as "in" rather than "out." Conversely, notes next to other counties that were awarded "out" status read "affluent" or "economic development" (Farren 1992).

Information like this was later summarized in a confidential public relations assessment by Epley Associates. The report focused exclusively on socioeconomic and political factors thought to distinguish certain potential sites as less likely to form active opposition. In general, the authors of the report tended to favor sites that were suffering from economic hardship. For example, they characterized one county that would become a candidate site in the following way: "Relatively poor and undeveloped, Richmond County would benefit immensely from the economic rewards of hosting the low-level radioactive waste facility ... Given Richmond County's less-than-thriving economy and the lack of environmental activism within the county, [here] might be among the less difficult of the potential sites." The authors also noted that "the county has no apparent history of environmental controversies or environmental activism" (Epley 1989: 6352). North Carolina state representative George Miller, who sponsored the original LLRW legislation and was intimately involved in the siting process, told me in a 2003 interview after his retirement, "the sites were not primarily selected or removed on scientific grounds; the site selection was political—they wanted to find sites that would not object."

In the New York siting process, a National Research Council review found that "[technical] performance and socioeconomic criteria were combined inappropriately during Candidate Area Identification and Potential Site Identification screening." The reviewers argued that this faulty practice enabled some sites with poor technical characteristics but favorable socioeconomic characteristics to garner a high enough total score to advance to candidate site selection.

The reviewers also found that a site that was volunteered by a landowner was named as a candidate site even though it did not meet the minimum cutoff score applied statewide. This violated the state regulation that required candidate sites to be at least as good as all other sites in the state. The reviewers found that the volunteered site in question should have been disqualified because of unsuitable soil composition (National Research Council 1996: 130, 145). The reviewers' conclusions match interview statements obtained from the landowner volunteering the site. In a 2002 interview, the landowner, Art Allen, described the commission's reaction to his proposal to sell his farm in the following way: "They'd already picked their five sites, and one of them just kind of glanced it over and they said, 'This is just what we've been looking for,' so they bumped the fifth site and put us on the list, and that's how we come to get on it. It was just a spur-of-the-moment thing." This occurrence typifies a flawed process that inserted socioeconomic factors and private property ownership into the search for technically suitable sites. The National Research Council reviewers argued that the New York State LLRW Siting Commission "did not always follow its own procedures as defined in the Siting Plan" (National Research Council 1996: 130).

One final example from Illinois reveals that the state's Department of Nuclear Safety (DNS) determined that at least one candidate site was suitable before the experts it hired to conduct this technical analysis had completed their reports. An Illinois Senate investigation found that Terry Lash, the director of the DNS, told personnel involved in the siting process that "site screening is more of an economic consideration than a safety consideration" (Illinois Special Counsel 1990: 8). Lash declared that safety would not be addressed by the DNS until after economic analysis of possible sites.

The Martinsville site in Clark County, Illinois, quickly became a favored site for nontechnical reasons, including economic factors, local political support, and access to a major interstate highway. However, the Martinsville area also had less-than-desirable groundwater hydrology characteristics. Every independent scientist working on the project, including contractors from Westinghouse, Earth Technology Corporation, and Battelle Corporation, agreed that the site sat on top of an aquifer and needed additional study. In spite of this evidence, Lash testified before the Illinois Senate that the site was, in fact, not located above an aquifer, and that "the facility could not conceivably pose a threat to the drinking water supplies of Martinsville." Lash then directed independent contractors to prepare a statement "that explains why the Martinsville Alternative Site is considered to be a 'technically excellent site.'" In the opinion of the contractors, Lash "sought to compromise the professional integrity of its independent consultants by directing which scientific conclusions they should reach" (Illinois Special Counsel 1990: 13, 15). The contractors refused to issue the report. The Senate Special Counsel ultimately chastised Lash and the DNS for their "premature and ambiguous insistence that Martinsville was 'technically excellent.'"

We might expect that the technical criteria required for LLRW sites would be associated with rural areas, and that more often than not such areas fit the demographic profile of the Cerrell report. However, the evidence from the three states that underwent independent reviews or court proceedings concerning the LLRW siting process indicates that demographic characteristics played a direct role in candidate site selection in ways often at odds with the technocratic language of the site selection guidelines and the siting authorities themselves. In some cases, demographic characteristics even trumped undesirable technical characteristics. Of course, as Fischer has noted, "In the 'real world' of public policy there is no such thing as a purely technical decision" (2000: 43). Even when "perfectly" applied, a technocratic approach must engage uncertainties and trade-offs among alternatives that necessitate value-laden decisions—despite the use of technical criteria employed by trained experts (Dahl 1989). As a result, a technocratic approach is exceedingly vulnerable in application. Any deviation from the technical criteria, or any indication of a value judgment on the part of the "experts," could undermine public trust in the process and the authorities charged to implement it. Demographic profiling in site selection had just this effect. Such profiling was an attempt to implement a "solution" that followed from the inclusion of local opposition as part of the LLRW problem definition. But the perception of injustice in these practices became the cornerstone of an alternative problem definition put forth by local opponents—the problem of environmental justice.

Environmental Justice

In the early 1980s, just as industry groups were popularizing the NIMBY acronym to describe local opposition, the activists comprising that opposition were popularizing the concept of environmental justice. In 1982, local activists joined with national leaders of the civil rights movement in acts of civil disobedience to oppose the construction of a hazardous waste facility in Warren County, North Carolina. The activists argued that the site was technically inferior because of its shallow water table, and that state authorities had targeted Warren County because it was home to a higher percentage of low-income and black residents than the rest of the state. Despite activists' marches, hunger strikes, and sit-ins in front of dump trucks, the facility was built.

However, the link between the siting of waste facilities and justice concerns gained momentum. Highly publicized studies by the U.S. General Accounting Office (GAO 1983) and the United Church of Christ's Commission on Racial Justice (UCC 1987) found that hazardous waste sites were disproportionately located near minority communities. In 1991, the National People of Color Environmental Leadership Summit convened a multitude of community activists in what could fairly be called a social movement around shared policy goals. A new field of academic analysis focused on the demographic distribution of existing sources of negative environmental consequences (Bullard 1983; Mohai and Saha 2007) and the development of an environmental justice movement (Pellow and Brulle 2005). In 1994, President Clinton signed Executive Order 12898 "to address environmental justice in minority populations and low-income populations." The EPA developed the following definition of environmental justice:

> The fair treatment and meaningful involvement of all people regardless of race, color, national origin, or income with respect to the development, implementation, and enforcement of environmental laws, regulations, and policies. Fair treatment means that no group of people, including racial, ethnic, or socioeconomic group should bear a disproportionate share of the negative environmental consequences resulting from industrial, municipal, and commercial operations or the execution of federal, state, local, and tribal programs and policies. (EPA 1998: 6)

The EPA guidance document on environmental justice defines two populations of concern: "minority populations," which are taken to mean all self-identified nonwhite people and Hispanics; and "low-income populations," which include those households that fall below the annual statistical poverty thresholds established in the Current Population Reports of the U.S. Census Bureau. The EPA's guidance is less clear on the thresholds of minority and low-income populations subjected to environmental hazards that should raise environmental justice concerns. It suggests that a population may be significant if it is "meaningfully greater" than the minority or low-income population in the general population or other "appropriate unit of geographic analysis" (EPA 1998: 11–12). Radion International, a private contractor that consults on environmental justice compliance issues, developed a formula of relative ratios, comparing the demographics of the immediate area hosting a given site to the larger area out of which the immediate site was selected (Crum et al. 1999). Following is the formula for the relative ratio strategy for environmental justice analysis:

R = relative ratio = ratio A/ratio B
ratio A = Mp/Mr
ratio B = NMp/NMr

where p is the proximate zone in the area within a given region of influence (in this case, the county), r is the reference area outside of the region of influence (in this case, the state minus the county), M is the minority population, and NM is the non-minority population. The same formula holds for low-income assessment, with the substitution of low-income population for minority population and non-low-income population for non-minority population.

This strategy applies the rule that if the relative ratio is less than one, there is no potential for disparate environmental harm. Table 4.1 presents the relative ratios for minority and low-income populations in the twenty-one counties facing a proposed LLRW facility.

The results of this assessment reveal that most counties selected as candidate sites for an LLRW facility were predominantly poor and white relative to their home states. There were just four counties with a relative

Table 4.1. *Relative ratio scores for counties facing a proposed LLRW facility*

County	Minority relative ratio	Low-income relative ratio
San Bernardino, CA	0.86	1.02
Montrose, CO	0.58	1.43
Hartford, CT	1.41	0.64
Tolland, CT	0.31	0.41
Clark, IL	0.02	1.59
Wayne, IL	0.03	1.87
Waldo, ME	0.53	1.37
Lenawee, MI	0.42	0.81
Ontonagon, Mi	0.08	1.81
St. Clair, MI	0.22	0.95
Boyd, NE	0.13	2.04
Nemaha, NE	0.18	1.37
Nuckolls, NE	0.06	1.48
Allegany, NY	0.05	1.18
Cortland, NY	0.05	1.04
Richmond, NC	1.35	1.37
Rowan, NC	0.62	0.99
Union, NC	0.63	0.69
Wake, NC	0.95	0.59
Hudspeth, TX	3.12	1.74
Windham, VT	1.03	1.13

ratio of one or greater in the minority column: Hartford, Connecticut; Richmond, North Carolina; Hudspeth, Texas; and Windham, Vermont. Hudspeth County has a very large score in this column, generated by its high minority population relative to the state of Texas. The most remarkable result is that fourteen of the twenty-one counties score a relative ratio greater than one in the low-income column, and three: Wayne, IL, Ontongon, MI, and Hudspeth, TX, scored nearly a two.

NIMBY or Environmental Justice? Framing the Site Selection Process

The exercises of determining whether the information above on the demographics of candidate counties for LLRW facilities and the use of such "nontechnical" characteristics in site selection processes are evidence of environmental injustice, and of assessing whether local opposition that emerged in these counties constitutes a NIMBY response, are not as essential to understanding implementation of the LLRWPA as is a grasp of what the dominant public perception of these siting processes came to be. NIMBY and environmental justice are not objective descriptors, but subjective and politically strategic frames of meaning reflecting competing definitions of the LLRW policy problem. Scholars have employed the term *framing* to help understand how political actors strategically create messages in an attempt to further their cause (Snow et al. 1986).

The NIMBY frame advanced the LLRW problem definition that federal and state decision makers came to share, centered on continued waste generation, the technical development of greatly expanded disposal capacity, and equity in siting across states. The LLRWPA solution to this problem assumed that state authority would select and, if necessary, impose upon local communities to host new LLRW facilities. The NIMBY frame advances this problem definition and solution. The NIMBY phenomenon is generally defined as the refusal of local populations to host the negative environmental consequences of a larger public good (Wolsink 1994; the Introduction of this volume). After reviewing the academic literature on NIMBY, Kraft and Clary summarized the NIMBY characterization of local opposition as "poorly informed, interested primarily in avoiding local imposition of risks, and emotive rather than cognitive" (1993: 96). Within this frame, local opposition is a problem that is at best avoided, or at least managed to prevent unqualified, self-interested, and emotional local actors from obstructing the technical process of creating new LLRW disposal capacity for the common good.

There is evidence that LLRW siting officials attempted to depict local opposition to proposed LLRW sites with NIMBY characteristics such as ignorance and selfishness. US Ecology, an LLRW contractor in Nebraska, wrote the following warning in a newsletter to people in the candidate county of Boyd:

> There is no question that there are individuals and groups, who because of their opposition to this project, have a vested interest in prejudging the sites and presenting their opinions as fact ... The possibility of such conjecture being popularly accepted as fact is prime evidence of why we must make environmental decisions primarily on scientific study rather than perception or politics. (qtd. in Snowden 1997: 117)

This quote depicts Boyd County opposition leaders as acting selfishly out of "vested interest" and ignorantly "prejudging" the site based on opinions. US Ecology argued that Boyd citizens should not be swayed by such "perception" or "politics." Instead, serious environmental decisions such as this should be based on "scientific study." Similarly, Angelo Orazio, chairman of the New York State LLRW Siting Commission, accused activists in Allegany County of treating local residents like "mushrooms." He claimed that activists were keeping residents "in the dark and feeding them manure … We have to remember that in spite of all our efforts, many people are suffering from information starvation" (Dickenson 1990).

However, the local political actors themselves had a very different definition of the LLRW problem that challenged the very generation of the waste, the feasibility of disposal technology at new sites, equity across communities, and democratic fairness in the site selection process. The environmental justice frame, with its emphasis on fair treatment, public involvement, and equity at the community level, advanced this problem definition. Once NIMBY and environmental justice were treated as strategic frames, it should come as no surprise that local opposition expressed itself with rhetoric that did not fit NIMBY characteristics, but instead latched on to environmental justice concerns.

Opponents responded to accusations of NIMBYism by generating counter-expertise on the issue of LLRW disposal. Opponents in Allegany County, New York, responded to Orazio's mushroom depiction with declarations like this: "Get involved. Get Informed … I do my own research. With access to the pros and cons of nuclear waste, I feel capable of making my own decisions" (Jefferds 1990). Another opponent explained, "What the Siting Commission does not seem to realize is that the citizens throughout these counties and throughout the world have educated themselves to the truth about so called 'low-level' radioactive waste" (Gardner 1990). An opponent in Boyd County, Nebraska, explained the self-education campaign this way: "'Well, you know, they [US Ecology] tell us one thing and then they say "get educated. You'll understand it." Well, you know the more educated we got, the less we wanted it. They didn't seem to understand that'" (qtd. in Snowden 1997: 121).

There is some evidence that LLRW opponents consciously moved away from NIMBY themes and strategically adopted alternative frames. During the course of the siting process, some letters to the editor published by local newspapers conveyed messages specifically to active LLRW opponents, urging them to avoid a NIMBY approach to the struggle. For example, in the days leading up to a public hearing on the LLRW siting, the following letter to the editor appeared in the *Richmond County Daily Journal*:

> It is important that people from Richmond County show up [to the hearing], show their concern, seek answers to their questions and state reasons why they don't want the facility here. It is also important that those present not get carried away by their emotions. It's an emotional issue, but rational arguments are more helpful for Richmond County's cause … Don't make it easy to portray Richmond County opposition to the site as the work of ignorant roughnecks. There are too many good and logical arguments against placing the site here to allow that to happen. (1989d)

This is clearly a message directed at LLRW opponents, with the purpose of moving away from the NIMBY characteristics of technically ignorant, personalized, and emotional opposition. During the same week, the *Salisbury Post* in Rowan County, North Carolina, printed a letter to the editor warning that emotional responses were "self-defeating":

> If I scream in your face, you tend to remember that I screamed in your face instead of what I said and whether it made sense ... If you were one of them [the state LLRW siting officials], which would sway you more: emotion and rudeness and mass hysteria? Or an attempt to persuade you, through a rational and respectful marshaling of facts, that another site would be more appropriate? (Bouser 1989)

A letter in the *Enquirer-Journal* in Union County, North Carolina, warned that outsiders viewed NIMBY groups "as being interested in self economic and social preservation and not [as] the concerned residents and citizens that they are." The author then suggested that opponents focus on technical issues such as transportation and groundwater (*Monroe [NC] Enquirer-Journal* 1989b). An opponent in St. Clair County, Michigan, chastised fellow opponents for writing letters to the editor that were "absolutely ridiculous, from uninformed people on this issue." The author urged citizens to provide "realistic solutions" rather than "misinformation, rumors and threats" (Bundy 1989). Messages like these demonstrate a strategic effort to adopt a less-personal and emotional response with a higher technical level of knowledge.

Opposition

State siting authorities and their contractors did not succeed in avoiding local opposition. Opposition was the dominant response to the LLRW issue in letters to the editors of the local papers across these cases. Letters of support for the LLRW failed to constitute a majority of letters on the issue in any of the twenty-one candidate counties. In the analysis that follows, I examine letters to the editor regarding the proposed LLRW facility in the closest daily newspapers to each of twenty-one counties named as LLRW candidate sites for the duration of the siting process. The duration of each case spans from the day the county was first publicly declared to be on a short list of candidate sites to the day the siting process effectively stopped. Public expressions such as letters to the editor are less an indicator of public opinion than a measure of how the issue was framed for public consumption by the "attentive public" engaged in the LLRW issue. My analysis found that 83 percent of the letters to the editor regarding LLRW expressed opposition (table 4.2).

Table 4.2. *Reaction to LLRW site proposals in letters to the editor*

Reaction	Percentage	N
Opposed	83	803
Neutral	6	54
Positive	11	108
Total		965

Note: Rounding error is present in the percentages.

Not only was the prevalence of an opposition frame to the LLRW sites overwhelming, but it was strongly expressed. The letters to the editor that expressed opposition to LLRW can be overwhelmingly categorized as "strongly opposed" (table 4.3).

Table 4.3. *Degree of public opposition to LLRW site proposals in letters to the editor*

Reaction	Percentage	N
Strongly opposed	87	698
Moderately opposed	10	80
Weakly opposed	3	26
Total		804

Note: Rounding error is present in the percentages.

The letters to the editor in candidate counties also reveal that local officials were predominantly opposed to the proposed LLRW sites. Table 4.4 shows that most of the letters penned by elected officials expressed opposition. In addition, local governments (municipal, county, or both) in eighteen of these twenty-one cases issued a formal statement of opposition to the proposed LLRW site.

Table 4.4. *Reaction to LLRW site proposals in letters to the editor authored by self-identified local government officials*

Reaction	Percentage	N
Opposed	84	43
Neutral	2	1
Positive	14	7
Total		51

Note: Rounding error is present in the percentages.

The predominant frame on the issue of LLRW as expressed in letters to the editor in candidate counties was one of opposition. If the state siting agencies and contractors were indeed trying to locate willing, or at least unopposed, candidate sites based on socioeconomic characteristics, these results indicate that they failed. Ironically, the way in which site selection processes injected socioeconomic characteristics into the technical considerations may have inspired significant opposition. As we will see below, opposition leaders often used the site selection processes to develop an injustice frame that effectively mobilized communities against the waste facilities.

Framing the Opposition: Avoiding NIMBY

But how exactly was the opposition framed? It did not easily fit a NIMBY characterization. Kraft and Clary, who summarized NIMBY characteristics in the literature as "poorly informed, interested primarily in avoiding local imposition of risks, and emotive rather than cognitive," developed a three-part categorization scheme to assess the technical awareness, geographic scope of concern, and personal and emotional claims made in public hearings on high-level radioactive waste disposal (1993). I apply this scheme to the letters to the editor on LLRW in the candidate counties. Table 4.5 presents the results of this content analysis.

Table 4.5. *Technical awareness exhibited in letters to the editor on the LLRW issue*

Technical knowledge	Percentage	N
High	45	196
Moderate	35	149
Low	20	86
Total		431

Note: Rounding error is present in the percentages.

I found 45 percent (431) of the letters addressed the technical suitability of the LLRW facility. Of these letters, 79 percent exhibited either a high or moderate level of technical awareness, with high awareness characterized by the proper use of scientific terminology or technical criticism of specific aspects of the LLRW facility, and moderate awareness exhibiting a general understanding of technical aspects of the LLRW facility or criticisms of the suitability of the site without scientific terminology. The remaining 21 percent of the letters addressing technical suitability exhibited a low level of technical awareness, evincing little understanding of the technical details relevant to suitability.

These letters expressed opposition to the LLRW facility based on the physical characteristics of the site, the properties of the waste stream, and the repository design. Thus, as in the other cases described in this volume, they do not easily fit the NIMBY stereotype of an uninformed public. In addition, these findings match those of Kraft and Clary, who found 67 percent of individuals testifying on facility suitability at high-level radioactive waste hearings demonstrating moderate to high levels of technical knowledge (1993: 97).

The geographic orientation of the opposition is measured by determining whether the focus of concern in each letter was exclusively local or expanded to a broader region of concern as well (table 4.6). The NIMBY response is characterized by an exclusively local concern.

Table 4.6 shows that 87 percent of the letters did convey some local concern; however, only 44 percent exhibited an exclusively local focus of concern. A majority of letters had a scope of concern that extended beyond the local area slated to host the LLRW site. Again, these findings match Kraft and Clary's analysis, which revealed that exclusively local concerns failed to constitute a majority of their responses.

Table 4.6. *Geographic focus of letters to the editor on the LLRW issue*

Geographic focus	Percentage	N
Local	87	836
State	42	406
Other states or nations	11	103
International	2	17
Local only	44	420

Note: Percentages refer to those demonstrating a given geographic focus. Letters could express multiple foci, and the total thus exceeds 100 percent.

Finally, table 4.7 shows that personalization of the LLRW issue and emotional claims in the LLRW letters to the editor were fairly rare, constituting just 14 percent and 15 percent of the total letters on the LLRW issue respectively. These findings also track those of Kraft and Clary.

Table 4.7. *Emotive themes expressed in letters to the editor on the LLRW issue*

Emotive themes	Percentage	N
Personalization of LLRW issue	14	134
Emotional threats made against siting authorities	15	144

Note: Percentage refers to the percentage of total letters expressing the emotive themes. Letters can fit into both of these categories.

The point here is not that the local response to the LLRW facilities was either NIMBY or not NIMBY, but rather that—at least in letters to the editor—it tended to be framed in a way that defies the stereotypical characterization of NIMBY. Taken as a whole, these letters do not reflect technical ignorance, exclusive concern with the local area, or personal and emotional expressiveness.

Framing the Opposition: A Sophisticated Injustice Frame

If the letters to the editor do not reflect a NIMBY frame, how were the opponents framing their concerns? Opponents predominantly employed a sophisticated injustice frame. As an example of the contrast, the following excerpt from an opposition letter in Richmond County, North Carolina, exhibits the hallmarks of a NIMBY response—a low level of technical sophistication, emotional and personal claims, and an exclusive concern with the local area:

> I am opposed to the state putting a low-level radioactive waste dump here in Hamlet. It could sink into the water and kill us all. It could cause all the people to move, or what little we have. Please put the dump somewhere besides Hamlet. (Robertson 1989)

Letters like this were the exception. Many more letters opposing site selection expanded the scope of concern beyond the candidate county. The following letter from Cortland County, New York, illustrates this in the simplest terms:

> I am not in support of the nuclear dump in Cortland County. With that fact in mind, I do not want the dump in other counties either ... The solution is to stop nuclear power. (Darling 1989)

Many letters showed a high level of knowledge and attacked the technical credibility of the siting agencies, as in this letter from Boyd County, Nebraska:

> Nebraska Department of Environmental Control title 194—Rules and regulations for the disposal of low-level radioactive waste, chapter 5, Section 001, states: "the disposal site shall be generally well drained and free of areas of flooding or frequent ponding. Waste disposal shall not take place in a 100-year flood plain or wetland as defined in Executive Order 11988, 'Floodplain Management Guidelines.'" The Butte site contains about 40 acres of federally certified wetlands. Ponding typically occurs during periods of normal precipitation. Do you wonder if US Ecology really cares about our safety when they blatantly disregard the rules and regulations of NDEC? Do you wonder if NDEC is really functioning as a watchdog for the welfare of the people? Do you wonder if the Butte site was picked because of suitability or availability? (Zidko 1989)

Letters like this affix blame to the siting agencies and contractors for failing to do a technically competent job choosing suitable candidate sites and imposing unacceptable risks on the community. Scholars of risk perception have shown that the general public ranks radiation risks from nuclear power and all types of radioactive waste as among the largest risks they might face (Slovic 1996). One of the factors these scholars associate with high risk perception in the general public is the degree to which the risk is perceived as involuntary. By attacking the technical credibility of the siting authority on an issue the public is already predisposed to fear as risky, opponents could easily paint the authorities as unjust. These kinds of arguments fit what Snow and Benford have identified as a "master frame" of injustice. Such a frame identifies "some existing social condition or aspect of life and define[s] it as unjust, intolerable, and deserving of corrective action." It also attributes "blame for some problematic condition by identifying culpable agents" (1992).

I found that the majority of letters to the editor (63 percent, or 586 of 931 letters) on the LLRW issue attacked the credibility of siting authorities or contractors. Nearly 85 percent (791 of 931) of the letters charged that the decision-making process was unfair, undemocratic, or improperly influenced by political rather than technical criteria, often latching on to the very kinds of demographic profiling practices authorities were using to avoid opposition. Opponents depicted their communities as victims of an unjust, technically flawed siting process.

Snowden's analysis of opposition rhetoric in Boyd County, Nebraska, demonstrates how an injustice frame is combined with an attack on technical credibility. She reported that members of the Save Boyd County opposition to LLRW "developed a perception of environmental injustice." She included the following quotation from an activist to exemplify this frame:

> They do not care about our safety or whether they kill us. We are a poor rural site, they thought we were ignorant. We are the fifth poorest county in Nebraska, we are expendable ... This was never sited on technical merit. (1997: 146)

Thomas's 1993 analysis in this same county revealed that the most pervasive theme was that the Boyd County site was a product of politics. Subcategories of this theme included the idea that the siting process was flawed, the siting officials were corrupt, and the need for community consent was promised but not given. He presented the following quotations from opponents as examples:

> [The siting process] appears to be, to me, largely political in the early stages. It appears that a site was chosen with the criteria in mind that it be a long ways away from the press, that it be against a state line ... the people on the other side of the state line, they can't vote. They don't have much access to your media. And, so it really eliminates political problems. (1993: 89)

> They didn't look at anything geologically when they picked that site, I don't believe ... why, [laughs] the water level's two foot below the ground or so. You know, forty some acres of wetlands, and it was just a half-section of land right along the highway that they could buy. I think that's all they looked at. If you look at the county

> maps, they'll tell you it's not a good building site, even to set a building on, because of the shrink and swell of the ground and the high water table and stuff. (1993: 86)

> The site selection was very poorly done. This site characterization appears to be a conspiracy of the Compact Commission, US Ecology, and the Nebraska Department of Environmental Control to site a dump in an area out of sight, out of mind, with no consideration of guidelines, rules, or regulations. (1993: 84)

> They [the governor's Citizen Advisory Committee] were to study this issue and listen to the concerns of the people ... This area was never ever represented on this issue. (1993: 111)

These quotes exemplify an evaporation of public trust in the LLRW facility siting processes, and a raw sense of injustice that was symptomatic across the candidate counties.

Often the authors of letters to the editor were able to frame opposition in ways that disavowed NIMBY characteristics, questioned the technical competence of the siting process, and leveled a charge of injustice against the siting authorities or government. The following excerpt from a letter in the *Hartford (CT) Courant* hits all of these themes:

> Calling us "NIMBY" is far from accurate. We don't want nuclear waste in anybody's backyard. To be sure, our concerns are about health and safety and about property values. But listening to residents speak at these meetings reveals the much larger moral issue of freedom itself. The American Revolution was fought because we could not stomach taxation without representation. We certainly did not like the taxes themselves, just as we don't like the ill effects of hazardous waste dumping. But then, as now, we are dealing with a more fundamental principle: that we the people must be considered and must be heard ... [T]he selection process claims to be blind. But blindness here does not equate to impartiality; it equates, instead, to not seeing, to a dismissal of values and, ultimately, to a real and figurative darkness. The selection committee did not set foot on the three sites or even in the three towns involved. Instead, the committee relied on evidence obtained from aerial photographs. As Americans we react in the only way we can when our rights are threatened: we protest ... States need to join together today to find a common solution to the nuclear waste problem, to find national sites away from homes and schools. But let no one, neither King George III in 1773, nor any superagency in 1991, impose a "solution" without our representation. (Policelli 1991)

Opponents in St. Clair County, Michigan, were able to stitch together a similar message, exemplified in this letter:

> The location of a so-called low-level radioactive waste disposal site in our cherished water wonderland may well be the worst of all blunders. Much of the criteria for site selection is already being ignored. But we can't rely on others to support us unless we offer convincing evidence as to why St. Clair County is a bad choice for a disposal site. Fortunately, there are good reasons for all Michigan residents to be concerned about dumping radioactive wastes in St. Clair County. For example, the

> proposed site's close proximity to Lake Huron and the St. Clair River is a problem. The main link of the Detroit Water Authority's Lake Huron pipeline passes through the site. This pipeline supplies 120 million gallons of water a day to residents of Southeast Michigan, and as far West as Flint. It seems remarkable to me that a team of scientists choosing the candidate areas "didn't know about the Detroit Waterline Oct. 4 when identifying 16,750 acres in Brockway, Emmett, Mussey and Lynn township as a potential home for the proposed site." (London 1989: 6a)

Letters like this show just how vulnerable the site selection processes were to contests over the dominant perceptions of the siting process in the candidate counties. Opposition leaders were easily able to shake the NIMBY label and instead create frames of meaning that discredited both the technical competence and democratic legitimacy of the state siting authorities.

Conclusions

For more than thirty years, political theorists have written about three dimensions of power (Gaventa 1980), and all three dimensions come into view in this intergovernmental conflict between state and local political actors. The first dimension of power is often described as political resources that can be brought to bear on decision-making processes—finances, organization, expertise, votes, authority (Dahl 1969). The LLRWPA assumed that state governments had adequate resources to establish new waste sites. Once implementation began, the states seemed to recognize that local communities were not without political resources. Although states had the legal authority to impose the facilities on local communities, the vast majority of elected officials at the federal, state, and local levels depend on the electoral support of local communities. The fear that politicians feel from NIMBY is the fear of applied local political resources.

The second dimension of power is less visible and includes the "rules of the game" that determine who participates, what is to be decided on, and how the decisions will be made (Bachrach and Baratz 1962). State siting authorities were operating in this dimension of power when they designed and implemented site selection procedures. In fact, in many cases, they may have been trying to minimize the likelihood of local application of political resources in the first dimension of power by using "rules of the game" that selected for demographics thought to be associated with acquiescent communities.

A third dimension of power flows from the strategic construction and communication of meanings by political actors (Gaventa 1980: 15). It is in this dimension that competing problem definitions and strategic frames vie for public adoption. In the LLRW siting process outlined above, local opponents to LLRW facilities worked strategically to avoid fitting the

NIMBY frame that siting authorities were applying, and instead created a sophisticated injustice frame. This latter frame of opposition seized on the ways siting authorities had strayed from technical criteria in the site selection processes, and worked to undermine the legitimacy of the processes by marking the authorities as technically incompetent, politically motivated, and fundamentally undemocratic. Social movement scholars have long considered collective action frames generally, and injustice frames particularly, as key factors facilitating mobilization (McAdam 1999).

Many environmental justice scholars use the concept of "injustice frame" to explain mobilization against environmental harms (McGurty 1995; Novotny 1995; Aronson 1997). In the LLRW siting struggle, the sophisticated injustice frame was a key component of early and intense local opposition in North Carolina, New York, and Connecticut (Sherman 2011b). Some state governments responded to this pressure by effectively joining the opposition and weakening the LLRWPA with court challenges and implementation refusal. This sparked a competition among states to avoid hosting an LLRW site. Even states that had made some implementation progress halted implementation. The LLRWPA goal of two dozen new sites was never realized. Instead, the waste shipments continued arriving at existing sites, with carefully negotiated agreements that empowered host states and communities with greater authority over where the waste came from, how it was managed, and the fees they could charge for disposal.

In the thirty years that states have spent avoiding implementation of the LLRWPA, the volume of waste has declined dramatically. Congress designed the LLRWPA with a view to expanding radioactive waste disposal needs, and sought to provide a virtually limitless supply of disposal capacity distributed evenly across the country. It failed to consider the predictable constraint that public opposition to nuclear power would have on the nuclear industry, as well as the predictable innovations in waste reduction strategies that would stem from limited LLRW disposal options. By making disposal availability scarce, the LLRW opposition indirectly raised the cost of disposal for this commercial waste stream. As the cost increased, waste generators pursued technological innovations that produced less waste and enabled short-lived waste to decay to less-harmful levels on-site before final disposal. Absent the scarcity of waste disposal availability that local opposition has caused, LLRW volumes would have likely continued to increase over the past three decades. Most recently, a similar intergovernmental drama played out over the struggle to open a geologic repository for spent nuclear fuel in Yucca Mountain, Nevada. Despite Congressional approval and Supreme Court decisions supporting the federal authority's decision to build the facility, the State of Nevada has successfully undertaken political maneuvers to defeat the project. In

2010 President Obama appointed a Blue Ribbon Task Force on America's Nuclear Future to reconsider nuclear waste disposal options. Perhaps the most significant finding of this task force was a political innovation inspired by opposition movements like the LLRW resistance—that future siting decisions be "consent based" and that "affected communities have an opportunity to decide" (Blue Ribbon Commission 2012: v).

References

Aronson, Hal R. 1997. "Constructing Racism into Resources: A Portrait and Analysis of the Environmental Justice Movement. Ph.D. diss., University of California–Santa Cruz.

Bachrach, P., and M. Baratz. 1962. "The Two Faces of Power." *American Political Science Review* 56: 947–52.

Bouser, Steve. 1989. "Trying Hard Not to Be Out-NIMBY'd." *Salisbury (NC) Post,* November 11, 2.

Bullard, Robert D. 1983. "Solid Waste Sites and the Black Houston Community." *Sociological Inquiry* 53: 273–88.

Bundy, Roger M. 1989. "Get the Facts on Radioactive Waste before You Protest." *St. Clair (MI) Times Herald,* November 13, 4.

Butler, Rodney. 1989. "More Opposition." *Richmond County Daily Journal,* November 28, 3.

Cerrell Associates. 1984. *Political Difficulties Facing Waste-to-Energy Conversion Plant Siting.* Los Angeles: California Waste Management Board.

Crum, Ron, Jason Sheely, and Raquel Jumonville. 1999. *Insights: Environmental Justice—A New Era in Environmental Permitting!* Baton Rouge, LA: Radion International.

Dahl, Robert. 1969. "The Concept of Power." In *Political Power: A Reader in Theory and Research,* edited by Roderick Bell, David M. Edwards, and R. Harrison Wagner, 249–68. New York: Free Press.

———. 1989. *Democracy and Its Critics.* New Haven, CT: Yale University Press.

Darling, Frances. 1989. "Stop Nuclear Power." *Cortland (NY) Standard,* April 25, 7.

Dear, Michael. 1992. "Understanding and Overcoming the NIMBY Syndrome." *Journal of the American Planning Association* 5892(3): 288–306.

Dickenson. 1990. "Protest Leaders Treat People 'like Mushrooms.'" *Olean (NY) Times Herald,* January 19, 11.

Epley Associates. 1989. *Public Relations Assessment.* Raleigh, NC: Epley Associates.

Farren, David. 1992. *Report on the Site Selection Process for the North Carolina LLRW Facility.* Raleigh, NC: Chatham County Board of Commissioners.

Fischer, Frank. 2000. *Citizens, Experts and the Environment: The Politics of Local Knowledge.* Durham, NC: Duke University Press.

Gaventa, John. 1980. *Power and Powerlessness: Quiescence and Rebellion in an Appalachian Valley.* Chicago: University of Illinois Press.

General Accounting Office/Government Accountability Office of the United States (GAO). 1983. *Siting of Hazardous Waste Landfills and Their Correlation with Racial and Economic Status of Surrounding Communities.* Washington, DC: GAO.

Griffen, Joy. 1989. "And Still More." *Richmond County Daily Journal,* November 28, 3.

Illinois Special Counsel. 1990. *Report of Special Counsel to the Illinois Senate Executive Subcommittee on Siting a Low Level Radioactive Waste Facility.* Springfield, IL: Special Counsel to the Illinois Senate.

Inhaber, Herbert. 1998. *Slaying the NIMBY Dragon.* New Brunswick, NJ: Transaction.

Kraft, Michael E., and Bruce B. Clary. 1993. "Public Testimony in Nuclear Waste Repository Hearings: A Content Analysis." In *Public Reactions to Nuclear Waste: Citizens' Views of Repository Siting,* edited by R. E. Dunlap, M. E. Kraft, and E. A. Rosa, 89–114. Durham, NC: Duke University Press.

"Let's Protest with Dignity." 1989. *Richmond County Daily Journal,* December 12, 4.

London, Terry. 1989. "Panel Must Offer Research Case against Waste Site." *St. Clair (MI) Times Herald,* November 8, 6A.

McAdam, Doug. 1999. *Political Process and the Development of Black Insurgency, 1930–1970,* 2nd ed. Chicago: University of Chicago Press.

McAvoy, George. 1999. *Controlling Technocracy: Citizen Rationality and the NIMBY Syndrome.* Washington, DC: Georgetown University Press.

McGurty, Eileen Maura. 1995. "The Construction of Environmental Justice: Warren County, North Carolina." Ph.D. diss., University of Illinois at Urbana-Champaign.

Mohai, Paul, and Robin Saha. 2007. "Racial Inequality in the Distribution of Hazardous Waste: A National-Level Reassessment." *Social Problems* 54: 343–70.

National Research Council. 1996. *Review of New York State Low-Level Radioactive Waste Siting Process.* Washington, DC: National Academies Press.

"NIMBY's Cause May Be Our Own." 1989. *Monroe (NC) Enquirer-Journal,* December 10, 4.

Novotny, Patrick John. 1995. "Framing and Political Movements: A Study of Four Cases from the Environmental Justice Movement. Ph.D. diss., University of Wisconsin–Madison.

New York State Low-Level Radioactive Waste Siting Commission (NYSLLRWSC). 1989. "Careful Study to Identify Sites." *LLRW Frontline*: 1.

O'Hare, Michael, and Debra Sanderson. 1993. "Facility Siting and Compensation: Lessons from the Massachusetts Experience." *Journal of Policy Analysis and Management* 12: 364–76.

O'Toole, Thomas, and Bill Peterson. 1979. "A-Wastes Rejected by South Carolina." *Washington Post,* April 12, A1.

Parker, Frank L. 1988. "Low-Level Radioactive Waste Disposal." In *Low-Level Radioactive Waste Regulation: Science, Politics and Fear,* edited by M. E. Burns, 85–108. Chelsea, MI: Lewis Publishers.

Pellow, David, and Robert Brulle. 2005. *Power, Justice and the Environment: A Critical Appraisal of the Environmental Justice Movement.* Cambridge: Massachusetts Institute of Technology Press.

Policelli, Eugene. 1991. "Radioactive Waste Shouldn't Be Dumped in Anyone's Backyard." *Hartford (CT) Courant,* June 27, A16.

Popper, Frank J. 1981. "Siting LULUs." *Planning*: 47:4 12–15.

Portney, Kent E. 1991. *Siting Hazardous Waste Treatment Facilities: The NIMBY Syndrome.* New York: Auburn House.

Robertson, Lynn Earley. 1989. "Coalition to Oppose Waste Site." *Salisbury (NC) Post,* November 14, 1.

Rosenberg, Gail. 1991. "Chem-Nuke Says Coverage 'Unfair.'" *Richmond County Daily Journal,* July 14, 5.

Sherman, Daniel J. 2011a. *Not Here, Not There, Not Anywhere: Politics, Social Movements, and the Disposal of Low-level Radioactive Waste.* Washington, DC: Resources for the Future.

———. 2011b. "Critical Mechanisms for Critical Masses: Exploring Variation in Opposition to Low-Level Radioactive Waste Site Proposals." *Mobilization* 16(1): 81–100.

Slovic, Paul. 1996. "Perception of Risk from Radiation." *Radiation Protection Dosimetry* 68(3/4): 165–80.

Snow, David, E. Burke Rochford, Steven Worden, and Robert Benford. 1986. "Frame Alignment Processes, Micromobilization, and Movement Participation." *American Sociological Review* 51: 464–81.

Snow, David, and Robert Benford. 1992. "Master Frames and Cycles of Protest." In *Frontiers in Social Movement Theory,* edited by A. D. Morris and C. M. Mueller, 133–55. New Haven, CT: Yale University Press.

Snowden, Monica A. 1997. *Low-Level Is Not Our Level: The Save Boyd County Association's Response to the Siting of a Low-Level Radioactive Waste Disposal Facility in Boyd County, Nebraska.* Ph.D. diss., University of Nebraska.

Szasz, Andrew. 1994. *Ecopopulism.* Minneapolis: University of Minnesota Press.

Thomas, Larry Lee. 1993. *Communication in the Public Sphere of a Community Conflict: The Case of Locating a Nuclear Waste Repository in Boyd County, Nebraska.* Ph.D. diss., University of Nebraska–Lincoln.

United Church of Christ (UCC), Commission on Racial Justice. 1987. *Toxic Wastes and Race in the United States.* New York: UCC.

U.S. Environmental Protection Agency (EPA). 1979. *Siting of Hazardous Waste Facilities and Public Opposition.* Washington, DC: SW-809.

———. 1998. *Final Guidance for Incorporating Environmental Justice Concerns in EPA's NEPA Compliance Analyses.* Washington, DC: EPA.

Williams, Bruce A., and Albert R. Matheny. 1995. *Democracy, Dialogue and Environmental Disputes: The Contested Languages of Social Regulation.* New Haven, CT: Yale University Press.

Wolsink, Maarten. 1994. "Entanglement of Interests and Motives: Assumptions behind the NIMBY-Theory on Facility Siting." *Urban Studies* 31(6): 851–67.

Zidko, Donna. ly 1989. "Some Questions." *Norfolk (NE) Daily News,* July 8, 4.

CHAPTER 5

Protecting Cultural Heritage

Unexpected Successes for Environmental Movements in China and Russia

Elizabeth Plantan

Whether positive or negative, NIMBY politics is often presented as a characteristic part of the democratic process (McAvoy 1998; Dahl 1989; Lindblom 1990). However, these same dynamics of citizen organization, protest, and government/corporate response can also occur in non-democratic contexts. Perhaps surprisingly, NIMBY politics in constrained political environments can still produce the types of positive innovation mentioned in the early chapters of this volume discussing Germany and the United States. The Gunter chapter on China and the Dalian power plant and the Haddad chapter on polluting factories in Taiwan and South Korea also illustrate the lasting effects that NIMBY politics can have, even in a politically constrained environment with a relatively weak civil society.

This chapter introduces two cases of NIMBY politics in politically restrictive societies with similar characteristics of environmental degradation: Russia and China. The comparison of Russia and China allows for a broader understanding of the factors that allow NIMBY politics to lead to innovation despite political constraints. While the political environments in both China and Russia are not traditionally conducive to collective action, there have been some important exceptions in which environmental movements have successfully challenged large infrastructural projects. The present study examines the factors that may account for the ability of these local NIMBY movements to foster innovative approaches to the policy process.

Previous studies have provided important insights into the divergent approaches to economic and political reforms in Russia and China (Pei 1994; Popov 2000). While several of the effects of the Chinese and Russian transitions have been explored in the literature (Hitt et al. 2004; Sun 1999), none of the research has compared the contribution of these reforms to environmental degradation in the two countries. Environmental degradation as a result of economic reform, while understudied in the literature, is an important factor in continuing political reforms in both China and Russia. As a generally "permitted" subject for expressing dissent, environmental issues provide members of the public with an unprecedented opportunity to voice their concerns to local, regional, and national governments. Environmental social movements, including NIMBY protest, are one of the most promising developments for improving state-society relations in both countries.

Shared History of Environmental Degradation and Political Constraints

Russia and China share a history of reforms that led to rapid industrialization and the large-scale exploitation of natural resources. At the height of Communist reforms in both countries,[1] the state of the natural environment was overlooked while natural resources were funneled into ambitious plans for industrialization and collectivization. From Stalin's push to complete the second five-year plan to Krushchev's Virgin Lands campaign to Brezhnev's Siberian river diversion, Soviet leaders endorsed policies that would "locate and exploit the empire's great natural and mineral resources" to expand development, simultaneously enforcing a Communist-era "political myth" that harnessing natural resources was "for the benefit of the masses" (Josephson 2010: 39; Ziegler 1985: 368). This Soviet ideological mantra of human control over nature was also reflected in Chinese policies under Mao Zedong. The dominant ideology at the time confirmed that "humans … could change nature and force it to serve them" (Bao 2010: 329). The idea that man could conquer nature inspired the huge irrigation projects, reservoirs, and dams constructed during the Great Leap Forward.[2]

During the Deng Xiaoping-initiated reform era (1976–1989) and Gorbachev's reforms of the 1980s, concern for the environment began to become a policy priority alongside economic development. In Russia, however, the environmental concern that followed the Chernobyl nuclear disaster was short-lived. After the fall of the Soviet Union, economic imperatives again elevated natural resource extraction to top priority. By the 1990s, any environmental gains from the post-Soviet economic collapse had been "offset by the growing extraction of natural resources, including the rapid development of the oil and gas sector" (Henry 2009: 49). As for China, though Deng's reforms led to the first constitutional provision for environmental protection in 1978, these laws were "rarely observed by polluters and seldom properly enforced by the authorities" (Bao 2010:

338; Lee 2005: 36). Local authorities focused more on increasing economic growth in their regions than on environmental protection. The regulatory structure remained ill-equipped to control environmental degradation at the local level while maintaining a national imperative for economic growth.

As a result of economic reforms and subsequent rapid development, chronic environmental problems persist in both China and Russia. In Russia, economic incentives for natural resource extraction have led to serious environmental degradation, such as deforestation from illegal logging and pollution from the extraction of iron ore, non-ferrous metals, and oil (Ostroverkh 2012; Tyutyunova et al. 2008). This strategy of placing economic development above environmental concerns has also led to serious environmental degradation in China. The pollution in China's major rivers is so serious that 80 percent no longer support fish, and nearly 300 million rural residents lack access to safe drinking water (Cann et al. 2005: 6; BBC Chinese 2012). In 2005, an estimated $112 billion was lost in economic productivity due to the human health impact of air pollution, including medical expenses, wage losses, and leisure losses (Matus et al. 2012). The legacy of reforms and rapid economic growth continue to contribute to environmental problems in Russia and China.

Despite the chronic environmental problems created in the last century, public ability to address these problems remains limited in both countries. While the Russian 1995 Federal Law on Ecological Expertise states that citizens and NGOs have the right to participate in environmental inspections, scientific experts and NGO representatives are largely excluded from policy making (Henry 2009: 59). Scientific experts in Russia have little faith in existing regulations. Even before Putin dissolved the Ministry of the Environment and gave its responsibilities to the Ministry of Natural Resources, an overwhelming majority of Russian scientific experts (73 percent) did not feel that the existing regulatory bodies were able to address environmental issues effectively (Protasov 1999: 605). Without credible regulatory agencies, Russian environmental organizations have begun to take on the responsibilities of monitoring and enforcement in "their own backyards."

Similarly, Chinese environmental enforcement mechanisms have led to citizen concern regarding environmental practices at the local level. The State Environmental Protection Administration (SEPA) is responsible for enforcement of national environmental laws at the national level, but implementation of these laws is predominantly local (Economy 2005: 104). Local implementation is much harder to monitor and enforce, which has led to many environmental transgressions at this level. While Chinese tolerance for political dissent is limited, citizens have been able, in some circumstances, to voice concern about poor local environmental practices, but not to launch larger complaints about national environmental policy. The environmental movement in China is, therefore, relatively limited to protecting "their own backyard."

Differences in Political Structure

The key similarities in political constraints and environmental degradation illustrate why Russia and China are appropriate cases for a paired comparison.[3] Besides these similarities, an important difference in political structure needs to be addressed. Some scholars have classified the Chinese political system as "fragmented authoritarianism," arguing that decision-making authority is allocated in a disjointed manner at all levels below the "very peak" of the Chinese political system (Lieberthal 1992: 8). This fragmentation of authority has important implications for the policy process, encouraging a system of "negotiations, bargaining and the seeking of consensus among affected bureaucracies" (Lieberthal and Oksenberg 1988: 3). This structure differs from the more centralized Russian political system. From competitive authoritarianism to elected or managed democracy, scholars agree that the Russian political system is far from embodying liberal democratic ideals (Diamond 2002; Colton and McFaul 2003; Fish 2005). The centralization of power for the executive branch under Putin has further derailed chances for a liberal democracy in Russia. Furthermore, while other political parties may exist, the dominant party, United Russia, strengthens the center's political power throughout the system. This distinction between fragmented and centralized authority contributes to nuanced differences in NIMBY politics in the two countries and is discussed in the analysis of the two cases.

Overview of Cases in the Present Study: Baikal and Dujiangyan

This chapter employs a paired comparison of two NIMBY movements to protect sites of significant cultural meaning in Russia and China—respectively, Lake Baikal and the Dujiangyan Irrigation System. In 2006, a local environmental movement successfully protected Lake Baikal, a UNESCO World Heritage Site since 1996, from the Eastern Siberia Pacific Ocean oil pipeline. In 2003, a local effort prevented the Yangliuhu dam project from destroying the 2,300-year old Dujiangyan Irrigation System (which was granted World Heritage status in 2000). Each case focuses on a central aspect of Russian and Chinese state economic interests: economic gain from the oil and gas industry in Russia, and further economic growth through the use of hydroelectric power in China. At the same time, both sites hold significant cultural and historical meaning for the local and national populations, which allows for the emergence of rhetoric concerning cultural heritage. These cases help focus the analysis on the strategies of local actors, national activists, and transnational networks to find innovative ways to influence the environmental policy-making process in China and Russia.

Shared Characteristics of the NIMBY Movements

As in many of the case studies in this volume, the two NIMBY movements explored here share a set of characteristics that led to innovation to protect the local environment. While the cases presented here reflect many of the factors outlined in the introduction to this volume, this chapter will focus on a few particularly salient ones. The Baikal and Dujiangyan cases illustrate the importance of developing counter-expertise through scientific information and advocacy. The two cases also show how this counter-expertise can be combined with local cultural resources to shape an alternative framing of the industrial/environmental conflict. Finally, the cases provide insight into the creation of broader networks to leverage political forces against one another.

For NIMBY movements to launch a campaign against an environmental challenge effectively, activists require scientific information on the possible effects of the proposed project. Often, the groups promoting the proposed project have their own scientific study or environmental impact statement. Harnessing alternative sources of scientific information allows NIMBY movements to develop counter-expertise. Scientists are sometimes caught in the middle between the two camps, and thus face a dilemma: to act purely as scientists in presenting "objective" information or to become advocates for a particular side of the issue.[4] The dangers of advocacy abound. The shift from science as information to science as advocacy reduces science to "a resource for enhancing the ability of groups in society to bargain, negotiate, and compromise in pursuit of their special interests" (Pielke 2007: 10).

The development of counter-expertise through science advocacy allows NIMBY activists to begin re-framing the situation.[5] Scientific information or knowledge is not the only available tool for this re-casting of the problem. NIMBY movements can also make use of local cultural resources and local knowledge to develop a broader lens through which to view the issue at stake. In the two cases presented here, the theme of cultural heritage is pervasive throughout the NIMBY movement. This cultural heritage theme is only possible given the special characteristics of the "backyard" in question. Both cases in this chapter are UNESCO World Heritage sites with significant cultural meaning for the broader population. The emergence of cultural heritage as a theme in the debate against the proposed project is an example of NIMBY activists harnessing local cultural resources.

From local actors to transnational groups, the NIMBY movements are able to create a network of diverse actors to support their efforts. One effect of emphasizing local cultural characteristics is the ability of NIMBY movements to attract diverse local actors to their cause, including formerly apolitical citizens or groups. Actors outside the domestic context of an environmental movement may also influence policy outcomes and the nature of the political debate. Transnational advocacy networks can emerge in support of the domestic NIMBY movement, including through a "boomerang" pattern in which domestic groups request that transnational advocacy networks put pressure on their government (or other targeted actor) to take favorable action (Keck and Sikkink 1998). Transnational networks are able to pressure targeted actors, often through a "mobilization of shame" (Keck and Sikkink 1998: 23). The political systems in China and Russia have barriers to political participation that may force domestic environmental activists to reach out to groups such as Greenpeace or the World Wildlife Fund. These broader networks, from formerly apolitical domestic allies to transnational advocacy groups, help NIMBY movements gain access to expanded resources. The following case studies explore the effect of integrating broader networks, mobilizing local cultural resources, and developing counter-expertise on NIMBY movements in Russia and China.

Case Study One: Protecting a Sacred Sea in Eastern Siberia

In his comprehensive study of the Russian movement to protect nature, Douglas Weiner (1999) includes a chapter on a 1960s campaign to protect Lake Baikal from the Baikalsk Pulp and Paper Mill that included the combined efforts of writers, scientists, and citizens. Although the movement focused on an ecosystem in a local "backyard," activists were able to communicate the goals of the movement to a wider audience and set the stage for the modern Russian environmental movement (Weiner 1999). This high level of environmental consciousness in the Baikal region persists, with several high-profile NIMBY-initiated protests featuring Baikal in the post-Soviet era. This section focuses on one such case, the 2006 NIMBY movement against the Eastern Siberia-Pacific Ocean (ESPO) oil pipeline.

Scientific Background: The Secret of Baikal's Pristine Water

Lake Baikal is located in southeast Siberia near the border between Russia and Mongolia. Lake Baikal is the oldest and deepest freshwater lake in the world. Formed on a rift valley, Baikal continues to deepen as the two plates move apart, which contributes to seismic activity in the region (Gulgonova and Rybalskogo 1996). Baikal's basin contains approximately one-fifth of the world's fresh water—more than all five of the North American Great Lakes combined (Grachev 2002). This deep basin is teeming with life. Approximately 1500 species are endemic to Baikal, including the world's only exclusively freshwater seal species.

Baikal is famous for its crystal-clear water, which allows for visibility of up to 40 meters in depth (Gulgonova and Rybalskogo 1996: 11). A species of tiny crustacean, Epischura baikalensis, is largely responsible for the pristine water, as it filters the surface layer of Baikal, removing impurities, and allowing the water column to remain oxygen-rich (Alferov 2005). Epischura depends on a narrow range of temperatures and on an abundance of other diatoms on which it feeds (Kozhov 1963: 246). Changes in temperature or the composition of the food web in Baikal's water column could endanger the creatures responsible for Baikal's pure water and complicate its use as a major source of drinking water. The 2.4 million residents of the Irkutsk region obtain 98 percent of their water resources (including drinking water) from the Angara River (the only river that flows out of Lake Baikal) and Lake Baikal itself (Irkutsk Oblast 2011).

Given Baikal's special characteristics and regional importance, it is no surprise that the region has sustained the environmental movement since the 1960s and earned international regard. Lake Baikal's unique properties and ecosystem were internationally recognized in 1996 when UNESCO added Lake Baikal to its list of World Heritage Sites (Grachev 2002). This status gives leverage to activists seeking to protect Baikal's pristine water.

The Eastern Siberia-Pacific Ocean Oil Pipeline

The Eastern Siberia-Pacific Ocean (ESPO) oil pipeline, a joint venture between Russia and China, was originally conceived as a means by which to supply Russian oil to northern China. In 2003, the Russian state-owned construction company Transneft began the planning stages for the route of the world's longest pipeline, stretching from Western Siberia through the Far East to China (Kommersant 2006a). Transneft's proposed route was planned to pass within the watershed of Lake Baikal, through its zone of seismic activity.

The first round of public hearings for the pipeline began in the fall of 2004. The most controversial of these meetings was in the Irkutsk region, the only region in which more than 100 comments, complaints, or questions were filed in its public hearing (Zhukov 2004). Aleksei Yablokov, former science adviser to the first president of the Russian Federation, Boris Yeltsin, recommended that the pipeline be moved at least 80 kilometers from Baikal's northern shore, citing the likelihood of a significant earthquake in the region that could rupture the pipeline (Polubota 2005). He also questioned the feasibility of employing Transneft's emergency plan in the event of a catastrophic oil spill (Polubota 2005). Given the pipeline's proposed capacity, some experts argued that it would take only 40 minutes for oil to reach Baikal's waters and cover a third of its surface (Khalii 2007).

In early 2006, Rostekhnadzor (the Russian Federal Service for Ecological, Technological, and Atomic Supervision) conducted a scientific study on the environmental impact of the proposed pipeline route. The committee, composed mostly of experts from the Russian Academy of Sciences, submitted the environmental assessment in January 2006, with 43 of 52 scientists giving a negative assessment of the proposed route (Kommersant 2006b). The head of Rostekhnadzor refused to ratify the assessment after rumored pressure from Transneft. Instead, the committee was restructured to add 34 additional members who were mostly experts in technical systems—not ecology or conservation (Zhukov 2006). This new committee produced a positive assessment that was quickly ratified, ruling in favor of the pipeline despite the concerns expressed in the original assessment. This example of the repeat environmental impact assessments shows how expert opinion was used to bolster the claims of industry interests, despite scientific opinion to the contrary. Scientific opinion developed parallel to the debate between pro-industry and pro-environmental activists—and both sides used scientific expertise to further their claims.

With Russia's environmental watchdog having failed to protect Baikal, the task fell to local environmental organizations, local community members, and concerned citizens across Russia. The work of the Irkutsk-based environmental organization Baikal Ecological Wave spearheaded the local movement against the pipeline, including organizing protests and collecting petition signatures (Weir 2008). The group itself was able to collect over 20,000 signatures from citizens who opposed the pipeline (Gulya 2008). Eventually, with the help of transnational groups World Wildlife Fund (WWF), Greenpeace, and Pacific Environment, Baikal Ecological Wave was able to collect more than 100,000 petition signatures and organize pan-Russian protests to build awareness of Baikal's plight (Mistiaen 2008; Kilner 2008). Throughout March and April 2006, protests were held in thirteen cities across Russia (Nikolaeva et al. 2006). One protest in Irkutsk attracted over 5,000 people; even the governor of Irkutsk, along with seventy State Duma representatives, supported the protesters' cause

(Orlova 2006; Kidenis 2006). Despite this flurry of activity in early 2006, a source within the Kremlin said that the ESPO project would not be reconsidered (Surzhenko and Nikolaeva 2006). The original pipeline route would go through as planned.

In a final attempt to pressure the Russian government to respond, activists appealed to UNESCO, hoping that international concern over Baikal's World Heritage status would provoke the desired reaction from the Kremlin. In March 2006, the chairperson of the World Heritage committee, Ina Marčiulionytė, sent Russian president Vladimir Putin a formal letter of concern, warning that the construction of ESPO would place Baikal on the List of World Heritage Sites in Danger (UNESCO 2006). Marčiulionytė's letter included an "urgent request" that Putin himself rectify the situation (Zhukov 2006). While there was no formal response from the Kremlin, the letter drew international media attention to Baikal's cause.

On April 26, 2006, Putin surprised everyone by coming to Baikal's rescue. Before a state visit with German Chancellor Angela Merkel in Tomsk, Putin met with a group on the economic development of the Siberian Federal District (okrug) (Nikolaeva et al. 2006). Present at the meeting was the vice-president of the Russian Academy of Sciences, Dr. Nikolai Laverov, who spoke for a few minutes about his concern for the ESPO pipeline (Kidenis 2006). After Laverov's appeal, Putin asked the director of Transneft whether the pipeline could be moved north. When the director stumbled in his response, Putin asserted that if there were any hesitation, then it must be possible to re-reroute the pipeline. The meeting was televised, a perfect set-up for publicity, showing Putin pointing a red pen at a giant map of Lake Baikal as he made his announcement. Later that spring, Transneft accepted a revised pipeline route that diverted ESPO a minimum of 400 km away from Baikal—a victory for the environmental movement (Sergeeva 2006).

Analysis of the Baikal Case

The NIMBY movement that arose to protect Lake Baikal against the Eastern Siberia-Pacific Ocean oil pipeline is an uncommon example of a successful attempt to reverse a previously set policy in post-Soviet Russia. While the NIMBY movement's success is surprising, that success is not the focus of this analysis. Successful or not, the NIMBY movement to protect Lake Baikal is an example of the ability of NIMBY protest to adapt to political constraints in innovative ways. The key factors in the NIMBY movement outlined in the introduction to this chapter—counter-expertise, local cultural resources, and broader leverage networks—are discussed in turn to trace the effects of these factors on this movement's innovative approaches to policy change.

Counter-Expertise, Science, and Advocacy

The Baikal case supports Pielke's (2007) warning that science is being used more often to advocate for special interests than to provide meaningful scientific information or recommendations for alternative courses of action. The environmental impact assessment for the pipeline is a clear example. The first set of scientists was asked to provide scientific information directly to a federal agency. However, when these scientists produced a negative assessment of the pipeline route, the agency, Rostekhnadzor, extended the assessment process and added thirty-four new members to the assessment team, most from technological systems backgrounds (Zhukov 2006). The new members were chosen to be advocates in the assessment process, and they unsurprisingly produced a positive environmental assessment of the proposed pipeline route.

On the other side of the debate, NIMBY activists gathered counter-expertise from scientists advocating against the proposed pipeline route. Perhaps the most influential scientific advocate on the side of the NIMBY protesters was the leader of Baikal Ecological Wave, Marina Rikhvanova. Rikhvanova, who co-founded Baikal Ecological Wave after working as a biologist at Baikal's Limnological Institute, used her scientific expertise to advance her cause (Weir 2008). Many other scientists offering their expert opinion in the media overwhelmingly expressed concern for the proposed route, perhaps intending to be purely scientific, but were portrayed by the media as strongly advocating against the pipeline. However scientists may have intended to portray their scientific information in the media, the point is that NIMBY activists harnessed this information to formulate credible arguments in opposition to industry advocates.

Local Cultural Resources

Framing the debate in terms of local characteristics and concerns became an important strategy for both advocates and opponents of Transneft's proposed pipeline route. When the pipeline route was first announced, industry emphasized the impact that the project would have on the region's jobs. The president of Transneft, Semyon Weinstock, even argued that the pipeline would solve Eastern Siberia's progressive economic crisis (Fadeev 2005). The media picked up on this theme of economics versus the environment, with some journalists siding with Transneft. One journalist agreed that it could be a powerful economic stimulus for the region by creating new jobs along the entire route (Vasil'yev 2006). Viktor Khristenko, the Industry and Energy Minister, argued that ESPO was important for Russia, both economically and as a strategic window to Asia (Slovo Kyrgyzstana 2006). The economic frame was supported by industry, members of the media, several federal agencies, and (at least up until April 26) President Putin himself.

The competing frame in the Baikal case, employed by the NIMBY movement, was the idea that Baikal was "more valuable than oil." Rikhvanova, the leader of Baikal Ecological Wave, referred to Baikal as the subject of legends, songs, and holy Orthodox and Buddhist-shamanistic rituals (Rikhvanova 2006). Besides invoking these spiritual characteristics, journalists covering the controversy repeatedly described the unique features of Baikal as the world's deepest and oldest freshwater lake (Skorlygina 2006). One journalist invoked the idea that the environmental movement's fight was a "holy war for the sake of [Siberia's] pearl" (Brovkin 2006). NIMBY activists harnessed local cultural resources to create a counter-frame for the debate around Baikal's special characteristics.

Baikal's UNESCO World Heritage status was often invoked as a way to justify the importance of Lake Baikal not only to Russia, but also to the entire international community. Emphasizing Baikal as an object of cultural heritage was quite a successful strategy. Rikhvanova also attributes the success of the NIMBY movement in protecting Baikal from the ESPO pipeline to the Internet, which allowed for the organization of protests across Russia and the former Soviet Union (Rikhvanova 2006). This allowed the cultural heritage message to reach a broader audience, mobilizing more people to the cause. Harnessing local cultural resources and developing counter-expertise allowed NIMBY activists to dominate the debate, overshadowing the alternative portrayal of the situation as economically positive and scientifically supported.

Broader Networks and Political Leverage

The emphasis on Baikal's local cultural characteristics, including its World Heritage status, was strengthened by the involvement of broader advocacy networks. NIMBY activists appealed to the chairperson of the UNESCO World Heritage Committee to put pressure on the Russian government. If Lake Baikal were listed as a World Heritage site in danger, Russia would be the first party to the World Heritage Convention unable to meet its obligations (Kuznetsov 2006). Activists hoped that this possibility would shame the Russian government into action. This strategy closely follows Keck and Sikkink's (1998) "mobilization of shame" and illustrates the "boomerang" pattern: when activists were not able to reach the national government through domestic public participation channels, they appealed to the international arena for assistance in pressuring their national government.

Besides the appeal to UNESCO, the NIMBY movement collaborated with other transnational environmental organizations. Greenpeace and the WWF were involved in the organization of Russian national protests, working directly with Baikal Ecological Wave (Rikhvanova 2006). This broader transnational network helped the local NIMBY movement attract people to participate in protests across Russia, and elevated the issue from a local concern to an international concern (Khalii 2007). In this way, the NIMBY movement came to achieve a wider significance and, as such, became more of a "not in *our* backyard" movement.

The Baikal Case as a Model

The Baikal case shows the ability of NIMBY activists to employ effective strategies to gather counter-expertise, harness local cultural resources, and appeal to a broader network despite constraints on public participation. Although all of these strategies were connected to the successful defeat of the ESPO pipeline, it is important to realize that these factors do not necessarily spell success in themselves. In an alternate case, the same NIMBY activists mobilized against another pollution threat on the southern end of the same lake and failed.

The Baikalsk Paper and Pulp Mill (BPPM) opened in 1966, despite growing opposition to the construction of the factory. BPPM discharged chlorinated water into Baikal's southern basin, without interruption (although its technology was obsolete from its inception) from the time that it opened until the global economic crisis in the fall of 2008. In 2008, environmental regulators finally enforced a ban on the discharge of chlorine and other chemicals into Lake Baikal. A combination of long-overdue environmental regulations and the international economic crisis caused the owner of the mill, Oleg Deripaska, to file for bankruptcy. His reasoning was that implementing the closed-loop cycle, as enforced by environmental regulators, would cost the mill too much to remain profitable. After BPPM closed, the single-industry town of Baikalsk lost over a thousand jobs. These unemployed workers protested the decision to close the mill and demanded severance wages from the mill's owners. Deripaska, well connected with Putin, appealed to Putin for some action to help people in Baikalsk who had lost their jobs when the mill closed (and to spare Deripaska from having to pay their back wages).[6]

In January 2010, Putin issued a decree lifting the ban on the disposal of chlorine waste in the Central Ecological Zone (CEZ) of Lake Baikal. This allowed the plant to reopen without implementing the closed-loop cycle that was part of the existing environmental regulations. Following the decree, there were protests from environmentalists, but also responses of relief from residents in the town of Baikalsk. The timing of this environmental battle, during a recession, without a transition plan for the town of Baikalsk, was fatal for the environmental movement. Economic issues trumped environmental concerns, and the factory reopened. Putin was again able to help his image, saving jobs during a time of economic crisis.

In the BPPM case, the NIMBY movement employed similar strategies used to mobilize against the pipeline route. They countered the government and industry argument that the chlorine was not affecting Baikal's ecosystem with their own counter-expertise showing that the chlorine was damaging the lake. Casting the issue as one of cultural preservation, the activists again appealed to UNESCO. However, these actions failed to produce a positive response from the national government. One explanation for the different result is timing. The economic argument that promoted the continual operation of the polluting paper mill resonated with the larger Russian population during a time of economic crisis. The idea that timing could affect the salience of local cultural resources is important to keep in mind when looking at other cases of NIMBY movements.

Even though the protest failed to stop the polluting activity, the development of counter-expertise led to social and political innovation as NIMBY activists and scientists united in pursuit of one goal. The emphasis on local cultural characteristics resulted in the involvement of formerly apolitical individuals and groups in the broader protest movement. Reaching out to broader networks was yet another political innovation aimed at leveraging transnational groups against the domestic government. The ability of a NIMBY movement to stimulate social and political innovation in a constrained political context, such as that of post-Soviet Russia, is an intriguing puzzle. What is more intriguing is that these same factors re-appear in the China case. The following section explores how the same NIMBY characteristics led to similar social and political innovation in a movement to protect the Dujiangyan Irrigation System.

Case Study Two: Protecting an Irrigation System in Southwestern China

China is the world's leading hydropower producer, followed by Brazil, Canada, the United States, and Russia (IEA 2010). The development of hydropower resources, specifically through damming the country's great rivers, is one of the fastest-growing ways to meet rapidly expanding demand for energy in China. The best-known case of hydropower politics in China is the infamous Three Gorges Dam. While the protest movement against Three Gorges ultimately failed, and the most prominent dissenters were imprisoned for their activism, the event served as a warning and a learning experience for dam activists across China (Sutton 2004). In particular, this section focuses on an anti-dam NIMBY movement against a proposed hydropower project that would potentially obstruct the ancient Dujiangyan Irrigation System.

Historical and Scientific Background: 2,000 Years of Irrigation

The Dujiangyan Irrigation System (DIS), located in Sichuan province in southwestern China, was built nearly 2,300 years ago during the Qin dynasty. It controls water from the Min River and delivers it to the Chengdu plain, enabling the Chengdu plain to become one of the most fertile regions in China. In 2000, the DIS was recognized as the world's oldest fully operational hydraulic engineering project when it was added to the UNESCO World Heritage list (Doar 2005).

Instead of changing the topography of the land to harness the Min River's water resources, the irrigation system was adapted to the existing characteristics of the river. The Chengdu plain slopes at about 0.4 percent from 730 m above sea level to 500 m, allowing the irrigation system to be run by gravity as the Min River flows downstream (Willmott 1989: 144). The three main features of the DIS, called Yuzui, Feishayan, and Baopingkou, work together to prevent flooding, filter out sediment, and provide water for irrigation. The DIS currently provides irrigation for about 737,000 hectares of land throughout the region (Li 2003).

The entire system has functioned with little reconstruction for over 2,000 years, including during natural disasters. In 2008, a magnitude 7.9 earthquake hit Sichuan province, causing widespread damage and massive casualties. However, the DIS never stopped delivering water to Chengdu, including on the day of the quake. Many buildings in the surrounding region were completely destroyed, but the headwork of the irrigation system was only cracked (Cao et al. 2010: 8). Despite natural disasters such as earthquakes, flooding, and mudslides, the DIS has managed to sustain the structural integrity conferred by its initial construction during the Qin dynasty.

The Yangliuhu Dam Controversy

Although neither plan materialized until the 2000s, two "sister dams" were proposed along the Min River during the Mao era: the Zipingpu and the Yangliuhu (earlier Yuzui) dam projects. The dams, part of a larger goal to develop western China, were proposed to "meet the triumvirate goals for large dam-building projects: hydropower, irrigation, and flood control" (Mertha and Lowry 2006: 9). In 2001, construction began on the Zipingpu dam about nine kilometers upstream from the DIS (Cao et al. 2010: 10). The Zipingpu dam project met with little opposition, since the dam helps to regulate the water flowing into Dujiangyan, reducing the risk of flooding for the entire Chengdu plain (Cao et al. 2010: 12). The Zipingpu dam is estimated to protect 720,000 people and 40,000 hectares of farmland from flooding (Mertha 2008: 98). While the Zipingpu project met national goals for both flooding prevention and economic development without interfering with the centuries-old irrigation system, the second dam project at Yangliuhu posed a threat to the Dujiangyan World Heritage site.

The first signs of the Yangliuhu (earlier Yuzui) dam project appeared in 2003. On April 28, the Dujiangyan Administration Bureau held a seminar to explore the feasibility of the project and to discuss the location of the Yangliuhu dam (Wan and Cao 2003). In attendance were eighteen experts in water conservancy, heritage, construction, environmental protection, and planning (Zhang 2003). Most experts agreed that Yangliuhu would affect flood and sediment diversion, and ruin the gravity flow of the DIS (Wan and Cao 2003). On June 5, another meeting was called—this time excluding those who had expressed reservations at the initial feasibility meeting (Wan and Cao 2003). The Dujiangyan Administration was trying to obtain support for a project that would bring revenue to the city (Zhang 2003). Proponents of the dam, who stacked the second expert meeting, argued that the Yangliuhu dam would help with the region's downstream water shortage (Xiao 2003). The Dujiangyan Administration assured the public that the Yangliuhu project would not cause substantial damage to the DIS (Feng et al. 2003).

Several journalists became interested in these meetings, and the opposing experts encouraged the journalists to speak with the UNESCO office in Beijing (Wan and Cao 2003). Zhang Kejia, a journalist for China Youth Daily, wrote an article condemning the Yangliuhu project. Zhang (2003) argued in his article that the Chinese people could not sacrifice their ancient heritage for a power station, and his article was widely reprinted or cited in other newspapers across China. Another prominent journalist, Wang Yongchen, wrote an article stating that the Yangliuhu dam project would embarrass China in the eyes of UNESCO and the entire international community (Wang 2003). Other prominent newspapers across China, including Worker's Daily (*Gongren ribao*), Southern Metropolis Daily (*Nanfang dushi bao*), Economic Half-Hour (*Jingji banxiaoshi*), and the Xinhua news agency, echoed the idea that a hydropower project at Yangliuhu did not merit the destruction of an important part of China's ancient cultural heritage (Feng et al. 2003). Each of these newspapers has wide distribution, both in print and online, and together they were able to broaden the debate over whether Chinese cultural heritage should be sacrificed for economic development in the region.

While activist-journalists were able to elevate the status of the threat to the Dujiangyan World Heritage site, other actors also helped to place pressure on government decision-makers. On June 27, Bian Zaibin, the Director of the Dujiangyan Municipal Cultural Relics Bureau, issued his own report to UNESCO opposing Yangliuhu (Mertha and Lowry 2006: 10). In early August, an investigation panel made up of experts from the Ministry of Housing and Urban-Rural Development, the State Administration for Cultural Heritage, and the Chinese National Commission for UNESCO urged another feasibility study to explore the potential impact of Yangliuhu on the DIS (Yan 2009). On August 4, the Dujiangyan Administration affirmed that the feasibility studies for Yangliuhu would continue (Long et al. 2003); however, on August 7, it was announced that all engineering and feasibility studies of the Yangliuhu dam were suspended (Chen and Zhou 2009). On August 29, the sixteenth executive meeting of the Sichuan provincial government unanimously rejected the Yangliuhu construction project (Yan 2009). The Yangliuhu project was abandoned, becoming the first successful case of policy reversal for a planned hydropower project of this scale in China.

Analysis of the Dujiangyan Case

The Dujiangyan case is an important anomaly in anti-dam movements in China, which have been typecast in the international sphere by the cautionary Three Gorges dam example. The end-goal success of the Dujiangyan movement is not the only important thing. In addition to achieving its goal, the NIMBY movement also fostered social and political innovation. The following section examines the three factors outlined in the introduction to this chapter—counter-expertise, local cultural resources, and broader leverage networks—to evaluate how these factors led to social and political innovations that protected the DIS from the Yangliuhu dam project.

Counter-Expertise, Science, and Advocacy

The contribution of counter-expertise to the Dujiangyan case is important, yet subtle. During the first meeting to study the site location and feasibility of the project, the eighteen experts assembled expressed their scientific opinions. When these experts produced an overwhelmingly negative assessment of the project, they were not invited to the second feasibility seminar. At that meeting, the Dujiangyan Administration Bureau included only experts hand-picked for their advocacy in support of the dam. This exclusion from the second meeting provoked the excluded experts to increase their involvement in the Yangliuhu dam debate.

Other scientists, excluded from official assessments, publicly voiced their objections to local media outlets. Engineers speaking on behalf of the Dujiangyan Administration Bureau informed journalists of the possible benefits of a dam at Yangliuhu for the entire Sichuan basin, including regulation of water resources to prevent a water shortage (Wan and Cao 2003). These experts also noted that government's financial investment in the project would be lost if it were to be cancelled. Meanwhile, other scientists on the opposing side informed journalists of the negative effects that Yangliuhu could have on the DIS. Experts from the Ministry of Construction, State Environmental Protection Administration, and State Administration of Cultural Heritage told reporters that the dam would reduce the flow of water through Dujiangyan's channels and disrupt the function of the DIS, while experts from the Sichuan Water Resources Bureau and the Ministry of Water Resources supported the dam project as necessary for the full functioning of Zipingpu (Zhang 2003; Li 2003). It is important to note that the Ministry of Water Resources and the Sichuan Water Resources Bureau had a 30 percent investment stake in the Yangliuhu project (Zhang 2003), so their positions could not be neutral. Many scientific experts mobilized as advocates in the Yangliuhu debate, whether on the opposing or supporting side. This shows the importance of developing counter-expertise in a NIMBY movement in order to have a stronger voice in the debate.

Local Cultural Resources

Similar to the Lake Baikal case, framing the problem as one of harm to local cultural resources became the most valuable strategy for NIMBY activists and other actors involved in the Yangliuhu dam controversy. In addition to scientific and expert opinion, the role of journalists and news outlets in disseminating frames was essential. Prominent journalist-activists Zhang Kejia and Wang Yongchen were two of the first journalists to frame the debate as one between (poorly-planned) economic development and the preservation of cultural heritage (Zhang 2003; Wang 2003). Other local, national, and international news outlets amplified this emphasis on cultural heritage preservation. In total, almost 180 domestic and foreign media reported the incident (Yan 2009).

The journalists and news outlets that helped distribute these opinions assisted NIMBY activists in emphasizing the importance of cultural preservation. This allowed the NIMBY movement's frame of cultural preservation to become dominant over the official Dujiangyan Administration Bureau's economic frame. In general, a decline in the strength of official state framing in China has allowed unofficial, alternative frames to emerge

(Mertha 2008: 13). In the Dujiangyan case, the official state view of the issue was less widely distributed and supported than the NIMBY movement's emphasis on local cultural resources due to the involvement of activists-journalists.

Broader Networks and Political Leverage

The broader network that NIMBY activists assembled included scientists and experts as advocates and activist-journalists. However, although cultural heritage preservation was the emphasis of the NIMBY movement, transnational influence remained less relevant, since the UNESCO World Heritage status of the DIS was mostly confined to a domestic debate. The UNESCO World Heritage Commission was never directly involved in the controversy, although the Beijing office was contacted regarding the matter by both journalists and local officials (Mertha and Lowry 2006: 10; Wan and Cao 2003). Although the Beijing UNESCO office is a regional branch of a transnational organization, it never made an official statement or appeal to the international organization to exert pressure on the Chinese government. China scholars agree that the opposition to the Yangliuhu dam project was not transnational in nature: "The opposition was not a transnational movement, but rather a domestic movement that adeptly utilized international symbols and related expectations on the part of the national authorities" (Mertha and Lowry 2006: 17). The opposition was domestic, but it did reach out to a broader network of scientists, experts, and journalists, lending the NIMBY movement broader legitimacy for political leverage.

The Dujiangyan Case as a Model

The ability of activists to protect the ancient Dujiangyan Irrigation System from the Yangliuhu dam project is a rare example of a successful NIMBY action against a hydropower project of its scale in China. In order to combat official expertise, scientists and experts lent their voices to the NIMBY movement's development of counter-expertise. The NIMBY movement was able to expand its message of local cultural preservation through amplification in the media. The broader network joined scientific experts, journalists, and local citizens in opposition to the proposed dam. However, the role of any transnational advocacy networks in the Dujiangyan case was absent. While the domestic NIMBY network used transnational symbols and threats of transnational pressure from UNESCO, a transnational body was never directly involved in the debate. Arguably, casting the Yangliuhu controversy as a matter of preservation of cultural heritage was the most important strategy for the NIMBY movement.

As a counter example, cultural heritage was also at stake in the far less successful anti-dam movement at Three Gorges. The Three Gorges project dates all the way back to the era of Sun Yat-sen (d. 1925), but various historical and financial hurdles delayed serious consideration and planning until the 1980s and 1990s, with construction beginning in 1993 (Jackson and Sleigh 2001: 60). Although not designated as a UNESCO World Heritage site, the hydropower project at Three Gorges threatened 1,208 historical sites, and while some were removed, others were submerged (Sutton 2004). Opponents of the Three Gorges dam expressed their concern about submerging these cultural relics that dated back to the same era as the DIS, but the idea of cultural preservation was less salient. The involvement of activist-journalists was not as prominent in the Three Gorges controversy. Without the same level of dissemination, it is possible that the theme of cultural preservation was unable to reach a broad audience. Another argument for the broad-based support and dissemination of the cultural heritage frame in the Dujiangyan case is that Hu Jintao, who became President in 2003, was perceived to be more open to critical media coverage (Doar 2005). This encouraged journalists to become more involved in the NIMBY movement and cultivate public concern for the fate of the DIS in a way that was not allowed at the height of the Three Gorges dam controversy in the mid-1990s.

The counter example points to the importance of timing for NIMBY protest. The Yangliuhu dam controversy benefitted not only from a perception of relative political openness, but also widespread knowledge of the consequences of Three Gorges in the Chinese national consciousness. In fact, one journalist compared the two dam controversies, urging those involved in the Yangliuhu dam debate to learn from the mistakes of the Three Gorges dam (Yao 2003). One such mistake was perceived to be the high level of international influence in the Three Gorges opposition movement. This may have also influenced the decision of NIMBY activists not to reach beyond the resources of local and domestic actors to protect Dujiangyan. Transnational involvement may not always be a boon to local activists, which suggests that there is a limit to the application of Keck and Sikkink's (1998) boomerang effect.

Even with these reservations about the "success" of the movement, it is clear that NIMBY movements can employ strategies that lead to social and political innovation, regardless of perceived political constraints. The development of counter-expertise brought scientists and experts together as advocates within the broader network of the NIMBY movement. Emphasis on local cultural resources allowed the NIMBY movement to find a resonating message for activist-journalists to circulate. This broad network brought together actors from many different backgrounds, including those who may have never previously been involved in politics. The fact that a NIMBY movement was able to voice its concerns to the media and freely appeal to various government bureaus shows a side of Chinese politics that is rarely studied. Even more valuable are its parallels with NIMBY movements in other politically constrained countries, such as Russia, and the lessons that can be learned through a comparison of the two.

Conclusion: Comparative Cases—The Success of NIMBY Protest

The two cases presented here encompass themes essential to understanding how NIMBY movements can generate positive outcomes even in a repressive political context. Both cases tackled issues at the center of China's and Russia's environmental concerns: the oil and gas industry in Russia and massive hydroelectric power projects in China. The ability of a NIMBY movement to fight these infrastructural giants in either country is an unexpected development that could indicate a gradual widening of political freedoms in China and Russia. From the development of counter-expertise to harnessing local cultural resources to building a broader network for political leverage, the NIMBY movements here found innovative new ways to approach environmental politics in both countries.

In each case, an initial expert panel was assembled to gather scientific information; however, when the experts overwhelmingly opposed the proposed project, the government agency gathered a second group of experts—this time chosen for their pro-project positions—to produce a positive assessment. The fact that the government agencies involved (Rostekhnadzor and the Dujiangyan Administration Bureau, respectively) discarded experts whose scientific conclusions were undesirable to government caused those scientists to be more likely to advocate in opposition to the infrastructural project. Russian scientists who were interviewed in the media overwhelmingly supported one side of the issue. Similarly, the discarded experts in the Dujiangyan case reached out to news outlets in order to amplify their advocacy against the Yangliuhu dam project. This has parallels with the German case in the Hager chapter. There, counter-expertise was also mobilized by the government's initial rejection of scientific arguments against the project. Developing counter-expertise fostered social and political innovation as scientists and experts became a part of the NIMBY movement to defeat the proposed project.

Harnessing local cultural resources was arguably the most important strategy for both NIMBY movements examined here. While the government was able to find scientists to claim that the projects were not ecologically harmful, it was politically impossible to deny the cultural importance of the two sites. In each case, the opponents and proponents of the projects attempted to reframe the debate. The media were involved in both cases, and in both cases the NIMBY movement's framing of the issue as one of cultural preservation was given greater distribution as it resonated with local, national, and international audiences. Lake Baikal and the DIS are both listed as UNESCO World Heritage sites, which allowed the use of local cultural resources to acquire international legitimacy. Rather than situate the debate as one of the environment versus economic development, both NIMBY movements focused on the idea that economic development was threatening the cultural heritage of the people.

The availability of these local cultural resources led to the political and social innovation of using these characteristics to create a broader network and involve previously apolitical groups. UNESCO World Heritage status offered greater legitimacy to the available local cultural resources, and gave the NIMBY movement a chance to connect to a transnational advocacy network for support. In the Baikal case, the transnational network included not only the UNESCO World Heritage Committee chairperson, but also the transnational environmental organizations WWF and Greenpeace. Although the movement remained domestic, the primary local environmental organization was able to network with these transnational organizations to influence the national government. As Keck and Sikkink (1998) explain, domestic movements that are unable to reach the national government (or other targeted officials) through political channels may appeal to transnational organizations for their influence through a "boomerang" effect. In this way, creating a broader network led to the political innovation of using that network to leverage domestic politics.

Although the domestic movement used transnational symbols in the debate over the Yangliuhu dam to pressure the government, an official appeal to the international UNESCO office never occurred, as it did in the Baikal case. However, the broader network of scientists, experts, and journalists was an important source of social and political innovation, lending legitimacy to the NIMBY movement. The exposure of the cultural heritage frame from this broader network was also a key innovation that helped the NIMBY movement to gain political leverage with the local and provincial governments. The fragmentation of Chinese authority helps to explain why political and social innovation in the Dujiangyan case was more locally focused, while activists in the Baikal case had to leverage politics at the very top level of government due to the centralization of power in the Russian political system.

While leverage through a broader transnational network was important in these two cases, it is also important to realize that the involvement of international advocacy networks can backfire, as Russian activists are now learning. The international influence that activists used to support their efforts to protect Baikal in 2006 has since become subject to new regulations from the Russian government, including restrictions targeting foreign-funded NGOs operating in Russia. Another example of international connections backfiring was the Three Gorges Dam, where activists' links to international NGOs enabled the Chinese government to frame the dam as a nationalist issue involving unwanted foreign interference. After the disastrous example of Three Gorges, Chinese activists became more cautious about international involvement in their local causes. Local NIMBY activists and journalist-activists hinted at the international shame that would come from losing UNESCO status, but never directly involved the international body in the matter. It is possible that the activists knew the dangers of too much foreign involvement in a domestic matter and thus kept international influence at arm's length.

NIMBY Movements in China and Russia

The Baikal and Dujiangyan cases presented here are important examples of effective NIMBY protest in places with relatively closed political opportunity structures originating from their respective regimes. As a generally "permitted" subject for expressing dissent, environmental issues provide the public with an unprecedented opportunity to voice their concerns to local, regional, and national governments. Baikal and Dujiangyan show that NIMBY politics can offer advantages for activists—especially in response to constraints on citizen access to policy making.

As illustrated by the Baikal and Dujiangyan cases, the concept of "Not In My Backyard" can be elastic. The NIMBY movement can expand and contract depending on the location or characteristics of the "backyard" in question. In both cases presented here, NIMBY movements mobilized to protect "backyards with special characteristics" that connected to broader narratives and national pride in cultural or natural heritage. These movements became, in essence, "not in *our* backyard" movements through a combination of developing counter-expertise, harnessing local cultural resources, and extending to a broader network. In turn, these factors resulted in NIMBY-led social and political innovation, such as engaging formerly apolitical groups and using networks for political leverage. Although NIMBY politics is often seen as oppositional, these cases show how NIMBY protests can create new avenues and methods for communication between citizens and their governments in places where state-society relations are often strained.

Notes

1. The time periods under discussion here are the Mao era (1949–1976) and the early-to-mid-Soviet period under Stalin, Brezhnev, and Khrushchev (1922–1982).
2. For a description of the impact of Mao's reforms on the Chinese environment, see Shapiro 2001.
3. For an explanation of paired comparison as a distinct strategy of analysis, see Tarrow 2010.
4. See Pielke 2007 for a breakdown of the four roles scientists can assume in policy-making, including issue advocacy. See Scott and Rachlow 2011 or Wilhere 2011 for the debate on scientists as advocates.
5. For a more in-depth discussion of how social movement groups use framing, see Snow et al. 1986 or Snow and Benford 1988.
6. This is a brief and simplified version of the BPPM case for the purposes of providing a counter-example. A full analysis of the BPPM case is beyond the scope of this chapter. For more information, see Trammell 2010.

References

Alferov, A. N. 2005. "Sokhraneniye ozera Bai'kal—e'to ustoi'chivoye razvitiye vostochnoi' Sibiri." *Uspekhi sovremennogo estestvoznaniya* 6: 71.

Bao, Maohong. 2010. "The Evolution of Environmental Problems and Environmental Policy in China: The Interaction of Internal and External Forces." In *Environmental Histories of the Cold War,* edited by J.R. McNeill and Corinna R. Unger, 323–40. Washington, DC: German Historical Institute and New York: Cambridge University Press.

BBC Chinese. 2012. "Yingmei: Zhongguo queshui yanzhong weixie jingji fazhan." February 17. Accessed February 18, 2012. http://www.bbc.co.uk/zhongwen/simp/chinese_news/2012/02/120217_press_china_water.shtml.

Brovkin, Ivan. 2006. "Padal sneg, no kazalos', plakal Bai'kal." *Vostochno-Sibirskaia Pravda,* April 19. Accessed December 2, 2014. http://www.vsp.ru/pisma/2006/04/19/426584.

Cann, Cynthia W., Michael C. Cann, and Gao Shangquan. 2005. "China's Road to Sustainable Development: An Overview." In *China's Environment and the Challenge of Sustainable Development,* edited by Kristen A. Day, 3–34. Armonk, NY and London: M. E. Sharpe.

Cao, Shuyou, Liu Xingnian, and Er Huang. 2010. "Dujiangyan Irrigation System—A World Cultural Heritage Corresponding to Concepts of Modern Hydraulic Science." *Journal of Hydro-Environment Research* 4: 3–13.

Chen, Cheng and Zhou Yi Xiang. 2003. "Poyu gefang yali Dujiangyan guanli ju jueding zanting Yangliuhu gongcheng." *Zhongguo xinwen wang,* August 7. Accessed December 2, 2014. http://www.chinanews.com/n/2003-08-07/26/333016.html.

Colton, Timothy J. and Michael McFaul. 2003. "Russian Democracy Under Putin." *Problems of Post-Communism* 50(4): 12–21.

Dahl, Robert A. 1989. *Democracy and Its Critics.* New Haven, CT: Yale University Press.

Diamond, Larry. 2002. "Elections Without Democracy: Thinking About Hybrid Regimes." *Journal of Democracy* 13(2): 21–35.

Doar, Bruce G. 2005. "Taming the Floodwaters: The High Heritage Price of Massive Hydraulic Projects." *China Heritage Newsletter* 1. China Heritage Project, the Australian National University.

Economy, Elizabeth C. 2005. "Environmental Enforcement in China." In *China's Environment and the Challenge of Sustainable Development,* edited by Kristen A. Day, 102–20. Armonk, NY and London: M. E. Sharpe..

Fadeev, Pavel. 2005. "E'konomika. Vostochnyi' proryv." *Rossiiskaia gazeta,* March 3. Accessed December 2, 2014. EastView Database.

Feng, Xing, Xiao Chuan, and Zi Feng. 2003. "Shijie yichan shifou chengwai shijie yihan?" *Zhongguo shuiyun bao,* August 11. Accessed December 2, 2014. EastView Database.

Fish, M. Steven. 2005. *Democracy Derailed in Russia: The Failure of Open Politics.* Cambridge: Cambridge University Press.

Grachev, M. A. 2002. *O Sovremennom Sostoianii E'kologicheskoi Sistemy Ozera Bai'kal.* Novosibirsk: Izdatel'stvo SO RAN.

Gulgonova, V. E. and N. G. Rybal'skogo. 1996. *E'kologicheskiye problemy Bai'kala i Respubliki Buryatiya.* Moscow: Rossiiskoye E'kologicheskoye Federal'noye Informatsionnoye Agentstvo (REFIA).

Gulya, Lisa. 2008. "Russia's Rabble-Rouser for the Environment." *Utne Reader*, April 15. Accessed December 2, 2014. http://www.utne.com/environment/russias-rabble-rouser-for-the-environment.aspx#axzz3KnQilt3S.

Henry, Laura. 2009. "Thinking Globally, Limited Locally." In *Environmental Justice and Sustainability in the Former Soviet Union,* edited by Julain Agyeman and Yelena Ogneva-Himmelberger, 47–69. Cambridge, MA and London: MIT Press.

Hitt, Michael A., et al. 2004. "The Institutional Effects on Strategic Alliance Partner Selection in Transition Economics: China vs. Russia." *Organization Science* 15(12): 173–85.

International Energy Agency (IEA). 2010. Renewable Energy Essentials: Hydropower. http://www.iea.org/publications/freepublications/publication/Hydro power_Essentials-1.pdf.

Irkutsk Oblast. 2011. "Kharakteristika pokazaleleij vodopotrebleniia i vodootvedeniia v 2010 godu." Ministry of Natural Resources and Ecology of Irkutsk Oblast. Accessed December 1, 2013. http://www.irkobl.ru/sites/ecology/working/woter/pokaz/index.php/.

Jackson, Sukhan and Adrian C. Sleigh. 2001. "The Political Economy and Socio-Economic Impact of China's Three Gorges Dam." *Asian Studies Review* 25(1): 57–72.

Josephson, Paul. 2010. "War on Nature as Part of the Cold War: The Strategic and Ideological Roots of Environmental Degradation in the Soviet Union." In *Environmental Histories of the Cold War,* edited by J. R. McNeill and Corinna R. Unger, 21–50. Washington, DC: German Historical Institute and New York: Cambridge University Press..

Keck, Margaret and Kathryn Sikkink. 1998. *Activists Beyond Borders: Advocacy Networks in International Politics.* Ithaca, NY: Cornell University Press.

Khalii, I. A. 2007. "Zashchita Bai'kala: Khronika Konflikta." *Sotsiologicheskie issledovaniia* 8: 26–34.

Kidenis, Aleksandr. 2006. "Prezidentskaia zagogulina spasla Bai'kal." *Russkii' kur'er,* May 1. Accessed December 2, 2014. http://www.ruscur.ru/archive.shtml?id=1326.

Kilner, James. 2008. "Russian Mother Who Took on Oil Giant and Won." *Reuters,* April 16. Accessed December 2, 2014. http://uk.reuters.com/article/2008/04/16/businessproind-russia-environment-dc-idUKL1499926200804l6.

Kommersant. 2006a. "Istoriia proekta VSTO." April 27. Accessed December 2, 2014. http://www.kommersant.ru/doc/670339.

———. 2006b. "Rostekhnadzor gotovit prikaz o prodlenii e'kspertizy VSTO." February 1. Accessed December 2, 2014. http://www.kommersant.ru/doc/645747.

Kozhov, Mikhail. 1963. *Lake Baikal and Its Life.* The Hague: Dr. W. Junk, Publishers.

Kuznetsov, Georgii'. 2006. "Bai'kal bolen. Diagnoz: truba." *Vostochno-Sibirskaia Pravda,* April 25. Accessed December 2, 2014. http://www.vsp.ru/ecology/2006/04/25/426431.

Lee, Yok-shiu F. 2005. "Public Environmental Consciousness in China: Early Empirical Evidence." In *China's Environment and the Challenge of Sustainable Development,* edited by Kristen A. Day, 35–65. Armonk, NY: M. E. Sharpe.

Li, Cathy. 2003. "Scientists Fear Dam Would Harm Ancient Wonder; Sichuan's 2,200-Year Old Dujiangyan Irrigation Scheme Could Silt Up, They Say." *South China Morning Post,* August 8. Accessed December 2, 2014. http://www.scmp.com/article/424140/scientists-fear-dam-would-harm-ancient-wonder.

Lieberthal, Kenneth, and Michel Oksenberg. 1988. *Policy Making in China: Leaders, Structures, and Processes.* Princeton, NJ: Princeton University Press.

Lieberthal, Kenneth. 1992. "Introduction: The 'Fragmented Authoritarianism' Model and Its Limitations." In *Bureacracy, Politics, and Decision Making in Post-Mao China,* edited by Kenneth Lieberthal and David M. Lampton, 1–31. Berkeley: University of California Press.

Lindblom, Charles. 1990. *Inquiry and Change: The Troubled Attempt to Understand and Shape Society.* New Haven, CT: Yale University Press.

Long, Can, Luo Jie, and Xu Zhuan Dong. 2003. "Buneng digu Yangliuhu gongcheng dui Dujiangyan de yingxiang." *Sichuan zaixian,* August 5. Accessed December 2, 2014. http://sichuan.scol.com.cn/bsxw/20030805/20038551245_hx.htm.

Matus, Kira et al. 2012. "Health Damages from Air Pollution in China." *Global Environmental Change* 22(1): 55–66.

McAvoy, Gregory. 1998. "Partisan Probing and Democratic Decision-Making: Rethinking the NIMBY Syndrome." *Policy Studies Journal* 26(2): 274–92.

Mertha, Andrew and William R. Lowry. 2006. "Unbuilt Dams: Seminal Events and Policy Change in China, Australia, and the U.S." *Comparative Politics* 39(1): 1–20.

Mertha, Andrew C. 2008. *China's Water Warriors: Citizen Action and Policy Change.* Ithaca, NY: Cornell University Press.

Mistiaen, Veronique. 2008. "Sacred Sea and Songs of Hope." *The Guardian,* April 15. Accessed December 2, 2014. http://www.theguardian.com/environment/2008/apr/16/activists.nuclearpower.

Nikolaeva, Anna, Ekaterina Derbilova, and Aleksei' Nikol'skii'. 2006. "Truby proch' ot Bai'kala." *Vedomosti,* April 27. Accessed December 2, 2014. http://www.vedomosti.ru/newspaper/article/2006/04/27/105871.

Orlova, Irina. 2006. "Protest. Irkutskaia oblast'—ne otstoi'!" *Vremia novostei',* March 21. Accessed December 2, 2014. EastView Database.

Ostroverkh, Olga. 2012. "V Primor'ye budut sudit' 'chernykh lesorubov.'" *Rossiiskaya Gazeta,* March 30. Accessed April 1, 2012. http://www.rg.ru/2012/03/30/reg-dfo/lesorubi-anons.html.

Pei, Minxin. 1994. *From Reform to Revolution: The Demise of Communism in China and the Soviet Union.* Cambridge, MA: Harvard University Press.

Pielke, Jr., Roger A. 2007. *The Honest Broker: Making Sense of Science in Policy and Politics.* Cambridge: Cambridge University Press.

Polubota, Aleksei. 2005. "Bai'kal—Truba?" *Trud,* November 16. Accessed December 2, 2014. http://www.trud.ru/article/16-11-2005/96604_bajkalu--truba.html.

Popov, Vladimir. 2000. "Shock Therapy versus Gradualism: The End of the Debate (Explaining the Magnitude of the Transformational Recession)." *Comparative Economic Studies* 42(1): 1–57.

Protasov, V. F. 1999. *E'kologia zdorov'ye i okhrana okruzhaiushei' sredy v Rossii.* Moscow: Financy i Statistika.

Rikhvanova, Marina. 2006. "Bai'kal—ne prosto ozero." *Neprikosnovennyi' zapas* 2: 233–40.

Scott, J. Michael, and Janet L. Rachlow. 2011. "Refocusing the Debate about Advocacy." *Conservation Biology* 25(1): 1–3.

Sergeeva, Yulya. 2006. "VSTO povernuli ne tuda." *Vostochno-Sibirskaia Pravda,* July 15. Accessed December 2, 2014. http://www.vsp.ru/economic/2006/07/15/424957?call_context=embed.

Shapiro, Judith. 2001. *Mao's War Against Nature: Politics and the Environment in Revolutionary China.* Cambridge: Cambridge University Press.

Skorlygina, Natal'ia. 2006. "E'kologicheskaia bezopasnost'. Bai'kal bol'she ne pomekha dlia VSTO." *Kommersant,* March 2. Accessed December 2, 2014. http://www.kommersant.ru/doc/654120.

Slovo Kyrgyzstana. 2006. "Rossiia segodnia e'konomika. Zolotoye secheniye truby." March 23. Accessed December 2, 2014. EastView Database.

Snow, David A., E. Burke Rochford, Jr., Steven K. Worden, and Robert D. Benford. 1986. "Frame Alignment Processes, Micromobilization, and Movement Participation." *American Sociological Review* 51(4): 464–81.

Snow, David A., and Robert D. Benford. 1988. "Ideology, Frame Resonance, and Participant Mobilization." *International Social Movement Research* 1: 197–217.

Sun, Yan. 1999. "Reform, State, and Corruption: Is Corruption Less Destructive in China Than in Russia?" *Comparative Politics* 32(1): 1–20.

Surzhenko, Vera, and Anna Nikolaeva. 2006. "E'nergoresursy. Kvashnin khochet perenesti VSTO." *Vedomosti,* March 27. Accessed December 2, 2014. http://www.vedomosti.ru/newspaper/article/2006/03/27/104501.

Sutton, Alan. 2004. "The Three Gorges Project on the Yangtze River in China." *Geography* 89(2): 111–26.

Tarrow, Sidney. 2010. "The Strategy of Paired Comparison: Toward a Theory of Practice." *Comparative Political Studies* 43(2): 230–59.

Trammell, Elizabeth. 2010. "Russian Political Reactions to a Changing Climate: Environmental Cases in the Arctic and Siberian Hydrosphere." Undergraduate honors thesis, Wesleyan University. http://wesscholar.wesleyan.edu/etd_hon_theses/391/.

Tyutyunova, F. I., K. E. Pit'yeva, and I. G. Shipakina. 2008. "Contsepyual'nye osnovy e'kologicheskoi' bezopasnosti osvoyeniia gidrolitosfery v usloviiakh postindustrial'nogo tekhnoreneza." In *Global'nye e'kologicheskiye problemy Rossii, Vypusk 3,* edited by A. L. Ianshina, 28–66. Moscow: Nauka.

UNESCO. 2006. "World Heritage Committee Chairperson Sends Letter to President of Russian Federation Concerning Lake Baikal." Press Release, March 24. Accessed February 20, 2012. http://whc.unesco.org/en/news/242.

Vasil'yev, Viktor. 2006. "E'konomika." *Sovetskaia sibir'*, February 9. Accessed December 2, 2014. EastView Database.

Wan, Jingbo, and Cao Yong. 2003. "Daba, li Dujiangyan 1310 mi." *Nanfang zhoumo,* August 1. Accessed December 2, 2014. http://news.sina.com.cn/c/2003-08-01/09321456226.shtml.

Wang, Yongchen. 2003. "Sichuansheng Dujiangyan Guanliju ni zai Dujiangyan jianshe Yangliuhu shuiku, ciju jiang dada pohuai Dujiangyan diqu de shengtai huanjing: jiujiu Dujiangyan." *Shengtai shikong,* July 29. Accessed December 2, 2014. CNKI China Core Newspapers Full-text Database.

Weiner, Douglas. 1999. *A Little Corner of Freedom: Russian Nature Protection from Stalin to Gorbachev.* Berkeley: University of California Press.

Weir, Fred. 2008. "Devoted to Saving Lake Baikal, She Won Even Putin's Ear." *The Christian Science Monitor,* April 14. Accessed December 2, 2014. http://www.csmonitor.com/World/Europe/2008/0414/p01s04-woeu.html.

Wilhere, George F. 2011. "Inadvertent Advocacy." *Conservation Biology* 26(1): 39–46.

Willmott, W. E. 1989. "Irrigation and Society in Sichuan, China." *The Australian Journal of Chinese Affairs* 22: 143–53.

Xiao, Longlian. 2003. "Zhuanjia xuezhe he minzhong dui Dujiangyan jianba shuo bu zhenglun ruhuo rutu." *Zhongguo xinwen wang,* August 7. Accessed December 2, 2014. http://www.chinanews.com.cn/n/2003-08-07/26/332883.html.

Yan, Yan. 2009. "Zhongguo 'fanba' yundong zhong de meiti de liliang." *Kexue xinwen,* October 22. Accessed December 2, 2014. http://discover.news.163.com/09/1022/10/5M7MGEKV000125LI.html.

Yao, Peng. 2003. "Cong Dujiangyan dao Sanxia: zun shong shui de benxing." *Zhongguo funu bao,* November 24. Accessed March 18, 2012. CNKI China Core Newspapers Full-text Database.

Zhang, Kejia. 2003. "Shijieyichan Dujiangyan jiang jian xin ba yuan mao zao po huai Lianhuguo guan zhu." *Zhongguo qingnian bao,* July 9. Accessed December 2, 2014. http://news.sina.com.cn/c/2003-07-09/1412348988s.shtml.

Zhukov, Boris. 2006. "E'kologiia. Velikaia Vostochnaia Truba." *Moskovskie Novosti,* March 31: 21. Accessed December 2, 2014. EastView Database.

Zhukov, Ivan. 2004. "Obschestvennye slushaniia po proektu VSTO zavershilis'." *Vostochno-Sibirskaia pravda,* September 1. Accessed December 2, 2014. http://www.vsp.ru/ecology/2004/09/01/439575.

Ziegler, Charles E. 1985. "Soviet Images of the Environment." *British Journal of Political Science* 15(3): 365–80.

CHAPTER 6

The Dalian Chemical Plant Protest, Environmental Activism, and China's Developing Civil Society

Mike Gunter, Jr.

China is probably not the first country that comes to mind when considering NIMBY protests. As an authoritarian state, it regularly invokes strict governmental control on everything from the Chinese equivalents of Twitter, Facebook, and YouTube to traditional civil society in the shape of nongovernmental organization (NGO) formation and individual membership in such social groups. Yet this omnipresent heavy hand of censorship is increasingly countered by evolving technology, namely access to information that challenges existing social and political structures (Xie 2011; Xie and Van der Heijden 2010). Microblogs such as Sina's *Weibo,* the Chinese counterpart to Twitter, continue to grow annually in popularity (Barboza 2011), and are a key political component in a country that struggles daily to reconcile its rapid economic growth with environmental protection and public approval for the Communist Party. According to a 2011 study by two scholars from north China's Nankai University, for example, over 90,000 mass strikes, riots, and protests took place in China in 2009 (Larson 2011). Another study by Sun Liping, Professor of Sociology at Beijing's Tsinghua University, claims that at least 180,000 incidents occurred in 2010 (Larson 2012). In their World Report for 2012, Human Rights Watch estimated that 250 to 500 protests occur each day in China (Human Rights Watch 2012).

Not all of these events are environmentally focused, of course, but many are. Indeed, until it stopped releasing official figures, the Chinese government itself reported tens of thousands of separate environmentally-related protests each year (Zissis and Bajoria 2008). Most of these historically involved industrial or agricultural workers reacting to atrocious working conditions, crop disasters, or illness and disease tied to environmental pollution—and most of these were blue-collar protests sparked by local grievances (Sun and Zhao 2008).

In August 2011, though, a decidedly different type of environmental protest took place, one that was more white-collar than blue-collar, and more proactive than reactive. The event, a protest to remove the Dalian Fujia Dahua Petrochemical Company plant from the northeastern coastal city of Dalian, was, in part, a classic NIMBY political protest. Dalian citizens did not want the petrochemical plant in their city, and publicly voiced their fears that a disaster would unfold if the plant continued to operate there. The Dalian protest also displayed characteristics that brought together individuals well outside Dalian City proper, extending the concept of "neighborhood" far beyond the Liaodong peninsula. Indeed, it is this combination of multiple geographic constituencies that makes Dalian such an interesting case study for environmental NIMBY movements in China.

This chapter thus looks at the existing landscape of civil society in China through an environmental lens, finding that NIMBY events like the Dalian protest are more and more likely to take place, even in a non-democratic country like China. Further, as the Dalian case illustrates, NIMBY politics is not simply oppositional in China, but incorporates important proactive components, drawing attention to public health and environmental justice when conventional channels, particularly at the local government level, are blocked. Finally, the Dalian case also demonstrates that NIMBY politics in China continues to evolve, leading to innovation technologically, socially, and, most importantly, politically.

It is critical to note that the PRC encouraged many of these developments itself. Implementing what a number of China experts (Economy 2004; Turner and Zhi 2006) consider a risky strategy to retain power, Beijing believes certain types of civic activism, ranging from nonpolitical environmental NGOs to unsponsored environmental protests like that in Dalian in August 2011, act as release valves for the general public and a mechanism for the Party to gauge public opinion. Indeed, as is well-documented, two decades of Chinese state-societal reform dominate its politics today. This combines with three decades of rapid economic growth, on the order of double-digit annual GDP increases, to create critical environmental and social consequences, and Beijing increasingly invites civil society to assist with these problems, at least in relatively non-controversial issue areas such as environmental protection. This stands notably in contrast to more politically sensitive issues such as human rights, in which civil society engagement is not welcomed, but instead is seen as a direct threat to the Party.

Beginning with Deng Xiaoping's economic liberalization movement in 1978, the Chinese Communist Party transitioned from a centrally planned to a more localized market economy, with more decision-making powers handed to local-level governments. This offered rapid economic advances, but also carried profound environmental and social consequences. Indeed, as the Chinese middle class grows, the government ironically becomes more of a victim, or at least potential victim, of its own success. A wealthier population in China, with jobs increasingly outside the governmental sector, can afford to worry more about environmental pollution and the longer-term economic impacts of that pollution. Beijing recognizes the basic contradictions tied to this breakneck-paced growth, especially as, according to some estimates, roughly 10 percent of GDP is lost annually to environmental pollution and degradation (Economy 2004; Economy and Lieberthal 2007). With the evolution of Beijing's "small state, big society" philosophy in the 1990s, such challenges convinced the government that it needed assistance, at least in relatively non-controversial development-related fields such as education, poverty alleviation, birth control, and environmental protection (Lu 2007). Chinese civil society began to evolve as a result, under direct encouragement of the government, with environmental groups such as the first domestic environmental NGO, Friends of Nature, leading the way with its founding in 1994 (Knup 1997). From these humble beginnings, a continually emerging civil society has moved beyond traditional, non-confrontational Chinese environmental activism to incorporate unique NIMBY protests like that of Xiamen in June 2007, Dalian in August 2011, and Ningbo in October 2012.

Perched in northeastern China on the tip of the Liaodong peninsula, opposite Taiwan, Dalian, in particular, is the focus in this chapter for a mixture of theoretical and practical reasons. The Xiamen PX protests on the first two days of June 2007 provide a second worthy case study, particularly as violence was, again, largely avoided, eight to ten thousand Chinese participated on the first day (half that on the second day), and bloggers such as *Southern Metropolis Daily* columnist Zhong Xiaoyong (writing under the persona Lian Yue) played a major role. That said, Xiamen is also a more conventional NIMBY in that protesters envisioned a traditional backyard in their opposition. The goal was to get the plant to move anywhere else but Xiamen. To this extent, protesters were successful. The government eventually, after drawing out the process for over a year, moved the PX (paraxylene) plant from the industrial and residential island of Haicang across the narrow strait from downtown Xiamen to someone else's backyard in the neighboring municipality of Zhangzhou, where sporadic protests were not nearly as effective.

Another example of NIMBY success occurred in October 2012 near Shanghai, in the prosperous southeastern coastal city of 3.4 million, Ningbo. Here, a week of at-times violent protests against the $8.9 billion expansion of a petrochemical plant run by one of the world's largest petrochemical companies, Sinopec, garnered a government commitment to halt the project pending "scientific review." Beijing-based environmentalist Ma Jun, who was honored in 2012 with the internationally prestigious Goldman Prize, links upsurges in middle-class protests such as Dalian, Ningbo, and Xiamen directly to technical, social, and political innovation through social media. "Social media is a game changer," according to Ma. "People can educate themselves and share information. The next leadership of China is going to face a challenge on these environmental issues, which the previous leadership had not seen so strongly for 30 years (Larson 2012)." Indeed, the demonstrations in Ningbo, Xiamen, and Dalian were organized to a great extent through text messages and microblogs, exploiting the use of brief posts or updates on social networking sites, and aided by the proliferation of mobile phones in China over the last decade.

From this introduction we now turn to a brief historical overview of Chinese civil society in the environmental arena, and then to four specific laws regulating NGO formation as well as operation. A third section then identifies three competing interpretations of how civil society operates in China, focusing on the degree of its autonomy from the state. Herein a unique twist on the role of NIMBY protest emerges, an iteration of sorts of the boomerang effect first described by Margaret Keck and Kathryn Sikkink (1998), whereby NGOs and civil society actors more generally cannot directly target the central authority in their protests and demonstrations, but instead use a variety of media to reach the ultimate decision makers indirectly. To explore this particular argument, the analysis turns in the fourth section to a focus on the Dalian chemical plant protest of August 14, 2011, explaining not only what happened that day in the northeastern coastal metropolitan area of six million, but also how technological tools such as microblogs like *Weibo* and the Chinese version of Facebook, *Renren*, made the event possible. This section also includes discussion of the subsequent restarting of plant operations in December 2011, and how those actions exposed initial praise for the role of NIMBY actions as premature, before then turning to some noted political ramifications. A concluding section examines what the larger implications for Chinese environmental activism might be, highlighting technical, social, and political innovations tied to the NIMBY movement in Dalian, as well as anticipated impact on democratic change within China.

Chinese Civil Society in the Environmental Arena

Over thirty different environmental laws have been enacted in China since 1989, including the Environmental Protection Law (1989), the Energy Conservation in Government Law (2006), the Water Pollution Prevention and Control Law (2008), the Air Pollution Prevention and Control

Law (2000), the Radioactive Prevention and Control Law (2003), the Regulation on the Environmental Protection Management of Construction Projects (1998), the Solid Waste Pollution Prevention and Control Law (2004), and the Marine Environmental Protection Law (1999), to name but a few. Implementation of this impressive legal framework, however, is weak and geographically uneven (Moore and Warren 2006). Even when instituted, the fining system in place is too meager to encourage more environmentally benign behavior (Zhao 2007). Even more specifically, what really encourages environmental degradation and debilitating pollution is the active collusion between governmental actors and polluting businesses, which is compounded by the fact that many of the businesses are state-owned. As in the West, civil society actors have emerged to address this fundamental problem, albeit with some uniquely Chinese characteristics.

According to Yu Keping, deputy director of the CPC Central Compilation and Translation Bureau, some 450,000 registered social organizations exist in China, with an astonishing estimated three million more unregistered. They are growing at a rate of 8 to 10 percent annually (Fu 2011). While these groups cover a range of issue areas, from health initiatives to education to poverty alleviation, environmental groups are arguably the most significant and most established of these social organizations (Ru and Ortolano 2009). During its tenure, the Communist Party has shifted its position as to how welcome these environmental groups are. Table 6.1 below spells out four key regulations in particular that have established the ground rules for civil society operations, with the 1998 regulations going into great detail about the qualifications required to register. In general, Chinese scholar Kang Xiaoguang sums up the sentiment over approximately the last two decades, "The government's rule in managing the NGOs has always been 'offer us more help and cause us less trouble.' NGOs need to be both exploited and reined in" (Kang 2008).

One of the great ironies here, and worth noting as more than an aside for the theoretical implications it presents, is the fact that the very term *non-governmental* is a linguistically difficult term, because the Mandarin translation is "anti-governmental organization" (Hsia and White 2002). Social organizations, as they are legally known, are not allowed to work *against* the government as alternative power sources like in the West, but instead are mandated to collaborate *with* the government. Semantics aside, unofficially the acronym NGO has been used since the 1995 UN conference on women in Beijing, a notable example of international-level influence upon the domestic. See table 6.1 for the four main regulations governing non-governmental organizations in China as well as key points of each.

Table 6.1. *Laws and regulations governing non-governmental organizations in China*

Year	Law	Key Points
1950	Interim Procedures on the Registration of Social Organizations	• First PRC legal document on NGOs • Nationalized many non-governmental associations and organizations, i.e. private hospitals, schools, charities • Virtually removed any and all NGO space in China

1989	Regulations on the Registration and Administration of Social Organizations	• Response to economic reform and changing NGO sector
		• Types of social organizations include:
		  ◦ Scholarly/scientific organizations
		  ◦ Professional associations
		  ◦ Trade/industrial associations
		  ◦ United organizations
		  ◦ Grant making institutions
		• Dual management system
		  ◦ Registration with Ministry of Civil Affairs
		  ◦ Annual reporting to relevant government or party sponsor
		• Large number of private non-profits not included in classification

1998	Regulations on the Registration and Administration of Social Organizations (revised) (State Council Order No. 251)	• Social organizations defined as "voluntary groups formed by Chinese citizens in order to realize a shared objective according to their rules and to develop non-profit making activities"
		• Criteria for establishment as a social organization
		  ◦ Over 50 individual members (or 30 unit members)
		  ◦ Standardized name and organizational structure
		  ◦ Permanent location
		  ◦ full-time staff
		  ◦ funding: national—100,000 Yuan; local—30,000 Yuan
		  ◦ ability to bear civil liabilities independently
		• Dual management system
		• Non-competition principle, i.e. only one organization of any type can operate in a region
		• Not allowed to operate outside of location where registered
		• Must submit an annual report to sponsoring government ministry

1998	Provisional Regulations on the Registration and Management of Popular Non-enterprise Work Units (State Council Order No. 251)	• Popular non-enterprise work units defined as "organizations carrying out social service activities of a non-profit nature, run by enterprise and institutions work units, social groups and other social forces, and also individual citizens using non-state assets" • Less rigorous than that for social organizations, i.e. no member, staff, or funding requirements

Source: Gunter and Rosen 2012

The conventional Western conceptualization of civil society as a countervailing power to government is thus inappropriate, or at the very least incomplete, in China. The relationship between these actors and government is decidedly different from that evident in the West, but civil society in China is not merely an extension of the Communist Party. China's civil society actors engage in more of a partnership with the government, in which they contribute important resources that the government lacks in order to help solve common public problems, often in the form of counter-expertise that expands knowledge of a difficult issue beyond that developed within the bureaucracy.

Schools of Thought on Chinese Civil Society

With this assertion in mind, there are three main schools of thought about Chinese civil society and its relationship to the government. A democratization school follows the traditional Western model, with its focus on autonomy from the government. A corporatist school emphasizes the restrictive legal framework in China and NGO dependence on the government—even outright co-optation by Beijing. Finally, a Chinese "third way" merges both of these schools, contending that civil society actors collaborate with government without co-optation (Howell 2007).

Western Democratization Approaches

As noted by Shui-Yan Tang and Xueyong Zhan, civil society is "the realm of organized social life that is open, voluntary, self-generating, at least partially self-supporting, autonomous from the state, and bound by a legal order or set of shared rules" (Tang and Zhan 2008: 429). The Western democratization school of thought builds on these parameters, defining civil society in China traditionally, whereby non-state actors operate independently from the state and offer countervailing power to state interests. Actors employ an array of strategies, including education initiatives, scientific research, government lobbying, and international monitoring, as well as protests and demonstrations.

Yet while civil society may "act as both allies and adversaries to states, forming networks that advocate policy changes and define ethical standards," (Gunter 2008: 95–99), democratization scholars such as Ann Marie Clark focus on the degree to which they "nearly always act in counterpoint with governmental actors" (Clark 1995). Information is gathered and presented to the wider public independently from government. With this autonomy, moreover, organizations are free to agitate for political change, speak out against governmental programs, and push for sweeping social reforms. In short, according to the democratization school of thought, civil society exists either to facilitate democratization or enhance existing democratic institutions, as articulated by prominent scholars from Alexis de Tocqueville (2004: 596) to Robert D. Putnam (1993). Of course, tight control and oversight by an autocratic Beijing government prevent an autonomous civil society from developing in China in the fully Western sense, with groups largely restricted from speaking out against the central government.

Corporatist or Co-optation Approaches

The corporatist or co-optation school focuses on this restriction. It disagrees with the idea that Chinese civil society acts autonomously from the state, and emphasizes the degree to which China "claims control over every social organization, on the premise that it is the ultimate guardian of the people and their good" (Hsia and White 2002: 332). The prevalence of government-organized non-governmental organizations (GONGOs) is a prime example of this approach. GONGOs are groups that have non-governmental organization legal status, but have very close ties with government. These ties may exist because the groups were established by the government, obtain all or most of their funding from the government, have key personnel who are current or former government officials, or have other characteristics that make it impossible for them to act as truly autonomous organizations even if they technically have independent legal status. As Fengshi Wu explains, GONGOs are "seen as organic parts of the government structure connected by a variety of financial, personnel, and operational ties" (Wu 2002: 47). This structure enhances and expands the efforts of government itself by allowing the two components to work towards a shared set of goals, a close relationship that has its benefits. For one, this closeness to government grants GONGO leadership better access to policy makers and policy making. Lu Yiyi, for example, points to "better bureaucratic connections, higher status, and superior knowledge of the way the state machinery operates" as critical assets in negotiating around government regulations and controls (Lu 2007: 109). Another benefit is that a well-connected membership also ensures priority treatment during funding allocations. Of course, democratization scholars are quick to critique these benefits as coming at great cost, sacrificing independence from government and, too often, bowing to Beijing's will.

But GONGOs are not the only evidence scholars point to when it comes to articulating the co-optation school of thought. Traditional civil society faces this as well. Several notable laws classify even popular groups that have been organized in seemingly independent Western fashion as under government control. Scholars of this corporatist school claim that because of the stringent application and reporting processes required by law, as outlined in table 6.1, all registered civil society groups are under government control (Ma 2002).

The first significant civil society legislation in 1950 was highly restrictive. Rules were then altered in 1989 in response to Tiananmen Square, and again in 1998 with the State Council's Regulations for Registration and Management of Social Organizations. Most notable of all, in both the 1989 and 1998 regulations, the Chinese government created a double registration, oversight, and accountability system. To operate legally, any civil society actor must find a government sponsor, i.e. "mother-in-law" organization, to oversee its activities, and then register officially with the Ministry of Civil Affairs.[1] Groups can only register, though, if they meet minimum financial numbers and have an appropriate office, membership, and staff. Finally, social organizations are restricted from operating in any region that already has a similar issue organization registered, with the express intent here being to bar construction of chapter affiliates and stymie national political networking (Hildebrandt 2011). What results is "a marriage of convenience rather than a catalyst for citizen resistance," as Renee Yuen-Jan Hsia and Lynn T. White II claim (Hsia and White 2002: 337). Civil society is thus co-opted, and exists only to advance government-approved agendas.

China's Third Way

While both the democratization and co-optation schools of thought offer key insights into civil society in China, neither fully describes the emerging civil consciousness there. Indeed, varying levels of autonomy exist in Chinese civil society. Different types of relationships with government prevail. A diverse range of goals and projects dots the landscape. Some NGOs fit the assumptions of the corporatist approach; a number of GONGOs, for example, serve as puppets to the government. On the other hand, popular organizations are able to maintain their individual identities, at times gaining various levels of autonomy that mimic what those in the democratization school emphasize. Moreover, despite what the co-optation school suggests, a GONGO might develop even more financial and administrative autonomy than a popular organization precisely because it is viewed as an extension of the government, as Fengshi Wu argues (Wu 2002: 47, 53). Furthermore, GONGOs offer a politically protected location where counter-expertise can be developed in order to inform, and sometimes even challenge, government policy. The government, for obvious reasons, has more interest in restricting non-GONGOs than GONGOs.

In any case, as Xiaohua Liu contends, "China's NGOs are becoming increasingly independent with the deepening of China's reforms" (Liu

2006). Jiang Ru and Leonard Ortolana concur, pointing to the unofficial role of some NGOs as "watchdog," enforcing national laws and policy at the local level (Ortolana and Ru 2009). This was the case with both Green Earth Volunteers and Green Watershed in their efforts to halt the Nu River Dam between 2003 and 2004. In each case, the indigenous NGO benefited from the international financial support of an organization called Global Greengrants, but consciously limited their activism efforts to developing public awareness. Green Watershed, for example, organized a tour of the Nu River for Chinese journalists and then uploaded their stories and images online (Global Greengrants Fund 2005). In this vein, most NGOs cooperate with government initially, by exploiting connections and expertise, before carving out independent identities.[2] Herein we see China's "third way" as one that effectively combines elements from both the democratization and co-optation schools to paint a more accurate portrait of China's emerging civil society. Indeed, the Dalian protest offers some insight into how NIMBY protests are being used to expand the Third Way in innovative ways.

The Dalian Chemical Power Plant Protest

Perhaps nothing illustrates the persuasiveness of this Third Way analysis of Chinese civil society better than a series of recent coastal city NIMBY protests, including Xiamen in June 2007, Dalian in August 2011, and Ningbo in October 2012. All are examples of local governments backing down quickly when faced with widespread public demonstrations against PX production plants. All are also examples of local governments, despite their initial promises, ultimately acting slowly, if at all, to meet protesters' demands. In each case, protests are not co-opted, but neither are they true democratization initiatives, and are instead hamstrung by authoritarian officials. Nevertheless, this new breed of NIMBY demonstrations stands in stark contrast to typical past disputes in which rural farmers or urban poor rose up over issues of financial exploitation. These three coastal cities, furthermore, represent innovative forms of protest because they represent proactive efforts to stop pollution before it starts rather than reactive demonstrations that break out only after damage has occurred.

NIMBY Protests

Beijing is deeply concerned by this new development in political action. As noted in the introduction to this chapter, with some 180,000 strikes, riots, and protests in 2010, amounting to approximately 500 per day according to the upward end of Human Rights Watch's estimates, increasing numbers of Chinese are deeply dissatisfied with their government. According to Yang Zhaofei, vice-chairman of the Chinese Society for Environmental Sciences, environmental protests have risen on average 29 percent each year since 1996 (Liu 2013), with the number of major environmental protests jumping an astounding 120 percent from 2010 to 2011 (Kennedy 2012). This clearly worries the central government, as reflected in its rising budget for *weiwen* or "stability maintenance." China is, in fact, now spending more on its internal defense than on its military (Xiaokang and Link 2013). Yang also notes that heavy metals and dangerous chemical pollutants like PX are particularly volatile, and frequent targets of protests by the Chinese populace. It does not take an expert to predict that with a rising middle class, more NIMBY protests are likely; within this crucible, our attention now turns specifically to the Dalian case.

The City of Dalian

Located in northeastern China, set on the tip of the Liaodong peninsula and jutting into the Yellow Sea, as noted in figure 6.1, Dalian is the country's northernmost warm-water port and boasts an ideal commercial location that shaped its development into an international shipping and logistics center. Indeed, in 2012 Dalian handled 303 million tons of cargo, according to the Consulate General of the United States, ranking it as third-busiest among Chinese ports and nineteenth-busiest in the world. This role has helped bring considerable wealth to the city, with a per capita GDP in 2012 of RMB 118,631, one that registers higher than even those of first-tier cities such as Beijing, Shanghai, and Guangzhou (Consulate General of the United States, Shenyang, China 2013).

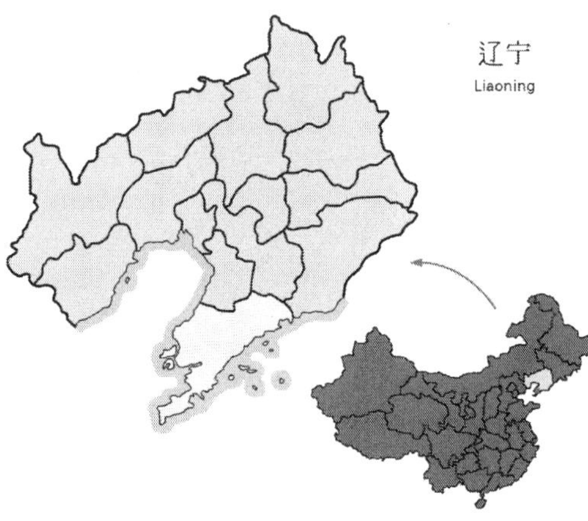

Figure 6.1. *Dalian Prefecture (lightly shaded) with Liaoning Province*

With this wealth and its emergence as the financial center of the northeast, Dalian is at times referred to as the Hong Kong of northern China, but the city is also unique for its architectural and demographic diversity. Although the British occupied the peninsula in 1858, Dalian's international flavor may be traced to its roots as a Russian port town in the late nineteenth century, before Japan defeated the Russians in the Russo-Japanese war and absorbed the fledgling port city as part of its mainland colony in 1905. Following a brief interlude of ownership after World War II, the victorious Soviets then presented the city to the Chinese Communist government in 1950.

It was not until the post-Mao era, however, that Dalian was truly able to exploit its geographic location to great economic profit. Dalian benefited significantly from designation as a Special Economic Zone, beginning in 1985, and investment poured into the city again in the mid-1990s when then-mayor Bo Xilai sought to develop it as a world-class port and destination for international events such as the September 2011 World Economic Forum. With its geographic proximity to Russia, Japan, and Korea, as well as an international flavor tied to the shipping industry, including a huge ethnic Korean population, Dalian also emerged as a popular holiday destination for foreign and domestic tourists alike (Livermore 2007). Famous beaches such as Tiger, Xinghai, Jinshitan and Fujiazhuang serve as prime attractions, and the city is widely acclaimed as one of the cleanest and most livable in China. In 2007, for example, Dalian was named one of China's top three cities for tourism and recognized by the United Nations World Tourism Organization for a range of attributes, from clean accommodation and friendly service to beautiful scenery and an unpolluted environment (*China Daily* 2007).

In some respects, Dalian is a Chinese Florida of sorts, where wealthy elderly couples retire (Larson 2011). But this city on the sea, with an urban population of 2.5 million and total metropolitan population of nearly 6 million, is also a major center of "food processing, machinery, IT, electronics, garments, petrochemicals, household goods, textiles, locomotives, shipbuilding, pharmaceuticals, chemicals, and petroleum refining" (Haft 2007). In particular, information technology, microelectronics manufacturing, oil refining, and petrochemical production provide the economic backbone for continued growth, which brings us to the now-infamous Fujia Dahua Petrochemical Company in the Jinzhou industrial complex. The Fujia factory first opened in 2007, fifty yards behind a seawall, and started full-scale production in June 2009, although according to official records the plant did not receive mandatory environmental approval from the Environmental Protection Bureau in Liaoning until April 2010.

This is a point worth emphasizing in that it illustrates the degree to which economic interests continually trump environmental safety concerns in China. It becomes all the more relevant when noting that the Dalian plant concentrates on production of paraxylene, or PX, a benzene-based chemical widely used in polyester clothes, plastic bottles, and cleaning products (Watts 2011). Vapor from PX can cause nose and eye irritation and, in high concentrations, nerve damage or death, but this toxic chemical has become even more politically poisonous in China, beginning with the aforementioned June 2007 protest walk in the southern city of Xiamen and continuing with Dalian in 2011 and Ningbo in 2012.

The 2007 Xiamen precedent was undoubtedly on the minds of many as Typhoon Mufia began to take shape in the Pacific in early August 2011. When a dike was breached in Dalian on August 8, 2011, and waves, some topping sixty feet, forced thousands to evacuate, concerns began to center on the Fujia chemical plant and the twenty metal tanks that were exposed to the elements. Interestingly, even before the breach, as Typhoon Mufia was still forming in the Pacific, state media CCTV had flown a film crew to Dalian to ask what would happen if a chemical storage tank were to leak during a storm. That film crew was not only denied entry to the plant, but also beaten up by workers there. News of that treatment began to circulate on microblogs, and CCTV itself ran a trailer for a planned segment on the Dalian chemical plant during a popular news program on August 9, 2011, the day after the dike breach. Authorities then second-guessed that decision and pulled the actual report from its scheduled airdate, which further frightened an already-alarmed populace and reinforced the belief that company and government financial interests would supersede any health risks. Memories of the Japanese Fukushima nuclear power plant disaster earlier that year, in March 2011, fueled a number of online rumors, one claiming that contact with contaminated seawater would kill a person in eight minutes (Larson 2011).

The 8-14 Event

On Sunday morning, August 14, 2011, roughly anywhere from 12,000 individuals (according to official estimates) to tens of thousands of protesters (according to reporters from *The Guardian* and *The Atlantic*) gathered in People's Square in Dalian opposite the city hall. This crowd then spilled onto the side streets around People's Square, becoming one of the largest protests in China in years. In fact, some locals now refer to the protest as the largest unrest since the Cultural Revolution. The Dalian chemical protest, or the "8-14 event" as it has come to be known in China, was advertised online, as many protests increasingly are, using the popular euphemism "stroll" instead of protest to avoid censorship.

In fact, a surprisingly diverse array of white-collar Dalian citizens shared information in the days leading up to the protest, using popular media such as Sina, *Weibo* (the Chinese word for microblog), and *Renren* (the Chinese version of Facebook). On the day of the event, and with the original organizer still unknown, a number of first-time protesters took part, according to numerous blog posts now deleted by the government. Throughout the morning, participants chanted revolutionary songs and held up banners that proclaimed slogans such as "PX Out!" Some even posed for group photographs in specially made T-shirts. The protest was largely peaceful, with riot police deployed to protect municipal government offices and periodic calls from within the crowd appealing to people to maintain order and reminding participants to avoid reacting radically so that the demonstration would be allowed to continue (Tang 2011). Indeed, only later in the day did scuffles break out between the crowd and riot police.

Postscript and Ramifications

As in the Lukang case in Taiwan highlighted in the Haddad chapter in this volume, the Dalian protest was different from most past protests in that its participants were mobilizing proactively before the plant actually caused damage. Traditional protests in China are reactive—strikes and protests that respond to health hazards that have already inflicted damage on the population, or, even more frequently, that have thrust tremendous financial loss upon rural farmers or urban poor. The protesters in those cases sought compensation for damage that already occurred. Dalian, like Xiamen in 2007 before it, took the form of an innovative, proactive political strategy. Citizens organized to pressure their government not to allow a petrochemical plant to continue to operate in their own backyards. The Dalian protest was also unusual in that it engendered an immediate response from local officials, with both the Dalian mayor Li Wancai and local Party secretary Tang Jun addressing the crowd on that Sunday and promising to move the plant. Such immediate concessions are rare in China for fear they will encourage future protests. This act of concession thus caught the attention of a number of international commentators, drawing widespread initial praise as an environmental victory along political lines of which Western democratization school scholars would approve.

As the Poulos chapter demonstrates, however, immediate "success" often means that NIMBY protests do not have long-lasting effects. Soon after the political leaders made their public statements, appearing responsive to popular opinion, additional riot police came in from outside Dalian, forcibly dispersing the remaining crowd. Photos of these actions appeared briefly online but were quickly taken down, and heavy censorship that Sunday evening made it impossible to obtain results from any search using terms related to the 8-14 event, such as "PX," "stroll," or "protest." On top of all this, the plant was quietly reopened in December 2011, calling into question the declared success of Dalian's NIMBY protest. A document leaked early in December 2011 suggested the plant would resume operations after passing a series of safety checks, and locals observed smoke coming from the factory chimney as well as workers commuting for their usual shifts before the close of the year (Larson 2011). International analysis of the event had thus shifted from the democratization school to the corporatist or co-optation school by early 2012. As explained by Lio Bo, Secretary General of the NGO Friends of Nature in China, "Previously, similar cases were reactivated without much scrutiny from the public. The public is much less organized, so when the crisis calms down it's difficult for them to monitor what's going on" (Ruwitch and Stanway 2012).

As is often the case, financial concerns drove the decision to reopen the plant. On the one hand, the local government feared Fujia would sue the city for breach of contract and Dalian would be liable for compensation, as the $1.5 billion plant is owned jointly by the city and Fujia. Additionally, the local government would lose approximately $330 million annually in tax revenue if it moved one of the ten biggest factories in Dalian to outside the city (which helps explain why it was promoting the plan to move the plant to Xizhong Island, which is still within city limits). As Yang Guang of the Dalian Propaganda office admitted, "We need to consider the profit of business. It takes time to move the plant. If the production is halted before the relocation, the business will be bankrupted" (Watts 2012). The Dalian case thus represents the classic quandary for Chinese leaders today in their efforts to create a more harmonious society, as they struggle with an increasingly difficult balance between economic growth and public anger over environmental pollution tied to this growth.

As with other cases, Dalian's value as a NIMBY protest rests less with the ultimate outcome for the plant and more in the ways that it created social, political, and technological innovations that became available to other citizens in China facing environmental hazards. To label Dalian a NIMBY failure, using Western democratization-school standards of civil society activity, is perhaps as much a rush to judgment as the initial international praise of the Dalian protest as a success. Much more interesting than the wins and losses of continuing plant operation is the process by which environmental activists let their displeasure be known—and the process by which governmental actors reacted. Dalian thus still serves as an example of countervailing political power in China. While the NIMBY protest itself was only initially successful and quickly dispersed, political engagement extended beyond the actual protest event. According to the Global Nonviolent Action Database at Swarthmore College, over the next year Dalian served as inspiration for a number of subsequent environmental protests, including the closure of a polluting solar panel plant in Haining in 2011 (Blount 2011). Additional instances of the middle class engaging in proactive environmental protests in 2012–13 alone include protests against the aforementioned PX plant expansion in Ningbo, a proposed smelting plant in Shifang, a proposed waste-water pipeline connected to a paper manufacturing plant in Qidong, and a proposed refinery for gasoline, diesel, fertilizers, and the petrochemical PX in Kunming. Thus, rather than being solely about one case, Dalian highlights the degree to which NIMBY events are much more complicated than the black-and-white rhetoric of victory and defeat. What are really interesting in the NIMBY arena are the grey areas in between, the political processes by which governmental actors and developing Chinese civil society interact—and the adjustments made in their aftermath.

The Dalian demonstration displays several key factors that characterize NIMBY innovation. For one, Dalian energized and engaged formerly apolitical actors, bringing white-collar and first-time demonstrators into the political arena, even when the actual organizer of the event was unknown. Second, Dalian involved the attempt to leverage different parts of government against each other, pitting national bodies such as the Ministry of Environmental Protection (formerly the State Environmental Protection Agency, SEPA) against local Party offices, and exploiting multiple access points. Highlighting Kenneth Lieberthal's (1992) fragmented authoritarianism, NIMBY in Dalian took advantage of inter-institutional and inter-governmental conflict, as discussed in more detail in Plantan's chapter in this volume on Russia and China. Third, Dalian illustrates the potential to widen interpretations of what constitutes "my" backyard. Participants were not worried only about personal health implications or motivated merely by the fear that their own long-term economic interests were being compromised by a short-term profit focus on the part of the local government and Fujia. Participants, and for that matter non-Dalian observers as well, were concerned about the cultural significance of the city of Dalian as a holiday and retirement destination. Fourth, timing was a crucial variable. Dalian followed on the heels of the international crisis in Fukishima, Japan, earlier that year, which primed public opinion and stoked fears of a natural disaster magnifying manmade problems. When the local crisis of Typhoon Mufia hit, the popular protest momentum became even more difficult to contain, and wild rumors began to spread about the lethality of PX. Taken altogether, with these four key characteristics, Dalian presented a powerful combination of factors that allowed this NIMBY movement to implement several noted technological, social, and, most importantly, political innovations.

In examining Dalian's case, these three closely connected types of innovation made through NIMBY deserve emphasis. For one, technological innovations through smart phones, texting, and microblogging made it possible to organize the Dalian protest, avoiding censors both before the event, and, to a lesser degree, after the protest as well. Indeed, Internet usage is increasing rapidly in China, and rose to 591,000,000 users by July 2013 (*BBC News and Technology* 2013), more than twice that found in the United States, according to China Internet Network Information Centre. That equates to 44 percent of China's population, nearly a quarter of the world's population, and a 10 percent rise from 2012. In contrast, the United States' 254,000,000 users represent a little more than 10 percent of the world's population. Of course, these numbers are geographically and demographically disproportionate within China, favoring younger city dwellers over older rural citizens.

Not only do these wealthy, urban Chinese have access to the Internet; they use it—a lot. In China's sixty largest cities, people spend 70 percent of their leisure time online, according to a 2010 *McKinsey Quarterly* study (Atsmon and Magni 2010). With these numbers, it is no wonder that scholars increasingly point to the role of the Internet in communicating dissent within China (Yang 2003), and perhaps even in pluralizing society (Zheng 2008). Blogs, discussion boards, and the Internet more generally allow activists to organize and communicate, to access information previously unavailable (Chase, Mulvenon, and Hachigian 2006). Jonathan Sullivan and Xie Lei, for instance, find that four primary functions for virtual environmental networks are emerging, including providing information, encouraging discussion, fostering online collaboration, and, perhaps most notably, developing campaign mobilization (Sullivan and Xie 2009).

These social networks pay real political dividends because China's political system, especially its local politics, is heavily influenced by social connections (Tsai 2007). The role of local politics has been strengthened by economic liberalization initiatives since 1979 that have transferred economic decision making to the local level. Further, political regulations in the aftermath of 1989 have encouraged the development of local environmental groups with loose links to one another and barred the formation of national groups with local chapters, largely due to the fear that these would present countervailing power challenges to government.

Middle-class Chinese citizens are considerably more socially empowered today with their smart phones and Internet cafés, even in the face of a mammoth state censorship apparatus. As Chinese "netizens" continually develop new social ties, there has been a dramatic expansion of public participation, which stands out as the most notable political innovation in the Dalian NIMBY case. Most environmental NIMBY protests in China have historically been in rural areas in cases in which farmers and fishermen find their livelihoods and the health of their families threatened by rising pollution of the air, water, and soil. These politically marginalized groups are generally excluded from elite politics and must take to the streets to be heard by their government. In contrast, Dalian's protest mobilized politically reticent middle-class urban populations, and helped publicize the ways that new technologies can be used to organize dissent.

White-collar citizens who had never before participated in a protest demonstrated in Dalian. They came to rally and promote grassroots democracy, even though the leader of the protest was unknown. Dalian's citizens, by challenging the government's story that PX was not dangerous, are helping to end a monopoly on knowledge about potential pollution from factories like Fujia (Zheng 2008). Furthermore, although NIMBY activities often emphasize the importance of "my" backyard, this protest emphasized how much the people of Dalian cared about not only their own personal health but also the larger community itself. As evidenced by microblogging activity across the country, the Dalian protest presented a culturally-framed argument that resonated well beyond Dalian city limits.

Proactive NIMBY protests by middle-class Chinese demanding that environmental damage be halted before it begins suggest that state-society relations are changing fundamentally in China. Citizens are no longer simply accepting development plans made by the government and are beginning to demand a say in how those plans are formed. Furthermore, a government that listens to these new kinds of citizens is a different kind of government. What remains unknown, of course, is whether these changes will continue to be incremental, largely non-violent, and guided by Party actions as they were on August 14, 2011, or whether they will be more dramatic and violent as was the case on June 4, 1989.

Conclusion

Academic attention to an emerging Chinese civil society continues to grow, particularly in the form of studies targeting indigenous NGOs and the unique breed of government-organized NGOs (GONGOs) developed by the Communist Party itself. In particular, environmental groups, with their largely non-confrontational posturing and technical emphasis, represent the first wave in this field. Few studies, though, analyze the role of environmental NIMBY initiatives in China, which have become widespread nationally and are becoming an increasing focus of government concern. This is a noted deficiency, as an expanding middle class has become more and more vocal over the last decade, increasingly expressing its displeasure about pollution and environmental degradation that damages its economic, ecological, and health interests. In contrast to what would be expected by the democratization school, but in common with the cases of Lukang in Taiwan and the Dujiangyan dam in China covered in this volume, Dalian's NIMBY efforts gained broader salience partly because they avoided targeting the central government and rather directed their focus toward local government and the general public, following the aforementioned boomerang-effect logic of Keck and Sikkink (1998). In short, environmental activism in China is more effective when it retains a local NIMBY character and does not grow into a national confrontation with government, as is often found in Western environmental movements. Those who challenge the state directly in an autocratic system such as China's have short lifespans—at times literally so.

As is the case with the preceding chapter examining Russia and China, this chapter argues that the Dalian chemical plant protest provides a model for improving state-society relations in the context of an authoritarian political structure. Dalian offered the Chinese people innovative forms of protest, using new technology, engaging previously inactive citizens, and transforming the character of citizen activism from merely reactive to proactive. These innovations were largely possible as a direct result of Dalian's NIMBY character, which was rooted in a particular community's backyard, but whose story resonated with many millions of Chinese facing similar threats across the country. As similar protests continue to spread across China, and as local governments grow more adept at dealing with protester demands to be part of policymaking, we can see how one backyard protest can contribute to the transformation of the overall politics of a country.

Notes

1. Registration is no easy task, as government organizations are typically reluctant to assume the potential liabilities of becoming a sponsor. As a result, social organizations often remain unregistered, which in theory ensures more autonomy, but in practice means basic operational tasks such as opening bank accounts, employing personnel, obtaining tax benefits, entering into cooperative arrangements, and establishing legal contracts are nearly impossible. Thus even unregistered organizations are controlled to great degree by the government.
2. According to a case study of the China Youth Development Foundation (CYDF), an extremely successful and largely autonomous GONGO, one of the interviewees "advised Chinese NGOs to make good use of government resources at the beginning, then to pay more attention to 'developing their individualities' later" (Yiyi 2007: 182).

References

Atsmon, Yuval and Max Magni. 2010. "China's Internet Obsession." *Harvard Business Review*. February 24. Accessed November 30, 2014. https://hbr.org/2010/02/chinas-internet-obsession.

Barboza, David. 2011. "Despite Restrictions, Microblogs Catch On in China." *The New York Times,* May 15. Accessed November 28, 2012. http://www.nytimes.com/2011/05/16/business/global/16blogs.html.

Blount, Pauline. 2011. "Chinese Residents Force Relocation of Chemical Plant in Xiamen, 2007." November 20. Accessed November 16, 2012. Global Nonviolent Action Database, Swarthmore College.

Chan, G., P. Lee, and L. Chan. 2008. "China's Environmental Governance: The Domestic-International Nexus." *Third World Quarterly* 29: 291–314.

Chase, Michael, James Mulvenom, and Nina Hachigian. 2006. "Comrade to Comrade Networks: The Social and Political Implications of Peer-to-Peer Networks in China." In *Chinese Cyberspaces: Technological Changes and Political Effects,* edited by Jens Damm and Simona Thomas. 64–101. New York: Routledge.

"China Protest Closes Toxic Chemical Plant in Dalian." 2011. *BBC News,* 14 August. Accessed December 1, 2013. http://www.bbc.co.uk/news/world-asia-pacific-14520438.

"China Smartphone Owners Swell Number of Internet Users." 2013. *BBC News and Technology,* July 17. Accessed December 1, 2013. http://www.bbc.co.uk/news/technology-23343058.

Clark, Ann Marie. 1995. "Non-Governmental Organizations and Their Influence on International Society." *Journal of International Affairs* 48(2): 507–25.

Consulate General of the United States, Shenyang, China. 2013. "Overview of Dalian City." November 25. Accessed December 1, 2013. http://shenyang.usembassy-china.org.cn/dl.html.

Economy, Elizabeth. 2004. *The River Runs Black: The Environmental Challenge to China's Future.* Ithaca, NY: Cornell University Press.

Economy, Elizabeth, and Kenneth Lieberthal. 2007. "Scorched Earth: Will Environmental Risks in China Overwhelm Its Opportunities?" *Harvard Business Review*, 85(9): 141–48.

Fu, Jing. 2011. "Better Use of NGOs Predicted." *China Daily,* May 14. Accessed July 1, 2011. http://www.Chinadaily.com.cn/cndy/2011-05/14/content_12509762.htm

Global Greengrants Fund. 2005. "China: Proposed Dam Project Suspended – For Now." Accessed November 18, 2012. http://www.greengrants.org/2005/09/08/china-proposed-dam-project-suspended-for-now/.

Gunter, Michael M., Jr. 2008. "Nongovernmental Organizations." In *Encyclopedia of Environmental Ethics and Philosophy,* edited by J. Baird Callicott and Robert Frodeman, 2: 95–99 Farmington Hills, MI: Macmillan Reference.

Gunter, Michael M., Jr., and Ariane Rosen. 2012. "Two Level Games of International Environmental NGOs in China." *William & Mary Policy Review* 3(2): 270–94.

Haft, Jeremy. 2007. *All the Tea in China: How to Buy, Sell, and Make Money on the Mainland.* New York: Penguin.

"Hangzhou, Chengdu, Dalian Named Best Tourist City." 2007. *China Daily,* February 10. Accessed November 20, 2012. http://www.china.org.cn/archive/2007-02/10/content_1199624.htm.

Hildebrandt, Timothy. 2011. "The Political Economy of Social Organization Registration in China." *The China Quarterly* 208: 970–89.

Howell, Jude. 2007. "Civil Society in China: Chipping Away at the Edges." *Development* 5(3): 17–23.

Hsia, Renee Yuen-Jan, and Lynn T. White III. 2002. "Working Amid Corporatism and Confusion: Foreign NGOs in China." *Nonprofit and Voluntary Sector Quarterly* 31: 329–51.

Human Rights Watch. 2012. "World Report 2012." Accessed December 5, 2013. http://www.hrw.org/world-report-2012/world-report-2012-china.

Kang, Xiaoguan. 2008. "On Chinese Government Control of NGOs." Duowei News [Hong Kong]. *China Digital Times,* December 15. Accessed November 30, 2014. http://chinadigitaltimes.net/2008/12/kang-xiaoguang-on-chinese-government-control-of-ngos/.

Keck, Margaret E., and Kathryn Sikkink. 1998. *Activists Beyond Borders: Advocacy Networks in International Politics.* Ithaca, NY: Cornell University Press.

Kennedy, John. 2012. "Environmental Protests in China on Dramatic Rise, Expert Says." *Clear the Air News Blog,* October 29. Accessed November 20, 2012. http://news.newclear.server279.com/?p=5417.

Keohane, Robert O., and Joseph S. Nye. 1977. *Power and Interdependence: World Politics in Transition.* Boston, MA: Little, Brown and Company.

Knup, Elizabeth. 1997. "Environmental NGOs in China: An Overview." *China Environment Series* 1: 9–15. Washington, DC: Woodrow Wilson International Center for Scholars.

Larson, Christina. 2011. "The New Epicenter of China's Discontent." *Foreign Policy,* August 23. Accessed November 20, 2012. http://www.foreignpolicy.com/articles/2011/08/23/the_new_epicenter_of_china_s_discontent.

———. 2012. "Protests in China Get a Boost from Social Media." *Bloomberg Businessweek,* October 29. Accessed November 26, 2012. http://www.businessweek.com/articles/2012-10-29/protests-in-china-get-a-boost-from-social-media.

Lieberthal, Kenneth. 1992. "Introduction: The 'Fragmented Authoritarianism' Model and Its Limitations." In *Bureaucracy, Politics, and Decision Making in Post-Mao China,* edited by Kenneth Lieberthal and David M. Lampton: 1–30. Berkeley: University of California Press.

Liu, Jianqiang. 2013. "China's New 'Middle Class' Environmental Protests." *China Dialogue,* January 2. Accessed December 5, 2013. https://www.chinadialogue.net/article/show/single/en/5561-China-s-new-middle-class-environmental-protests.

Liu, Xiaohua. 2006. "NGOs in China: An Overview." Sept. 2002. International Community Foundation. Accessed June 2, 2009. http://www.icfdn.org/publications/NGOsinChina-ICFWhitePaper.doc.

Livermore, Adam. 2007. "An Investor's Guide to Dalian." *China Briefing News,* September 26. Accessed November 26, 2012. http://www.china-briefing.com/news/2007/09/26/an-investors-guide-to-dalian.html.

Lu, Yiyi. 2007a. "The Autonomy of Chinese NGOs: A New Perspective." *China: An International Journal* 5(2): 173–203.

———. 2007b. "Environmental Civil Society and Governance in China." *International Journal of Environmental Studies* 64(1): 59–69.

Ma, Qiusha. 2002. "The Governance of NGOs in China since 1978: How Much Autonomy?" *The Nonprofit & Voluntary Sector Quarterly* 31(3): 305–28.

Moore, Allison, and Adrian Warren. 2006. "Legal Advocacy in Environmental Public Participation in China: Raising the Stakes and Strengthening Stakeholders." *China Environment Series* 8: 3–26.

People's Republic of China, State Council. 1998. *Regulations for Registration and Management of Social Organizations.* Accessed November 30, 2014. http://www.cecc.gov/resources/legal-provisions/regulations-on-the-registration-and-management-of-social-organizations.

Putnam, Robert. 1993. *Making Democracy Work: Civic Traditions in Modern Italy.* Princeton, NJ: Princeton University Press.

Ru, Jiang, and Leonard Ortolano. 2009. "Development of Citizen-Organized Environmental NGOs in China." *Voluntas* 20: 157.

Ruwitch, John, and David Stanway. 2012. "China struggles for solution to growing NIMBY movement." *Reuters,* November 1. Accessed November 30, 2014. http://www.reuters.com/article/2012/11/01/us-china-environment-idUSBRE8A01L020121101.

Sui-Lee, Wee. 2011. "China Says Will Shut Plant as Thousands Protest." *Reuters,* August 14. Accessed November 26, 2012. http://www.reuters.com/article/2011/08/14/us-china-protests-idUSTRE77D0EK20110814.

Sullivan, Jonathan, and Lei Xie, 2009. "Environmental Activism, Social Networks and the Internet." *The China Quarterly* 198: 422–32.

State Council Order No. 251. 2009. Translated by China Development Brief. June 11. Accessed November 30, 2014. http://chinadevelopmentbrief.cn/wp-content/uploads/2014/08/PROVISIONAL-REGULATIONS-FOR-THE-REGISTRATION-AND-MANAGEMENT-OF-CIVIL-NON-ENTERPRISE-WORK-UNITS1.pdf..

Sun, Yanfei, and Dingxin Zhao. 2008. "Environmental Campaigns." In *Popular Protest in China,* edited by Kevin J. O'Brien, 144–62. Cambridge, MA: Harvard University Press.

Tang, Hao. 2011. "Public Storm in Dalian." *China Dialogue,* September 6. Accessed November 18, 2012. http://www.chinadialogue.net/article/show/single/en/4511-Public-storm-in-Dalian.

Tang, Shui-Yan, and Zhan Xueyong. 2008. "Civic Environmental NGOs, Civil Society, and Democratization in China." *Journal of Development Studies* 44(3): 425–48.

Tocqueville, Alexis de. 2004. *Democracy in America.* Translated by Arthur Goldhammer. New York: Library of America.

Tsai, Lily L. 2007. "Solidarity Groups, Informal Accountability, and Local Public Goods Provision in Rural China." *The American Political Science Review* 101(2): 355–372.

Turner, Jennifer L., and Lu Zhi. 2006. "Building a Green Civil Society in China." In *State of the World 2006: A Worldwatch Institute Report on Progress Toward a Sustainable Society.* Worldwatch Institute, 152–170. New York: W.W. Norton & Company.

Watts, Jonathan. 2011. "Tens of Thousands Protest against Chemical Plant in Northern China." *The Guardian,* August 14. Accessed November 11, 2012. http://www.guardian.co.uk/environment/2011/aug/14/china-protest-against-px-chemical-plant.

Watts, Jonathan. 2012. "Controversial Chinese Chemical Plant Believed to have Resumed Production." *The Guardian,* January 13. Accessed November 10, 2012. http://www.guardian.co.uk/environment/2012/jan/13/chinese-chemical-plant.

Wu, Fengshi. 2002. "New Partners or Old Brothers? GONGOs in Transitional Environmental Advocacy in China." *China Environment Series* 5: 45–58.

Xiaokang, Su, and Perry Link. 2013. "A Collapsing Natural Environment?" In *Restless China,* edited by Perry Link, Richard P. Madsen, and Paul G. Pickowicz, 213–36. Lanham, MD: Rowman & Littlefield Publishers, Inc.

Xie, Lei. 2011. "China's Environmental Activism in the Age of Globalization." *Asian Politics & Policy* 3(2): 207–24.

Xie, Lie, and Hein-Anton Van der Heijden. 2010. "Environmental Movements and Political Opportunities: The Case of China." *Social Movement Studies* 9(1): 60–61.

Yang, Guobin. 2003. "The Co-Evolution of the Internet and Civil Society in China." *Asian Survey* 43(3): 405–22.

Zhao, Dagong. 2007. "The Xiamen Demonstrations and Growing Civil Consciousness." *China Rights Forum* 3:104–107.

Zheng, Yongnian. 2008. *Technological Empowerment: The Internet, State and Society in China.* Palo Alto, CA: Stanford University Press.

Zissis, Carin, and Jayshree Bajoria. 2008. "China's Environmental Crisis." *Council on Foreign Relations,* August 4. Accessed November 26, 2012. http://www.cfr.org/china/chinas-environmental-crisis/p12608.

Chapter 7

Local Activism and Environmental Innovation in Japan

Takashi Kanatsu

Japan's environmental performance has been stunning, to say the least, considering that the country was dubbed a "pollution archipelago" (*Kogai Retto*) in the 1960s. Some of the pollution-related diseases suffered by Japanese people are still remembered vividly in Japan and the rest of the world. Since 75 percent of Japan's terrain is mountainous, almost half of its natural seashores were lost in order to construct industrial complexes.

Japan changed its approach to the environment dramatically circa 1970, becoming one of the most environmentally conscious countries in the world. Japan is leading the world particularly in the field of efficient, environmentally friendly technologies. The studies conducted by Scruggs (2003) and Jahn (1998) ranked Japan high among OECD countries, particularly in the field of air pollution and also as an economy that expanded but performed well. Scruggs ranked Japan between West Germany (538 and the highest in the study) and the United States (291), with a total score of 414 in the indicator that includes SOx, NOx, waste, recycling, fertilizer, and water treatment (Scruggs 2003: 51). Jahn's study ranked Japan's environmental performance seventh, between those of Germany (second) and the United States (fifteenth), although energy use in Japan expanded during the study period while it shrank in Germany (Jahn 1998: 113). The most recent Environmental Performance Index (EPI)[1] (2012) ranked Germany 11th, Japan, 23rd, and the United States 49th (Emerson et al. 2012: 10). Furthermore, the most recent OECD data shows that Japan beats both Germany and the United States in greenhouse gas emissions: 2011 total greenhouse gases, tons per capita were—Japan 10, Germany 11, United States 21 (OECD 2014). Thus, after its dramatic policy shift in the early 1970s, Japan has continued to be a global leader in environmental performance.

One of the most remarkable of Japan's achievements was the reduction of automobile CO, HC, and NOx emissions. Air pollution originating from the car became a focal point in 1970 in the United States, when Japanese auto manufacturers started venturing into the U.S. market. At that time, Japanese automobile technologies lagged behind those of American manufacturers by a wide margin. Japan was challenging the largest and most formidable automobile giants in the world: the Big Three of the United States. By 1978, Japan had achieved all of the standards—CO, HC, and NOx—mandated by the U.S. Clean Air Act of 1970, while the U.S. fleet did not achieve this standard until 1997. Even California, which imposes much stricter standards than the U.S. federal government, did not catch up to Japan's own standard for HC emissions until 1980 and for NOx until 1983 (Nishimura and Sadakata 1989: 116).

This chapter argues that NIMBY protest was a key factor shaping Japan's air pollution policies. Local advocates took advantage of the opportunities created by the Japanese macro-political structure, including party politics and inter-ministerial disputes, to push their demands for cleaner air. Contrary to traditional recipes for environmental policy success, such as strong pro-environmental political parties and nationally or internationally organized strong environmental NGOs, the Japanese experience demonstrates the effectiveness of NIMBY activism even where macro-political structures would have predicted a major failure.

The NIMBY-Inspired Solution to Japanese Environmental Problems

One of the main reasons that Japan was able to overcome collective action problems common to environmental issues was that NIMBY mobilization transformed clean air, often perceived as a collective good, into a non-collective good. Local communities identified their pollution problems as local problems and sought local solutions. Those local solutions, because they involved national and multinational corporations, became national and, indeed, international solutions. Local Japanese became aware of environmental problems because industrial pollutants were killing people in their own communities, most notably in Minamata, Yokkaichi, Toyoma, and Niigata. These pollution problems were not considered to be a diffuse, national issue but rather a collection of local problems. This stands in stark contrast to the German case, where one of the first major pollution issues was the problem of acid rain, initially observed in the Scandinavian countries rather than inside Germany in the early 1970s. From the beginning, pollution problems were international issues for Germany, while for Japan they were not.

Traditionally, NIMBY has been considered a common reaction to private "bads" that accompany collective "goods" (Aldrich 2008). For example, while everyone recognizes the need for garbage-free streets for the entire nation, no one wants to have a landfill in her or his backyard. This is why NIMBY protest is commonly seen as a hindrance to the pursuit of a common interest. However, as the case of Japan will demonstrate, NIMBY can contribute to solving collective action problems by sharing information about costs and clearly identifying project beneficiaries. In other words, "I don't want pollution in *my* backyard," can become "pollution shouldn't happen in *anyone's* backyard."

In the case of Japan, the history of NIMBY-inspired solutions to pollution problems goes back to the early twentieth century. Hashimoto explains: "Local initiatives provided the first programs of pollution control and compensation upon which later national programs were modeled ... Although the Imperial Constitution of 1889 did not grant autonomy to local governments, the ministry of the interior in fact permitted a measure of local autonomy" (Hashimoto 1989: 8). In post-World War II Japan, the Local Autonomy Law of 1947 fortified this autonomy, as it allowed local governments such as prefectures, cities, and others to make ordinances as long as they did not violate national laws. The first post-World War II pollution-related regulations were promulgated in Tokyo in 1949, decades ahead of any national pollution laws.[2] By 1971, all prefectural governments had established pollution prevention ordinances. At the same time, local governments started making pollution prevention contracts with businesses, the first of which was between Shimane Prefecture and local paper and textile companies in 1952 (Ogata 2008: 8). Since then, frequent bargaining has taken place at the construction sites of many power stations (Lesbirel 1998). Although this bargaining resulted in additional costs, initially, in the form of compensation to fishermen etc., in the end, this bargaining allowed for effective monitoring, which lowered the overall cost to the businesses involved and to Japanese society.

A further indication of how the Japanese perceived pollution problems to be local issues rather than national ones is the fact that many of the early pollution issues came to be known by the name of the town or city where they occurred, rather than by the chemical that was causing the problem—Ashio, Besshi, Hitachi, Osaka, Yahata, Tokyo, Kanagawa, Fukuoka, Mishima-Numazu, Nishinomiya, Isogo, and Sapporo, among others. All four major pollution-related diseases in Japan also came to be known by the specific places where they occurred rather than by their pollutant names—Minamata disease (mercury poisoning), Niigata Minamata disease (mercury poisoning), Yokkaichi asthma (caused by sulfur dioxide and nitrogen dioxide)—or the feeling they caused—Itai-Itai (Ouch! Ouch!) disease (cadmium poisoning). Air pollution caused by automobile emissions was concentrated in large cities, and people identified those pollution problems with their cities—Tokyo, Osaka, etc—as this chapter will explain in detail later.

NIMBY Issue Framing in Japan

Japanese political institutions provided the framework to channel environmental problems into NIMBY issues. First, one-party dominance encouraged the framing of environmental problems as non-partisan technical issues. Second, inter-ministerial disputes shifted the solution to the local level even where the problems were broader in scope. Third, local government leaders, particularly of major cities where pollution is generally concentrated, tended to be opposition leftists, who were more sympathetic to the health and environmental concerns of residents. These local governments picked up on local concerns well and provided various policy innovations in spite of their limited budgetary resources.

LDP's Dominance Contributed to NIMBY Framing

After ten years of volatility following the end of World War II, Japan had extremely stable national party politics, with the LDP in power continuously from 1955 until 2009.[3] What Hall (1993) calls a "third-order change" (279), or "a radical change in the overarching terms of policy discourse," did not take place in Japan until 2009. In 1955, three years after the end of the Allied occupation of Japan, two conservative parties merged into the Liberal Democratic Party (LDP). This was a response to the rising power of the Japan Socialist Party (JSP), which benefited from rapid urbanization and lingering social and economic confusion in the wake of the war. The merger of 1955 marked the beginning of more than a half-century of political dominance by the LDP. Under the so-called 1955 system, even the largest opposition party—the JSP—was ridiculed as a half-party. Although they lost the majority 1993, the LDP regained power in less than a year, while opposition parties were in disarray.

The environment was not framed as a partisan issue at the national level, given the LDP dominance of the government. This means that environmental issues were *not* "politicized" as much as they were in Germany and the United States, where leading political parties fought bitter campaigns centered on environmental policy issues. Therefore "the difficulty of building *sufficient consensus among the ministries*" (Schreurs 2002: 173, emphasis added) was quite distinct from the national level political consensus, which Japan had sustained for half a century since 1955. Election results as well as public opinion polls of the half-century until 2009 clearly indicated continuing public support for the LDP. Thus, the two most important battlegrounds for environmental issues were (1) inter-ministerial, when different ministries with overlapping jurisdictions competed for favored policy solutions, and (2) local government, where actors at the local level (citizens, corporations, local government officials) fought to improve their positions in a specific local community.

Inter-ministerial Battles led to NIMBY Framing

Although there was consensus in the legislative branch of government because of LDP dominance, different ministries diverged significantly and competed for favored policy solutions to environmental problems. Inter-ministerial conflicts helped promote NIMBY solutions because they created openings for local policy innovation. It is important to realize that policy making is just a part of politics overall. Implementation or enactment is also a key process of politics, and this is where the coordination of various ministries matters (Reed 1981: 255).

Japan's environmental policy faced significant collective action problems at this level because turf battles among ministries were very fierce. It is commonly observed that "Japanese administration is characterized by vertical fragmentation (*tate wari gyosei*), with each ministry jealously guarding its jurisdictions and exercising a virtual veto over any proposals that would impinge upon its prerogatives" (Reed 1981: 255). As in many other countries, we can conceptually divide Japanese ministries into pro-environment and pro-economic growth groups, based on respective jurisdiction. Traditionally, the Ministry of Health, Labor, and Welfare (MHLW)[4] has represented the pro-environment side. On the pro-economic growth side has been the Ministry of Economy, Trade, and Industry (METI).[5] The Ministry of Land, Infrastructure, Transport and Tourism (MLITT)[6] and Ministry of Agriculture, Forestry, and Fishery (MAFF) have usually been centrist on the issue, but the MAFF has tended to be more environmentally protective. Since 1971, pro-environment policy has typically been represented by the Environment Protection Agency, which was finally upgraded to ministry status in 2001, becoming the Ministry of Environment.

This general division of ministries between pro-environment and pro-economic growth, however, does not always hold. METI's role, while always pro-business, has been much more ambiguous with respect to the environment than its name suggests. In the past, in cases in which METI shared interests with a pro-environment ministry such as the Ministry of Health and Welfare, it has not hesitated to collaborate, as can be seen in the case of Dr. Kiyoshi Kurokawa's Investigative Task Force regarding the Yokkaichi case in 1964 (Hashimoto 1989, 16). When the MHLW found an increase in levels of asthma in the city of Yokkaichi, the ministry contacted METI to ask if it would like to set up a joint research commission to investigate the matter. METI agreed, and the joint commission was created, led by Dr. Kurokawa, the Director General of METI's Institute of Industrial Technology. In that case, all of Dr. Kurokawa's recommendations, many of which concerned technical improvements, were implemented.

METI has been an ardent supporter of anti-pollution and energy-saving technology and policies. For example, when oil prices declined in 1986, the petroleum sector put strong pressure on METI to allow more imports of petroleum to Japan with a lower market price. METI usually supported the petroleum industry's demands, but in this case it was able to shift its support to alternative energy such as liquefied natural gas (LNG), nuclear, and coal, and thus resisted this pressure from petroleum companies (Lesbirel 1988: 295).

Although METI is concerned primarily with national-level politics and policy, sometimes it can become directly engaged in NIMBY conflicts. For example, in 1963 the Shizuoka prefectural government presented a project to build a huge petrochemical factory complex straddling the cities of Mishima and Numazu (Mishima-city). Citizens' groups immediately organized demonstrations against the construction and held numerous public study sessions in the community. Eighty-two percent of the citizens of Mishima signed petitions against the construction of the petrochemical complex. In response, two scholarly groups were created to assess the environmental impact of the complex, one formed by METI and led by Dr. Kurokawa (the same person who had led the Yokkaichi case mentioned above) and the other organized by Mishima City and led by Dr. Matsumura. In the end, not only did METI give up on the construction project, it changed its national policies to reflect the lessons it learned in the Mishima conflict.

This Mishima-Numazu local dispute also mobilized the national government, another example of NIMBY's contribution to Japan's environmental policy innovation. In the same year as the Mishima-Numazu case, METI started a large national desulfurization project under one of its research institutes, the Agency of Industrial Science and Technology (AIST), to reduce the pollution produced by petrochemical production across the country (MOE 1971). It developed a dry desulfurization technology in 1966, and continued to work on the project until 1969[7] (NEDO 2002: 2–15). This was probably METI's largest contribution to environmental technology to date. The business / technology-government (METI) linkage was a big factor in Japanese environmental technology development, and this project was one of its most important cases. Four major corporations joined the project, which had been led by METI from the beginning: Hitachi, TEPCO, MHI, and Chubu Electric Power Co. (NEDO 2002: 2–17). This project represents one of the top environmental technology exports from Japan to various developing countries. According to JETRO, the largest portion (44 percent) of air pollution prevention technology exports from Japan between 1997 and 2006 was flue gas desulfurization equipment—a direct descendant of METI's 1963 project (JETRO 2007).

Local Governments Were Key Battlefields in Environmental Policymaking

Local governments are the main battlefields in environmental policy making in Japan, and the battles usually take the form of NIMBY politics. Citizens organizing around NIMBY issues target local governments first. They have often been able to partner with local governments to resolve their issues. There are four reasons for this. First, Japanese local governments can engage in a wide range of actions without the involvement of the national government. As discussed above, under the 1947 Local Autonomy Law, Japanese local governments can enact various ordinances as long as there are no national laws that overlap in jurisdiction. Also, local governments are allowed to make agreements with businesses when they construct factories and other facilities. Furthermore, METI is usually disinclined to get involved in local disputes related to pollution issues, widening the scope within which local governments can make policy. Although local governments must operate within limited budgets, known as the "thirty percent of autonomy" (McKean 1981: 23) or *Sanwari-Jichi,* they have quite significant leeway within those parameters to establish legal mechanisms related to environmental management.

Second, implementation of environmental policies usually depends on local politics. No matter how well-crafted a central government's policies are, their effectiveness will be significantly compromised if local governments do not have the willingness and ability to implement them. Thus, local governments can influence not only the creation of policy at the local level, but also the implementation of national policy that affects their communities.

Third, local leaders are elected in a different way than national leaders in Japan. Japan has a parliamentary democracy at the national level, but governors of prefectures and mayors of cities, towns, and villages are directly elected.[8] The individual governor or mayor, rather than the party, has a major effect on policy choices. In the case of Japan, several governors and mayors played key roles that led to the success of environmental policies in the 1970s, and many of them were not from the LDP but from left-wing parties (Hashimoto 1989: 27). It is important to note that major innovations came from the local governments whose leaders were leftists.

Finally, and most importantly, local governments were the battlegrounds because local environmental issues can avoid many collective action problems when they are addressed at the local level. Local environmental issues in Japan tend to be viewed as NIMBY issues, which allows activists to overcome the collective action problems that often plague environmental politics at national and global levels. At the local level, both polluters and project beneficiaries are clearly defined, information can be obtained relatively easily, and sanctions can be applied against violators. Thus, coordination is much easier at this level. In short, this is the strength of NIMBY, which the Japanese have used to positive effect to address major environmental challenges. Local NGOs, or citizens' movements, were able to remain local partially because of their effectiveness in working with local governments to solve collective action problems related to the environment (Haddad 2012; McKean 2008). Citizens' movements are described below for several specific cases, and in greater detail for the case of innovations in auto emission controls, which began with various local incidents.

In the Japanese case, the inter-ministerial bickering at the national level was overcome by sound policy making at the local level. Starting in the mid-1960s in the city of Yokohama, local governments were able to force corporations to agree on pollution control measures, or pollution prevention contracts (McKean 1981: 149). In December 1964, Mayor Asukata of Yokohama, responding to citizen concerns, asked the electric company J-Power to agree to fourteen environmental conditions upon the construction of a power plant in Isogo in Yokomaha. J-Power agreed. This type of private agreement between local governments and corporations regarding pollution control became known as the "Yokohama Formula" and spread to other siting cases in Japan (Matsumoto 2004: 3). The number of pollution prevention contracts between local governments and corporations, or "Yokohama Formulas," rose to 800 by 1970 and to more than 25,000 by 1984. The enforcement was effective at this level because the corporations helped to craft the pollution restrictions, and local government officials were able to insist on time-consuming environmental impact studies because the demands were coming from local fishermen and residents whose lives were at stake due to the environmental impact of the planned facilities, a typical NIMBY scenario (Eguchi 1980: 269).

Now, as then, the local bargaining process is very different from national-level environmental policy making because local governments have considerable leeway to negotiate with corporations, and those corporations must gain local government approval in order to operate in any given jurisdiction, as was the case in Yokohama. It is common in Japan for local governments to impose more stringent environmental ordinances than the national government requires (Hashimoto 1989: 74). In 1969, the Tokyo Metropolitan Government under Governor Minobe began the trend of enforcing more stringent local pollution regulations than required at the national level (Schreurs 2002: 41). This pattern, in which NIMBY protest led to local policy innovation, which in turn led to national policy change, can be seen in the automobile industry, to which we turn next.

Case Study: NIMBY-Inspired Solutions for Automobile Emissions

How did NIMBY contribute to the adoption of stringent automobile emission standards in Japan? Automobile emissions were framed as NIMBY issues in Japan despite their relevance at the national level. The concentration of air pollution in major cities caused automobile emissions to be treated within a NIMBY framework. Eventually, local activism redounded to the national government when the mayors of seven major cities created a powerful committee to investigate automobile emissions nationwide.

Local governments and counter-experts played a major role in this process of developing strict pollution controls in the Japanese automobile industry. The sequence was the following: Local residents in numerous Japanese cities faced various negative consequences of air pollution, and suspected automobile emissions to be the cause. Their unrest encouraged local medical professionals to conduct studies. Then, certain media picked up the issue and broadcasted it nationally. Local governments, which tended to be led by leftist leaders (in contrast to the national government), responded by establishing ordinances and setting up various committees, led by academics, to study the matter. This eventually led the relevant national ministries to propose tougher national laws and adopt new regulations. Thus, although air pollution affected the entire nation, it started as a NIMBY issue and developed into a case of NIMBY changing national politics.

The most typical example of NIMBY promoting political innovation in the field of automobile pollution started with the Ushigome-Yanagi-cho crossing case in 1970. There was a shocking report in May of that year that alkyl-lead was accumulating in the blood of people living near the Ushigome-Yanagi-cho intersection, where traffic was very heavy. Medical doctors belonging to the HeW CO-OP (Japanese Health and Welfare Co-operative Federation) conducted medical tests of the residents and reported on May 21, 1970 that the alkyl-lead levels in their blood were higher than the acceptable limits set by the national workman's compensation insurance body. The residents of Yanagi-cho complained to the Tokyo Metropolitan Government. Major media picked this case up, and "lead poisoning" dominated the headlines. Although the link between auto emissions and lead poisoning was later disproved by a study conducted by the Tokyo Metropolitan Government, the incident mobilized the national government, including METI and MHLW (MOE 1972). The report that concentrated lead was found in the blood of Tokyo residents shocked the nation, as it was reminiscent of previous heavy metal disease incidents (Kadowaki 1992: 115). Only one week after the "lead" report appeared in the media, METI announced that it would study lead-free gasoline at its Industry Structure Deliberation Council meeting on May 28, and it decided to make regular gasoline lead-free by 1974. Two days later, on May 30, 1970, the MHLW decided to revise the Air Pollution Prevention Law to include lead as a part of emission regulations because lead was a heavy metal, much like those implicated in the aforementioned "Big Four" pollution disease cases (Kadowaki 1992: 47, 50). This clean-air victory is an especially strong case of NIMBY effectiveness because the will of local residents became national policy even when the scientific evidence that had initiated the local mobilization was disproved.

Another dramatic case was the Rissho High School case, which also occurred in 1970. On July 18, 1970, forty-eight female students participating in a physical education class outside of Rissho High School in the Suginami Ward collapsed, and nine of them were hospitalized (Kadowaki 1992: 32–33; MOE 1972). The media reported that their collapse was a result of photochemical smog, and later it was found that high levels of NOx in the air were the reason for the dangerous smog. Responding to this shocking event, various NIMBY actions arose. First, local resident groups organized to fight this pollution. For example, as early as September of the same year, the Nerima Ward, right next to the Suginami Ward where the incident took place, set up a pollution prevention committee (Nerimaku Kogai Taisaku Renraku Kyogikai). In the same month, the residents of Nerima started a citizen's group to oppose the construction of roads No. 35 and 36 in the Nerima Ward. After the Rissho High School incident, a series of photochemical pollution incidents took place in Tokyo, resulting in various resident and local government actions.

The Tokyo Metropolitan Government also responded to these residents' and wards' actions. In the same month as the Rissho High School incident, the Tokyo government started issuing photochemical smog warnings. The second extraordinary session of the Tokyo Metropolitan Government in August 1970 was dubbed the "Metropolitan Government Pollution Diet [Parliament]" ahead of the so-called National Pollution Diet in December in the Suginami Ward. In October of the same year, the Tokyo Metropolitan Government set up a pollution bureau. The Rissho High School incident was followed by numerous complaints of photochemical smog in Tokyo and other places in Japan, including at Shakujii-

Minami Junior High School in May 1974, an incident in which more than 100 students got sick, although its scientific correlation to photochemical smog was again doubted (Nerima Ward 2007).

As with the Ushigome-Yanagi-cho crossing case, the root cause of the dangerous air pollution may not have been automobile emissions. In an interview with the JGI, former transportation ministry officers Hisashi Kageyama and Kazusuke Yorihara claimed that the root cause of the smog was, in fact, garbage incineration rather than automobile emissions. The Tokyo Metropolitan Government, seeking to deflect the blame for photochemical smog from its own garbage incinerator, had put the blame on automobiles instead, according to these officers (JGI 1997: 240–41). The Ushigome-Yanagi-cho crossing and the Rissho High School incident both served to mobilize local residents, media, and local governments around the issue of auto emissions, and their activism spurred the development of a new national emissions policy even when it was later proven or suspected that auto emissions were not the root cause of the pollution in those cases.

Given the strong NIMBY activism in these cases, the Ministry of Transportation, which is in charge of operation of vehicles, strengthened national emission regulations. Similarly, METI—which was in charge of regulating and developing the automobile industry—also responded to citizens' concerns by claiming that Japan's levels of technical expertise made even stricter controls possible, and declaring that the new regulation should be applied to used cars as well as new ones. The Ministry of Welfare used the incidents to claim that the scope of its health regulations should be widened (Kadowaki 1992: 43). In this case, all relevant ministries agreed to head in the same direction of strengthened environmental standards. This consensus was a rare exception in a milieu in which inter-ministry bickering in policy making had been common. The NIMBY political sequence was critical in this success story. First, the pollution problems occurred in limited local areas. The residents complained to local government, and the media picked up on the cases. Local governments then enacted anti-pollution ordinances and set up various policy mechanisms, such as a bureau for pollution issues. Finally, the national government took action.

In May 1974, another significant milestone regarding the effectiveness of NIMBY activism on environmental protection was reached. Dissatisfied with the rhetoric being promoted by the national ministries and, especially, leading auto manufacturers that the upcoming 1976 emission standard was going to be technically impossible to achieve on time, the mayors of seven of Japan's major cities[9] joined in creating the Research Committee of Automobile Emission Regulation Issues of Seven Major Cities, hereafter called the Seven Major Cities committee. The committee produced an expert report that stated that the so-called 1976 standard was technologically feasible to achieve on time (Hashimoto 1989: 39). The members of this committee were Tokue Shibata (leader of the group and director of the Tokyo Environmental Pollution Research Institute); Hikaru Shoji (Professor, Engineering Department, Kansai University); Hajime Nishimura (Associate Professor, Engineering Department, Tokyo University); Kanichi Kondo (Technology Consultant); Sachio Mizutani (Associate Professor, Engineering Department, Osaka University); Ken Hanayama (Associate Professor, Engineering Department, Tokyo Institute of Technology); and Katsumi Kataoka (Assistant Professor, Engineering Department, Osaka Prefecture University).

This Seven Major Cities committee performed two important functions. First, it played the role of counter-expert on pollution, generating local government-sponsored science that offered a different perspective from that sponsored by METI and the large corporations. This group intentionally included experts who had no connection to Japanese automobile manufacturers. Initially, the Governor of Tokyo, Minobe, had gone so far as to suggest a commission composed of foreign experts so as to be free from the industry's influence (Nishimura 1976: 59), although this proposal was ultimately not adopted. This group also represented a political bridge between local-level NIMBY mobilization and national political mobilization around air pollution issues. It helped bring local air problems to the attention of the national government.

The fact that the mayors of these seven major cities were all members of opposition parties is important. Although national politics was still controlled by the LDP majority, the opposition wielded significant political clout in urban, local politics, led by Tokyo governor Minobe (Kadowaki 1992: 111). Through their mayors' influence, the seven cities' NIMBY movements started moving the nation.

According to the committee, Toyota and Nissan were the major opponents of pollution control measures. One of the committee members, Kondo, backed up this claim by pointing out that, while Toyota was pretending that it could not make a catalytic converter, its new Corolla model already included a space for a catalytic converter in its body panel (Nishimura 1976: 62).

At the time the committee was set up, the major issue was whether the 1976 standards would be achievable by 1976. The committee decided to assess each automobile manufacturer's readiness to develop technology that would meet the 1976 standard. In a June 1974 hearing at the Environment Agency, the predecessor of the current Ministry of Environment, all manufacturers unanimously denied the plausibility of the 1976 standard for NO_x (0.25g/km). Both Honda and Toyo Kogyo (Mazda), however, stated that they would be able to achieve NO_x levels of 0.6g/

km to 0.7g/km. The other automakers suggested they might be able to reduce NOx emissions, but avoided providing specifics (Nishimura 1976: 63–64).

The Seven Major Cities committee interviewed Mazda (Toyo Kogyo) first. The committee found it strange that Mazda insisted on being held to a NOx standard of no less than 0.6g/km despite the fact that its Luce model, which had a rotary engine, already cleared 0.4g/km at that time. It turned out that the Japan Automobile Manufacturers' Association (JAMA), a powerful automobile industry organization whose leadership was dominated by Toyota and Nissan, had pressured Mazda to support the more lenient standard. However, Mazda later distanced itself from JAMA and claimed that it would be able to achieve less than 0.4g (Nishimura 1976: 69–70). The seven-city mayors' political strategy was to highlight the divisions among manufacturers within JAMA, and then take advantage of those divisions to promote their policy preferences.

Following Mazda, the committee interviewed Honda. Honda, along with Mazda, would have benefitted from a stricter emission policy, because they already had technologies to meet the standard. Yet to argue directly against the Big Two—Toyota and Nissan—was not easy. Honda thus answered the interviewers' questions in an ambivalent way. It stated that NOx emissions of 0.25g/km or even 0.20g/km would be possible, emphasizing the technological superiority of its CVCC technology (Nishimura 1976: 71). Yet Honda did not forget to add that drivability would become an issue in selling a 0.25g/km engine, showing its concession to the Big Two's opposition to the 1976 standard. However, when Honda presented its CVCC technology in the United States, it clearly stated that the drivability would not be an issue (Nishimura 1976: 73), suggesting that it was equivocating on this point to the Committee.

Toyota was the committee's next interviewee. Toyota was clearly opposed to the 1976 standard. It claimed that the standard would be impossible to achieve, and asked for leniency. According to committee members, Toyota was not interested in developing this kind of new technology. Toyota claimed that it had doubled the number of engineers working to develop the clean emission technology, but still would not be able to meet the standard. The committee accused Toyota of trying to unload as many of its pre-standard vehicles as possible in order to increase its market share before the stricter control was imposed. This maneuver was so glaring that even the president of Mitsubishi Motors, Mr. Tomio Kubo, complained about it at the meeting of JAMA. Nissan was also very uncooperative, refusing to show its data to the committee (Nishimura 1976: 75–83).

The Seven Major Cities committee's actions broke apart JAMA's collective bargaining position, making it impossible for them to remain united when called to the National Diet to testify on this matter. The Diet held a hearing in September 1974 to review the 1976 standards. At the hearing, according to Hashimoto, "Toyota and Nissan stated that a standard of 0.9 g/km for NOx emissions would be feasible in 1976; Honda and Mazda stated that 0.6 g/km is feasible" (1989: 39). Once the division was made between the Big Two and the rest, the battle between the Big Two and medium-sized companies intensified. When Nissan's president criticized Mazda for claiming that it was possible to develop a vehicle with NOx emissions of 0.4g/km, Mitsubishi Motors' president defended Mazda and accused Toyota of bullying its competitors (Kadowaki 1992: 64). The Big Two failed to force the medium-sized manufacturers to follow their lead, and instead they had to follow the lead of the smaller manufacturers. In the end, all manufacturers were able to meet the stringent NOx emission standard by May 1976, and the mass production of the improved cars started in October of the same year (Hashimoto 1989: 86). Although the implementation of this act took years in Japan, the United States only imposed this level of emission control in 1997. Even California achieved this standard only in 1983 (Nishimura and Sadakata 1989: 115). Thus, because of pressure exerted on automakers, first from below and eventually from above, Japan was nearly two decades ahead of the United States in this field.

In examining the automobile emission case, it is clear that the issue started with a few significant but geographically limited incidents such as the Ushigome-Yanagicho crossing case and the Rissho High School case. Although neither local residents nor NGOs organized any national campaigns, local governments picked up residents' concerns, and moved ahead of the national government to implement various policy innovations. This movement culminated in the Seven Major Cities committee, which eventually forced the national government and auto manufacturers to adopt the world's most stringent automobile emission controls.

Conclusion

The conundrum for analysts of Japanese environmental policy is to explain how Japan, which lacks various factors traditionally considered necessary for success in environmental policy making, managed to transform itself from the "pollution archipelago" of the 1950s and 1960s to a global environmental leader. It lacks strong, national environmental NGOs. A single pro-business party—the Liberal Democratic Party—dominated its democracy for more than half a century at the national level. Its focus on economic development has been strong. A key answer turns out to be the origin and framing of environmental advocacy as NIMBY protest, which helped solve collective action problems and was able to take advantage of divisions among national ministries and leading manufacturers who might otherwise have prevented the development of cutting-edge environmental policy.

NIMBY contributed to both political and technological innovations in Japan. The LDP dominance of national party politics made environmental policy disputes into non-partisan issues at the national level. Under the LDP's dominance, the environmental battle shifted downwards to inter-ministerial conflicts. Due to the lack of coordination among ministries, the real decision making moved in turn to local governments, where NIMBY mobilization helped shape policy choices.

Prefectural and city governments, many of which were led by governors and mayors from opposition parties, were often able to respond to NIMBY protests against air pollution by imposing stricter standards than those set at the national level. As was the case in other countries highlighted in this volume, these local governments used additional resources, such as counter-expertise, to promote their environmental agendas beyond their local communities. Local governments, supported by counter-experts, used the Seven Major Cities committee to create a collective action problem for the automobile manufacturers' association, JAMA, by identifying automakers that were able to meet higher pollution-emission standards and finding ways to ally them to the cause of pollution control. Although the environmental technologies themselves were not innovated at the local level, unlike in the German case, it was NIMBY activism that pressured the auto manufacturers to develop new, clean technologies. Now those manufacturers lead the world in auto sales, particularly of green technology-related automobiles (Reuters 2013; Chen 2014). The rapid implementation of these technologies was certainly aided by the continuing threat of NIMBY mobilization.

Japanese policy is usually made by elites in the national bureaucracies working closely with the LDP and leading corporations. Policy-relevant advocacy NGOs are virtually non-existent (Pekkanen 2006). This is not a context in which one would expect NIMBY to have much relevance. And yet, as the emissions case makes clear, NIMBY protest was critically important to turning Japan into the environmental leader that it is today. Facing dire pollution consequences in their own communities, local advocates took advantage of the opportunities created by the Japanese macro-political structure, including party politics and inter-ministerial disputes, to push their demands for cleaner air. And they succeeded. Local policy change led to national policy change. Contrary to traditional recipes for environmental policy success, such as strong pro-environmental political parties and nationally or internationally organized strong environmental NGOs, the Japanese experience demonstrates the effectiveness of NIMBY activism even where macro-political structures would have predicted a major failure.

Notes

1. The Environmental Performance Index, the first of which was published in 2002, followed the Environmental Sustainability Index, which was published between 1999 and 2005. EPI ranking is based on twenty-five indicators including air pollution, water, biodiversity, natural resources, and climate change. These indexes were developed by Yale University.
2. The first national environmental law was not promulgated until the latter half of the 1950s.
3. Except for an eight-month period in 1993.
4. This was the Ministry of Health & Welfare and Ministry of Labor until 2001.
5. This was MITI or the Ministry of International Trade and Industry until 2001.
6. This was the Ministry of Construction and Ministry of Transportation until 2001.
7. After this, METI continued to help develop this technology further by providing funding to private corporations as a part of industrial policies.
8. SMDP (Single Member District Plural) is a method of voting mainly adopted in the United States and Great Britain for national congressional/parliamentary elections. Each district has one seat, and whoever receives the highest number of votes (plurality) wins the election. This system is much more widely used in local elections in countries where national elections take place via a different method such as proportional representation.
9. Tokyo, Kawasaki, Yokohama, Nagoya, Kyoto, Osaka, and Kobe.

References

Aldrich, Daniel. 2008. *Site Fights: Divisive Facilities and Civil Society in Japan and the West.* Ithaca, NY: Cornell University Press.

Chen, Lily. 2014. "Toyota Prius Continues to Dominate the Hybrid Category." *Asian Fortune,* January 6. Accessed January 10, 2014. http://www.asianfortunenews.com/2014/01/2014-toyota-prius-continues-to-dominate-the-hybrid-category/.

Eguchi, Yujiro. 1980. "Japanese Energy Policy." *International Affairs* 56(2): 263–79.

Emerson, J. W. et al. 2012. *2012 Environmental Performance Index and Pilot Trend Environmental Performance Index.* New Haven, CT: Yale Center for Environmental Law and Policy.

Evans, Peter C. 1999. "Japan's Green Aid Plan: The Limits of State-Led Technology Transfer." *Asian Survey* 39(6): 825–44.

Forsythe, David P. 1989. *Human Rights & World Politics,* 2nd ed., revised. Lincoln: Nebraska University Press.

Haddad, Mary Alice. 2012. *Building Democracy in Japan.* Cambridge, MA: Cambridge University Press.

Hall, Peter. 1993. "Policy Paradigms, Social Learning and the State: The Case of Economic Policymaking in Britain." *Comparative Politics* 25: 275–96.

Hashimoto, Michio. 1989. "History of Air Pollution Control in Japan." In *How to Conquer Air Pollution, A Japanese Experience,* edited by H. Nishimura, 1–93. Amsterdam: Elsevier.

Hollingsworth, J. Rogers, and Robert Boyer, eds. 1997. *Contemporary Capitalism: the Embeddedness of Institutions.* Cambridge: Cambridge University Press.

Jahn, Detlef. 1998. "Environmental Performance and Policy Regimes: Explaining Variations in 18 OECD Countries." *Policy Sciences* 31: 107–31.

Japan External Trade Organization (JETRO). 2007. *Nihon-no Kankyo Gijutsu, Chosa Houkoku (Taiki Osen Boshi) (Japan's Environmental Technology Research Report [Air Pollution Prevention]).* Accessed January 11, 2014. http://www.jetro.go.jp/ttppoas/special/env_rep2/env_rep_05_1j.html.

Jidosha Gijutsu-shi Iinkai (JGI). 1997. Jidosha Gijutsu-no Rekishi-ni Kansuru Chosa Kenkyu Houkoku-sho (The Research Study Report Regarding the History of Automobile Technology in 1996). Tokyo: Jidosha Gijutsu-kai.

Johnson, Chalmers. 1982. *MITI and the Japanese Miracle: The Growth of Industrial Policy, 1925–1975.* Stanford, CA: Stanford University Press.

Kadowaki, Shigemichi. 1990. *Kuruma-shakai to Kankyo-Osen: Jidousha Haikigasu-Kisei no Ashidori. (Motorized Society and Environmental Pollution: The Evolution of Automobile Emission Regulations).* Hiroshima, Japan. Keisuisha.

———. 1992. *Gijutsu-Hattatsu no Mekanizumu to Chikyuu-Kankyou no Oyobosu Eikyou (The Mechanism of Technology Development & the Influence of Earth Environment).* Tokyo, Japan: Sankai-do.

Krasner, Stephen D. 1984. "Review: Approaches to the State: Alternative Conceptions and Historical Dynamics." *Comparative Politics* 16(2): 223–46.

Lesbirel. S. Hayden. 1988. "The Political Economy of Substitution Policy: Japan's Response to Lower Oil Prices." *Pacific Affairs* 61(2): 285–302.

———. 1998. *NIMBY Politics of Japan: Energy Siting and the Management of Environmental Conflict.* Ithaca, NY: Cornell University Press.

Mason, Robert J. "Whither Japan's Environmental Movement? An Assessment of Problems and Prospects at the National Level." *Pacific Affairs* 72(2): 187–207.

Matsumoto, Reishi. 2004. "Development of Social Capacity for Environmental Management: The Case of Yokohama City." Discussion Paper Series Vol. 2004-4. Paper presented at COE Study Group of International Cooperation Study Division of Hiroshima University Japan.

McKean, Margaret. 1981. *Environmental Protest and Citizen Politics in Japan.* Berkeley: University of California Berkeley.

Ministry of Environment (MOE). 1971. *Kogai Hakusho: Annual Report on Pollution.* Accessed January 11, 2014. http://www.env.go.jp/policy/hakusyo/hakusyo.php3?kid=146.

———. 1972. Kankyo-Hakusho: Annual Report on Environment.

Mishima-city. *The Struggle Against the Petrochemical Complex.* Accessed March 3, 2013. http://www.city.mishima.shizuoka.jp/ipn001983.html.

Moore, Curtis, and Alan Miller. 1994. *Green Gold: Japan, Germany, the United States, and the Race for Environmental Technology.* Boston, MA: Beacon Press.

New Energy and Industrial Development Organization (NEDO). 2002. *The Research on Next Generation Coal Technology Development "Co-Environmental Coal Burning Technology Field [Advanced Exhausting Treatment Technology]" Mid-term Report.* Accessed March 4, 2014. http://www.nedo.go.jp/content/100089423.pdf.

Nelson, Richard R., and Sidney G. Winter. 1982. *An Evolutionary Theory of Economic Change.* Cambridge, MA: Belknap Press of Harvard University Press.

Nerima Ward. 2007. Nerimano Kankyo Heisei 19 Nendo Houkoku (*Nerima's Environment 2007 Report*). Nerima-Ward, Tokyo.

Nishimura, Hajime. 1976. *Sabakareta Jidosha. (Automobile Adjudged).* Tokyo: Chuokoron-sha.

Nishimura, Hajime, and Masayoshi Sadakata. 1989. "Emission Control Technology." In *How to Conquer Air Pollution: A Japanese Experience,* edited by H. Nishimura, 115–56. Amsterdam: Elsevier.

Noble, Gregory W. 1998. *Collective Action in East Asia: How Ruling Parties Shape Industrial Policy.* Ithaca, NY: Cornell University Press.

North, Douglass C. 1990. *Institutions, Institutional Change and Economic Performance.* Cambridge: Cambridge University Press.

OECD. 2002. *OECD Environmental Performance Reviews: Japan 2002.*

———. 2014. OECD.StatExtracts. Accessed November 22, 2014. http://stats.oecd.org.

Ogata, Toshinori. 2008. *Nihono-no Kankyou Gyosei to Jichitai-no Yakuwari (Japanese Environmental Governance and the Role of Local Governments).* Tokyo: GRIPS.

Olson, Mancur. 1971. *The Logic of Collective Action.* Cambridge, MA: Harvard University Press.

Ostrom, Elinor. 1990. *Governing the Commons: the Evolution of Institutions for Collective Action.* New York: Cambridge University Press.

Pekkanen, Robert. 2006. *Japan's Dual Civil Society: Members Without Advocates.* Stanford, CA: Stanford University Press.

Ramseyer, J. Mark, and Frances McCall Rosenbluth. 1993. *Japan's Political Marketplace.* Cambridge, MA: Harvard University Press.

Reed, Steven R. 1981. "Environmental Politics: Some Reflections Based on the Japanese Case." *Comparative Politics* 13(3): 253–70.

Reuters. 2013. "Toyota Keeps Top Spot in Auto Sales Rankings, Outselling GM, VW." October 28. Accessed January 10, 2014. http://www.reuters.com/article/2013/10/28/us-global-autos-toyota-idUSBRE99R04K20131028.

Schreurs, Miranda. 2002. *Environmental Politics in Japan, Germany, and the United States.* Cambridge and New York: Cambridge University Press.

Scruggs, Lyle. 2003. *Sustaining Abundance: Environmental Performance in Industrial Democracies.* Cambridge and New York: Cambridge University Press.

Streeck, Wolfgang, and Kathleen Thelen, eds. 2005. *Beyond Continuity: Institutional Change in Advanced Political Economies.* Oxford: Oxford University Press.

Suginami Ward. 2013. *Suginamiku Kankyo Hakusho Heisei-25-nenban (Suginami-Ward Environment White Paper 2013).* Tokyo: Suginami-Ward.

Wilkening, Kenneth E. 1999. "Culture and Japanese Citizen Influence on the Transboundary Air Pollution Issue in Northeast Asia." *Political Psychology* 20(4): 701–23.

CHAPTER 8

From Backyard Environmental Advocacy to National Democratization

The Cases of South Korea and Taiwan

Mary Alice Haddad

This chapter examines the link between NIMBY protests and democratization movements, focusing on the cases of South Korea and Taiwan. In both of these countries,[1] mobilization around local environmental issues fed into broader discussions about political reform and eventually culminated in successful national democratization movements that ended decades of military/authoritarian rule. The two cases are "hard" cases because the political contexts in which the NIMBY movements emerged were ones in which successful environmental advocacy was least likely to occur. The cases also work as "outlier" cases in which local environmental advocacy contributed to the most extreme result possible: complete regime transformation. Examining these two cases offers insights into the interplay between NIMBY activism and national democratization.

There are two key findings from this study of NIMBY activism in South Korea and Taiwan. First, there are many linkages that can and have been made between local environmental advocacy and broader discussions about democratic governance. Rather than being doomed to parochial political goals and organizations, NIMBY politics can contribute to major political transformation at the national level. Second, connecting NIMBY politics to national democratization movements can have a paradoxical effect on environmental advocacy: In both South Korea and Taiwan, linking environmental and democratization movements politicized the environmental movement in ways that ultimately undermined the political efficacy of environmental organizations to influence environmental policy when conservative parties returned to power.

This chapter will be divided into three parts. The first section offers a brief review of the literature on civil society and environmental politics in

South Korea and Taiwan. The second section examines the two countries and presents the main arguments of the chapter: that (a) NIMBY environmental movements are well-placed to begin and contribute to national conversations about democratic governance; and that (b) linking environmental and democratization movements can have a paradoxical effect on environmental advocacy once democracy is achieved. The final section discusses the ways that the experience of NIMBY protests in South Korea and Taiwan can help us understand the connections between NIMBY and political, technological, and social innovation.

South Korean and Taiwanese Environmental Politics

As in many of the other cases covered in this volume (e.g., radioactive waste in the United States, water pollution in Russia, water and air pollution in China, and air pollution in Japan), engagement in environmental issues in South Korea and Taiwan emerged directly in response to the negative human health and economic consequences of industrialization. Following the same pattern discussed in the introduction to this volume, environmental activism began when local residents living near polluting industrial facilities began to feel the effects of various forms of industrial pollution. Residents would organize to try to get, for instance, a factory to stop polluting their local environment. Initial governmental and corporate responses were predictably resistant to change, and often violent in their attempts to coerce communities to accept the costs of pollution in exchange for a variety of economic and other benefits. When residents refused to be bought off, government and corporate actors engaged in a wide spectrum of responses, ranging from violent suppression, coercion, and co-optation to compromise and even innovation. Citizens then found innovative ways to push for better environmental outcomes, and in both South Korea and Taiwan these efforts were not only successful, they led to political, social, and technological innovations that contributed to broader democratization movements that eventually resulted in national political transformation.

The Republic of Korea (commonly known as South Korea) and the Republic of China (commonly known as Taiwan) share many historical, political, and social features. Both places were occupied/ruled by the Japanese: The Taiwanese from 1895–1945 and the South Koreans from 1905–1945. Both are parts of divided countries, one part of which is ruled by Communists and the other part by non-Communist political parties, and debates about how to deal with the "other" side dominate politics in both places. South Korea and Taiwan have both adopted Japanese-influenced "developmental state" models of economic development, leading to very rapid industrialization and high-speed economic growth (Johnson 1982; Woo-Cummings 1999). In 1960, South Korea's per capita GDP was $291 and Taiwan's was $346. By 1980 those figures had jumped more than tenfold to $2,500 and $3,800 respectively, and by 2010 per capita incomes were more than one hundred times greater than they had been in 1960, standing at $28,800 and $32,300 for South Korea and Taiwan, respectively.[2] Both countries have security agreements with the United States and enjoy significant economic and military support from that country (Kan 2012; Manyin et al. 2010).

Although they share many common features, South Korea and Taiwan are also distinct from one another. Their populations speak different languages, eat different food, have different dominant religions, and enjoy (or suffer from) different roles in global politics. As the following pages will explain, while the two countries experienced successful pro-democracy movements at a similar time, and environmental NIMBY protests played into the democratization efforts in both places, the role that the protests played and how that linkage has subsequently affected politics have been quite different.

South Korea

South Korea's NIMBY protests and its environmental movement more broadly have grown out of and have contributed to a long history of protest politics. South Korea's tradition of mass protests can be traced back more than a century, beginning with the 1894 Donghak Peasant Movement protesting government corruption. Other famous mass movements in South Korea include the March First Movement protesting Japanese rule in 1919, the April Revolution when student and labor organizations successfully ended the autocratic rule of Syngman Rhee in 1960, the failed student-led pro-democracy protests in May 1980, and the successful democracy movement of June 1987. This long history helped normalize protest, even violent protest, as a regular method by which civil society organizations could engage the state. Although considerably less violent than their predecessors, contemporary South Korean civic organizations, of which environmental organizations are one group, continue to favor confrontational modes of political engagement (Oh 2012; Kim 2009b).

Scholar and environmental activist See-Jae Lee argues that South Korea's environmental movement has passed through four stages: (1) negation (1960s and 1970s), meaning neither the state nor civil society viewed the other side as legitimate; (2) resistance (1980s), meaning the state acknowledged the existence of civic actors but did not view them as partners for dialogue and sought to suppress them; (3) negotiation (1990s), meaning both sides recognized one another and struggled against one another for policy influence and public support; and (4) participation (2000–present), meaning environmental organizations have been incorporated into the state's decision-making process and participate in jointly developed policy projects (Lee 2000).

Early environmental organizations in South Korea were generally located in churches and universities and were focused primarily on raising environmental consciousness among the population (Lee 1999: 143). However, as had been the case in Japan, the high-speed growth policies of the 1960s led to rapidly deteriorating environmental conditions that began to threaten human health and livelihoods. Early environmental protest movements in South Korea, like their counterparts in Japan, China, Russia and elsewhere, began with residents' demands for compensation for damages. The first major case to generate national attention was in the Ulsan and Onsan areas of Gyeongsangnam-do province. Construction on the government-approved Ulsan Industrial Complex began in 1962, and in 1967 farmers began to demand compensation for agricultural losses. In 1971 they formed a pollution countermeasures committee, and 1978 they increased their demands to include financial aid for relocation as well as compensation for residents experiencing health damages. Urban residents in large cities such as Seoul and Inch'on also began to protest against noise and air pollution (Lee 2000: 144; Ku 2002: 76).

Responding to growing public concern, a small number of environmentalists, religious leaders, and pro-democracy activists formed the Pollution Research Institute (PRI) in 1982 in order to conduct pollution-related research independent of the government. In contrast to the local NIMBY protesters, who were usually farmers, fishers, and local residents living near factories, PRI had connections to national church leaders, leading academics, and student groups. It was the first professional environmental organization in South Korea with dedicated staff and office space (Lee 1999: 93). However, because of its close connection with student groups involved in the democracy movement, the anti-pollution movement was also seen as an anti-government movement, so the government tried to prevent the formation of connections between local grassroots NIMBY groups and the professional environmental organization (Ku 2002: 76).

In 1983, heavy metal pollution made the water near the Ulsan complex so toxic that the government suspended fishing rights. Immediately the people took to the streets to demand financial compensation for lost revenue, and the PRI began an independent investigation into the situation. In much the same way as the counter-experts did in Germany, the United States, Russia, and Japan, PRI's first contribution was to embark on independent scientific study of the environmental problem, challenging the government-industry story that the water was safe. In 1985 PRI released a very detailed report claiming that more than 500 people in Onsan suffered from cadmium contamination. The press offered considerable public exposure for the findings, and the issue became one of national interest. Soon after the PRI report, the Environment Administration conducted its own tests and reported that the illness spreading among the Onsan population was not a pollution-related disease. Residents and the PRI refuted the official test results and engaged in a series of public protests. Eventually the government was forced to concede to the growing pressure from environmental groups and the public, and resettle about forty thousand residents to new areas (Ku 2011: 211–13; Lee 1999: 94).

In the wake of the successful efforts in Onsen, South Korea saw the proliferation and institutionalization of environmental groups in the capital, in major regional cities, and also in local communities. Examples of these groups include the Association for the Preservation of Youngsan Lake (founded in 1983), the Anti-Pollution Citizens' Movement Association (formed in 1986), and the Youth Association of the Anti-Pollution Movement (founded in 1987). Some of these groups formed first as environmental organizations and then merged and/or supported pro-democracy groups that were forming at the same time, and some of the groups formed with a dual environmental and democracy purpose from the start. Much of the leadership for both the environmental movement and the democracy movement was intertwined (e.g., Yul Choi of PRI), and anti-pollution movement groups recruited members from students and anti-government activists (Ku 1996; 162).

The political actions of groups also indicated the interconnectedness of the two movements and the ways that activists were framing pollution issues as fundamentally political problems. During the Ulsan and Onsan evacuation, PRI published a declaration that clearly articulated the link that activists saw between the two issues. "The pollution problem was created by a few government-supported conglomerates and military dictatorship. Thus … people all over the nation have to commit themselves to a more basic and broad anti-pollution movement in order to terminate the anti-nationalist and anti-popular conglomerates and military dictatorial regime causing the problem." Less than a year before the end of military rule, PRI issued its Anti-Pollution Declaration, which stated, "If the pollution problem can be solved only by a mass movement, democratization including the implementation of a local autonomy system and freedom of speech is the inevitable condition to solve the pollution problem. Democratization has an inseparable relationship with the solution of the pollution problem" (quoted in Ku 1996; 162, 167).

In June 1987, through a series of events that has come to be known as the June Democracy Movement or the June Uprising, President Chun Doo-Hwan acceded to public demands for direct presidential elections and a restoration of civil liberties. In February 1988 South Korea's revised democratic Constitution was promulgated simultaneously with the inauguration of democratically elected Roh Tae-woo, ushering in a new era in South Korean politics, one that was far more democratic than its predecessor. Democracy, however, is never instantaneous (Haddad 2012). Indeed, South Korea's first directly elected president was, in fact, the chosen successor of his predecessor (anti-government opposition was too fragmented to coalesce on an electorally viable alternative). Thus, although February 1988 represented a major victory for South Korea's environmental and democracy movements, activists continued to struggle for greater governmental accountability, transparency, and enhanced citizen participation. NIMBY protests continued to create important opportunities for political, social, and technological innovations that promoted the public good.

The next major environmental protest erupted in March 1991 in response to the discovery that Doosan Electro-Materials had leaked 325 drums of phenol into the Nakdonggang River in 1990. Since the Nakdonggang is the main source of drinking water for citizens in Daegu, the third largest city in South Korea, public outrage erupted as soon as the news leaked out. Primed by growing media attention to environmental issues, and fueled by the concerted efforts of new groups such as the Citizens' Coalition for Economic Justice (CCEJ), protests spread (Lee 1999; Haddad 2013: Lee 2000: 145). Citizens hit the streets, individuals and grocery associations boycotted Doosan products, and residents refused to pay their water bills. President Roh Tae-woo condemned the leak as a crime against society, and Mak Yong-gon, chairman of the Doosan Group, pledged a 20-billion won (about $13.5 million) donation to local governments along with a public apology. After shutting the factory down in March, the government allowed it to reopen in April. A mere five days after it reopened, another leak was reported, and the Environment minister and vice minister were removed from their posts (Ku 2011: 13–14).

A month later, a chemical leak from Hwasŏng industrial waste disposal plant in Kyŏnggi-do province threatened nearby communities. This set off another round of protests, and residents blocked the roads to the plant, prohibiting any new waste from being deposited there. To resolve the dispute, a joint investigation team was formed, bringing together experts from the government and environmental organizations in equal numbers. From that point forward, creating joint investigation teams in which government and environmental organizations' experts are equally represented has become a common formula for resolving pollution disputes in South Korea (Lee 2000: 147).

The 1990s saw further incorporation of nongovernmental organization (NGOs) into the environmental policy making process. As was the case for China and other countries, the 1992 Earth Summit in Rio de

Janeiro offered an opportunity for government officials as well as local environmental activists to connect with international environmental organizations, and the anti-pollution movement began its transformation into a broader environmental movement (Lee 1999: 106; Ku 2002: 77). The South Korea Federation for Environmental Movements (KFEM) formed the following year and began to expand its membership. KFEM is now the largest environmental organization in Asia, boasting 80,000 members, 250 staff members, and 50 local branch offices.[3]

Throughout the 2000s, South Korean environmental organizations expanded their membership and broadened the scope of their issues, moving beyond merely responding to situations of environmental degradation to initiating preventive campaigns. The anti-Doggang Dam Campaign was one such campaign, led by KFEM, which aimed to prevent the construction of a new dam. The campaign had a sophisticated strategy that included the development of counter-expertise, reframing the issue, drawing on indigenous cultural resources, and reaching out to new constituencies for support. KEFM began by conducting detailed research on the ecological damage the proposed project would cause, and proposed concrete cost-effective policy alternatives that would protect the environment, which included plans for how to promote tourism to the river. It also used cultural symbols, such as the annual Jeongseon Airirang festival, as well as ecological symbols, displaying rare species of fish and otters that live in and along the river. In 1999 Kim Dae-jung's government formed a citizen-government joint investigation panel to research the dam, and a year later the committee recommended that construction be canceled. On Environment Day, June 5, 2000, President Kim announced a New Millennium Vision for the Environment, and pledged to repeal construction plans. (Kim 2010; Ku 2011).

In the 2000s, South Korea's environmental groups grew increasingly politically involved and enjoyed closer connections to the government, serving on joint panels and being appointed to key government positions. They joined several other NGOs in forming the Citizens' Alliance for the 2000 general elections, which was a pro-transparency, anti-corruption campaign that blacklisted candidates with records of political corruption or illegal activities and succeeded in defeating 56 of the 89 candidates it targeted. President Roh Moo-hyun of the Millennium Democratic Party pledged to create a "participatory democracy" in South Korea, appointing many civil society activists to government positions and expanding NGO participation in policy making (Oh 2012: 547; Choi 2010: 17–22; Kim 2004).

This situation changed dramatically when a growing global economic crisis brought a wave of conservative parties back into power. In late 2007 South Korean voters elected Myung-bak Lee of the conservative Grand

National Party, and he assumed his post as President in February 2008, ending more than a decade of liberal government.[4] Lee built a national campaign from a highly successful four-year term as mayor of Seoul in which he completed a very popular urban renewal project, Cheonggyechon, that removed an elevated highway from the center of the city, restored the stream that lay underneath, and created a long, connected area of green spaces and a number of cultural spaces in the center of downtown Seoul. His campaign focused on creating a Grand South Korean Waterway, which would have been a much larger version of the project he had done in Seoul, developing river waterfront from Seoul in the north to Busan in the south.

As the world financial crisis grew during 2008, the Lee administration, along with many other governments in the region, promoted "green growth" as a key component of a strategy for economic recovery. The Grand South Korean Waterway was scaled down and reframed as the "Four Rivers Project," becoming the core of South Korea's Green New Deal, an economic stimulus package that pledged $40 billion dollars (equivalent to 4 percent of total GDP) for four years to promote sustainable economic growth (Chang et al. 2011).

However, even as the conservative government and businesses promoted environmentally friendly economic development, environmental activists felt completely shut out. In interviews, several suggested that the election brought back the very same people who had been in charge under the military government of an earlier era, and activists felt that the political leaders had not yet adjusted to the new democratic system. As one South Korean activist stated in an interview in 2010, "The ex-government valued governance and wanted to hear civil society. It didn't decide everything on its own but always had channels with civil society. This government doesn't."

Environmental activists are not just sitting back and allowing themselves to be excluded from politics. KFEM and other environmental groups are able to be involved in politics at national and local levels, and they are also well-positioned to take advantage of political opportunities when they arise. Mere months after the new conservative government had assumed office, it reversed the decision of the earlier administration and re-allowed the import of U.S. beef, which had been banned since 2003 after evidence of bovine spongiform encephalopathy (BSE or mad cow disease) had been identified in the United States. Playing on food safety fears spurred by BSE and the concurrent tainted milk scandal in China, building on rising anti-U.S. nationalist sentiment among youth, and capitalizing on national discontent with the new conservative leadership, KFEM joined other environmental and social groups to support public protests against the national government. The protests, which came to be called the Candlelight Protests because they were usually held at night and protesters brought candles, grew to be national in scope and attracted hundreds of thousands of protesters from late May through August. Since conservative parties have retaken control of the national government, it appears that national environmental organizations may be reverting to the kinds of protest repertoires common in the past (Choi 2010; Oh 2012).

Building from their roots in local NIMBY protest, South Korean environmental organizations have become institutionalized in South Korea politics, playing important roles in electoral politics and policymaking, which have contributed to the consolidation of South Korean democracy. As one scholar has phrased it, "[some] NGOs established in recent years have greatly participated in the political process and played significant roles as policy initiators. Their policy-related activities have, in turn, placed a substantial feedback effect on the process of consolidating democracy" (Kim 2010: 604). Although their participation in governmental policymaking has been challenged in recent years by a more conservative government, South Korea's environmental organizations, which grew directly from local NIMBY protests, will continue to play important roles in South Korea's democracy.

Taiwan

Taiwan's environmental movement shares many characteristics with South Korea's: its root in NIMBY protests against toxic waste, the involvement of religious organizations, and its close ties with the successful democratization movement. Although Taiwan's environmental organizations also engage in public protests, Taiwan's political history does not have as strong a tradition of mass protests, so large-scale public protests and violent confrontations with the government have played much less of a role in the environmental movement on the island. Furthermore, in contrast to the movement in South Korea, Taiwanese environmentalists are still striving to become an institutionalized part of politics, and are therefore seeking more ways to cooperate with government and businesses on a regular basis, rather than confront them as part of electoral politics.

Taiwan has been a hub of international trade since the seventeenth century, and has been focal point of global politics ever since. During the seventeenth, eighteenth, and nineteenth centuries the island experienced total or partial occupation by the Dutch, Spanish, French, Chinese, and Japanese as the global powers competed with one another for regional dominance. After the defeat of the Qing Dynasty in the first Sino-Japanese war (1895–95), Taiwan (called Formosa at the time) was formally ceded to the Japanese, who occupied and ruled the island until their defeat in World War II in 1945. For a variety of reasons, including proximity to

Japan, size of the native population, level of racism, experience of prior occupation, relative level of economic development, and the personality of the Japanese governors, Japanese rule in Taiwan was less repressive than its occupation of South Korea. As a result, while the period of the Japanese occupation created a tradition of violent mass resistance in South Korea, the same was not true in Taiwan (Myers and Peattle 1987; Caprio 2009; Tsurumi 1977).

After the Japanese surrendered to Allied forces in 1945, General Chen Yi of the Republic of China (ROC) assumed responsibility of the island. On the mainland, the Chinese Communist Party (CCP), led by Mao Zedong, resumed its civil war against the nationalist Kuomintang Party (KMT), led by Chiang Kai-shek, eventually driving the latter off the mainland. Chiang evacuated his government to Taiwan in December 1949, with the expectation that his forces would retake control of the mainland after regrouping. Chiang's government declared martial law in May of 1949, which continued until it was eventually repealed in 1987.

As had been the case in South Korea, for half a century after the Japanese surrender, Taiwan was run as a U.S.-supported, authoritarian, single-party government focused on economic growth. Although the Communists controlled mainland China from 1949 onward, the United States did not resume relations with Beijing until President Richard Nixon's visit there in 1972. The United Nations had switched China's seat from the Republic of China (ROC) to the People's Republic of China (PRC) the year before. In 1979 the United States recognized the PRC as the sole legitimate government of China and terminated relations with the ROC as the government of China (U.S. Department of State Office of the Historian). The United States closed its embassy in Taipei and established the American Institute in Taiwan as a private, non-profit organization to handle consular services, among other activities (American Institute of Taiwan). The United States, PRC, and ROC all have an official policy that there is only "one China," which means that the ROC often does not have official representation or official relations with international organizations or foreign governments, although it does maintain relations with some. Currently it has official membership in twenty-seven intergovernmental organizations, including the World Trade Organization, the Asia Development Bank, and the Asia-Pacific Economic Cooperation (APEC) forum, and it has observer status or associate membership in twenty-one intergovernmental organizations (Official ROC Foreign Relations Overview). Taiwan's ambiguous position in international politics impacts environmental politics in a number of complex ways. On the one hand, its participation in international organizations and agreements can be difficult (it is often a non-voting member, or a participant but not a member/signatory). On the other hand, it can often plug directly into international discussions without having to negotiate layers of national and state-level bureaucracies.

As was the case for the rest of the region, Taiwan's environmental movement began as local protests against industrial pollution, and similar to South Korea, the rise of pollution protests emerged simultaneously with the democracy movement. In South Korea, national organizations such as the KFEM formed to help connect local NIMBY environmental protesters with pro-democracy student and intellectual activists in the capital. In Taiwan, that bridging did not occur,[5] so successful NIMBY protests helped contribute to national discussions about governance, but protesters made strategic decisions not to become organizationally linked to national groups.

The first NIMBY protesters were victims of industrial pollution: farmers, fishers, and local residents who had their health and livelihoods threatened by nearby industrial production. From 1980 to 1987, 97 percent of environmental protests were reactive—victims seeking redress against damage that had already occurred (Tang and Tang 1997: 284). Examples include a lawsuit launched in 1981 when villagers in Hua-t'an village demanded compensation from local brick manufacturers for damage to their nearby rice paddies. They eventually won NT$1.5 million (U.S. $375,000).

In a context in which newspapers were increasingly reporting on local pollution issues, Taiwanese citizens were also affected by international events. Although not as geographically widespread as the Chernobyl explosion that would follow two years later, in 1984 a disastrous gas leak from a Union Carbide factory in Bhopal, India killed two thousand people and made major headlines across the globe. Taiwanese were already feeling sensitive to the damaging effects of chemical pollution in their own communities, and they immediately recognized that they were similarly vulnerable. The very next year, protests and threats of violence against pesticide companies in Hsin-chu and T'ai-chung forced the closing of both factories for cleanup (Reardon-Anderson 1997: 11–12).

The largest turning point for Taiwan's environmental movement occurred in 1986, when the sleepy fishing village of Lukang began a protest against a planned titanium dioxide plant. The protest represented a shift away from a strategy of reactive protests against damage already done to proactive political action aimed at preventing damage that had not yet occurred. According to James Reardon-Anderson, who wrote an excellent book analyzing the protest in Lukang, if the protest had happened earlier, it would have been crushed; if it had happened later, it would not have been noticed. "But it came just at the time when environmental consciousness in Taiwan had reached a critical mass and as the government was introducing political reforms that gave unprecedented scope to new forms of civic action." In that context, a small group of determined local activists "focused the attention of the entire island on this sleepy provincial town, raised the national consciousness about threats to the natural environment, and challenged the rules that government officials and industrial leaders in Taiwan had come to take for granted" (Reardon-Anderson 1997: x).

In late 1985, DuPont Taiwan Ltd. received permission to build a titanium dioxide plant near Lukang, a small fishing village on the west coast of Taiwan. Community members got wind of the decision and began to mobilize against the plant. Committed to non-violent tactics, opponents of the plant began their protest using regular political channels. The leader of the protest movement, Li Tung-liang, began with a petition, and then he ran for political office, pledging to block the plant if he were elected to the Chang-hua Country Assembly. He won a seat on the Assembly and formed the Chang-hua Nuisance Prevention Association to help coordinate and finance the opposition movement. The association began a sophisticated public relations campaign that involved presentations at town halls and informal community gatherings in villages near the proposed plant site, and within a month after Li's election it had collected 16,000 signatures. A small group of protest leaders delivered copies of the petition to the Executive Yuan, the Legislative Yuan, and the KMT party headquarters in March. When he stopped by the DuPont office in Taipei, DuPont President Paul Costello invited the group in for a conversation about the project, about which DuPont had yet to make any public statements.

When three months passed with no apparent modification of the construction plans, the protesters shifted tactics to increase the visibility of their opposition. They targeted a major folk arts festival held in the region as their venue. Because Taiwan was still under martial law, all of their planning had to be done in secret, and actions had to be closely coordinated. First, Li recruited elementary and middle school children to make posters highlighting the dangers of environmental pollution, and he arranged to have the emotionally evocative images prominently displayed on the main street during the festival. When word came that TV crews were going to film the children's posters, leaders thought the opportunity too good to pass up. Over the course of twenty-four hours, they printed up T-shirts, constructed homemade banners and posters, and contacted reporters and film crews. The morning of June 24, 1986, 500 to 1000 protesters began walking the one-mile course down the main road, chanting slogans and waving banners. The TV crews shot their footage, and the protesters quickly cleared out. The publicity stunt worked: the national media carried pictures and stories of the event for several days. The mass demonstration "challenged not only the plan to locate a chemical factory on the

Chang-hua coast, but the very authority of the government to make and implement policy in this arena" (Reardon-Anderson 1997: 40–41).

After the demonstrations, the protesters continued their efforts to spread the word about the dangers of the proposed plant, and in doing so spread counter-expertise to the public. They organized study tours for residents and local leaders to visit other towns that had suffered from pollution, conducted many information sessions highlighting the dangers of pollution, and engaged in a few short-but-visible public demonstrations in Taipei. With general elections looming in December, political leaders and candidates responded to public sentiment, although the Lukang leadership remained completely non-partisan, refusing to endorse any candidates for the general elections. In stark contrast to their South Korean counterparts, activists wanted to avoid any taint of politics. "We wanted to remain pure and keep environmental protection separate from politics" (Reardon-Anderson 1997: 60).

While the Lukang leadership may have resisted becoming formally linked to party politics, the newly forming Democratic People's Party (whose official foundation date was September 28, 1986) was actively reaching out to all of the democratic, human rights, environmental and other social movements on the island in an attempt to support a broad-based democratic transformation of the country. The party created a department of social movements for the express purpose of reaching out to these groups and incorporating them into the democracy movement. Furthermore, just as had been the case in South Korea, key environmental leaders were brought into the party and later given important leadership positions in government (e.g., Chang Kuo-lang and Lin Jun-yi) (Lyons 2009; 61–2).

Concurrent with the protesters' attempts to gain sympathy with the public, DuPont had also begun, belatedly, to try to do some of its own public relations, finding employees native to Lukang willing to go back and say good things about the company to build public trust. In the end, though, it was not enough. On March 12, DuPont President Paul Costello called a press conference and announced that DuPont would not build the proposed plant near Lukang. Ten days later, Lukang residents celebrated their victory with dragon dancers, marching bands, high priests, clowns, and other hallmarks of a community celebration.

As Reardon-Anderson has phrased it, "Lukang emerged as a symbol of civic action, at a time when political reforms were being introduced and the standards of public conduct redrawn" (1997: 58). Although the protesters in Lukang resisted overt ties to national politics, they profoundly influenced it. Nien His-lin, a former school teacher who was a leader in the movement, used that successful venture to launch a career of civic activism, and many other Lukang activists joined him in spreading the technique of grassroots mobilization across the island. Lukang's success "convinced the opposition leaders that they could challenge the Kuomintang effectively on environmental issues," and, indeed, the DPP candidate won a landslide victory in Lukang in the elections (Ho 2013), setting the stage for greater electoral victories in the years to come.

Less than two months after Lukang's celebration festivities concluded, President Chiang declared an end to martial law, and the Environmental Protection Bureau was elevated to cabinet-level status before the year was out. Important national environmental organizations such as the New Environment Foundation, Taiwan Greenpeace, the Taiwan Environmental Protection Union (TEPU), and the Homemaker's Union Environmental Protection Foundation were founded shortly thereafter (Weller 1999: 112). Lukang's NIMBY movement not only gained them the local outcome that they wanted—a halt to the proposed DuPont plant—it helped change the institutional framework of environmental policy making, and ultimately made a fundamental contribution to the democratization of Taiwanese politics.

Perhaps ironically, the biggest single "winner" of the battle in Lukang may have been DuPont. DuPont today is one of the world's largest and most profitable companies. It took the lessons it learned from its "loss" in Lukang and put them to good use. It changed the company protocol for development, including more community relations with residents of potential factory sites and higher environmental standards. It now leads the industry not just in profitability, but it regularly wins environmental awards for its products and its corporate practices.[6] Thus, technological, political, and social innovations emerging from NIMBY protests do not just accrue to the activists but also to their opposition.

After the spectacular success in Lukang, Taiwan's environmental NIMBY protesters had more mixed success, partially because government and corporate actors became more sophisticated in finding ways to prevent NIMBY organizations from consolidating (Aldrich 2008). In 1987, the year that DuPont announced its withdrawal from Lukang and also the year that martial law was lifted, residents in Kaohsiung began protesting against a proposed naphtha cracker (petrochemical processing capacity) that was going to be added to the government-owned Chinese Petrochemical Company plant in a nearby industrial complex. In response to community protests, the government promised more extensive environmental assessments, the petrochemical firm began public relations campaigns that promised local jobs and beautification projects, and the firm made large donations to local temples. The government promised to establish a fund for compensating victims of pollution, and the opposition to the project broke up (Tang 1997: 286–87).

While individual NIMBY protests have had mixed success, Taiwan's environmental policy-making process has been dramatically improved since Lukang. The Environmental Protection Bureau was elevated to cabinet-level status in 1987, new laws requiring environmental impact assessments have been put in place, pollution control regulations have become more stringent, and tax incentives for industrial investment in pollution reduction have been put in place. KMT and government-owned businesses have developed better community relations and have begun to invest more in pollution control (Tang 1997: 289; Hsiao 1999: 48).

Similar to their counterparts in South Korea, Taiwanese environmental organizations worked closely with leftist political parties to facilitate a change in government. In 2000, their hopes were realized when Shui-bian Chen won the presidency, and the DPP gained control of the legislature two years later. With a friendly government in office, environmental leaders were asked to serve on government committees and were placed in positions within the government, and environmental legislation was put forward. However, even though they had access, many activists felt like their interests were pushed aside in favor of big business once the parties they had supported gained power. As one Taiwanese activist phrased it, "The DPP changed when it took power. When in power, then it didn't like the environment anymore." From another, "They want the votes, but they don't want to hear the voices" (interviews in Taipei 2010). Remarking on the paradoxical effect of democratization, David Lyons writes, "The impact of the new structural order, while appearing to provide greater opportunities for advancement of environmental protection, did not, however, translate easily into progress on such issues" (Lyons, 2009: 64).

However disappointed environmental leaders may have been with the DPP, they felt even more shut out when the KMT regained control of the government in 2008. Just as in South Korea, Taiwan promoted "green growth" as part of the economic stimulus packages created in the wake of the global economic crisis. However, most activists felt shut out of government, and, like their counterparts in South Korea, felt that the "green growth" strategy promoted by the KMT was just old-style new-construction-based development with very high consideration for the "growth" and very little consideration for the "green." As one activist bluntly phrased it, in Taiwan, "corporations are a shadow government. Our government is their puppet" (interviews in Taipei 2010).

In 2009, waiting a bit longer than his counterparts in South Korea, President Ma lifted the ban on U.S. beef. In contrast to the reaction in South Korea, where the beef issue was used as a rallying cry for all opponents of the resurgent conservative government, the response in Taiwan was rather tepid. Whether it is because of their much smaller organizational structure or because of differences in public and governmental responses to public protests, Taiwanese activists did not engage in mass demonstrations. Indeed, it appears that environmental activists are beginning to shift their tactics away from protests and partisan politics. Environmental leaders talk about how the public and policymakers have become anesthetized to public protests, such that they are no longer effective as a mode of advocacy. Instead, scientific and policy reports that give policy makers new information about an environmental problem and create an opportunity for dialogue about solutions appear to be more effective (interview with Echo Lin and Kuang-Jung Hsu, Taipei 2010). As a result, Taiwan's environmental politics may be moving closer to the model found on the Chinese mainland, where advocacy has been aimed more at working with the government than against it (Ho and Edmonds 2007; Xie 2009; Hildebrandt and Turner 2009; Haddad 2013).

Conclusion

The cases of South Korea and Taiwan offer a strong counter-narrative to the dominant discourse that suggests that NIMBY environmental protests are doomed to remain local events, concerned only with their parochial worries and never growing beyond the boundaries of their local neighborhoods. In these cases, local people anxious about the conditions of their own communities were able to stand up to powerful governmental and business interests. Their bravery inspired others to do the same, and as communities and organizations were able to copy their successful strategies, calls for political reform spread. No longer confined to their small neighborhoods, these local activists helped fundamentally transform national politics.

While South Korea and Taiwan are certainly unusual in the extent of the relationships between local NIMBY protests and national regime change, there are many lessons that others can and should learn from their experience. First, small victories that compel powerful actors to bring environmental improvements to a single village can reveal preexisting fissures in social and political systems, helping to contribute to political change at the national level. Second, advocates should be careful what they ask for. Winning a NIMBY battle and even contributing to national democratization may not leave one with as much progress as expected. Success breeds its own set of challenges, and environmental advocates must be able to adjust to new political conditions to promote continuing success.

In the cases of South Korea and Taiwan, we see all three types of innovations discussed in this volume—political, technological, and social. By far the most important innovations were the political, the ways that South

Korean and Taiwan NIMBY battles in the mid-1980s contributed to the democratization movements in those countries. In both places, ordinary citizens defied authoritarian governments to confront polluters who were threatening their health and livelihoods. While their actions were begun due to parochial motivations to protect their own communities from threat, they tapped into broader national frustrations with the political status quo, and they were able to take advantage of international events, such as the deadly Union Carbide gas leak in India, that put their own small battles into a broader political context. Their bravery and political strategies inspired other communities to take similar measures to protect their own communities, demanding changes in the insular and undemocratic decision-making practices of their governments. In both countries, new organizations formed at both the local and national levels to help promote both democracy and environmental protection.

Not only citizens learned from the experiences of the early NIMBY protesters. The South Korean and Taiwanese governments responded quickly to the new citizen demands, creating more robust environmental policy institutions and working to identify better ways to include citizens in the policy making process. Corporations, too, improved their methods of community engagement. Sometimes, as was the case for DuPont, companies discovered that making more environmentally friendly products in a more environmentally friendly way was actually profitable. For these companies, a NIMBY "loss" resulted in technological and social innovations that ultimately generated high-profit returns.

Success is contagious. When a sleepy fishing village led by a high-school educated shopkeeper can defy martial law and stand up to a multi-billion dollar international corporation and an authoritarian president and win, others take notice. Other communities tired of polluted water and air, poor health and education, and corrupt politics gain hope and start to resist. As this volume has shown, although each NIMBY case is unique, led by individual personalities who are able to take advantage of particular opportunities and draw on the cultural resources of their own specific communities, in many ways their struggles and triumphs are shared by others.

As we have seen in the case of Russian workers, American farmers, strolling Chinese, and countless others, one of the most potent reasons NIMBY protests are powerful lies in the very ordinariness of the protesters and the parochial nature of their demands. These are not professionals championing someone else's cause. They are not making pie-in-the-sky demands. They just want to be able to live decent lives. To keep their families healthy. To continue earning a living as their parents, grandparents, and great-grandparents have. These are not revolutionary demands; they are the same demands that people have been making of their leaders for centuries, perhaps millennia.

When these basic demands are made by the right people in the right context, however, they can lead to dramatic transformation. Whether the protesters ultimately win or lose their particular fights, the processes they set in motion can reach far beyond their small communities. They can transform the politics of an entire nation. They may change the ecology of an entire planet. Although they do not always lead to the positive outcomes one might dream for them, NIMBY can be beautiful.

Notes

Research for this project was made possible by an Abe Fellowship from the Japan Foundation and the Social Science Research Council, a fellowship from the East Asian Institute, and grants from Wesleyan University.

1. There is considerable dispute about whether Taiwan should "count" as an independent state. It has most of the features of an independent state, such as printing its own currency, a national military, and sovereign control of its territory. However, it is missing some key symbols of contemporary statehood, such as recognition by the United Nations as an independent state, and the People's Republic of China also claims that it is one of China's territories. Therefore, I am using the label "country" in this chapter largely for rhetorical ease and not as a political statement about Taiwanese statehood.
2. Penn Data Tables. https://pwt.sas.upenn.edu/php_site/pwt71/pwt71_retrieve.php. Accessed December 12, 2012. Using cgdp figure—PPP Converted GDP Per Capita, G-K method at 2012 prices in U.S. dollars.
3. Interview with Sae-Jae Lee, co-president of KFEM and professor of Sociology at The Catholic University of South Korea in November 2010 in Seoul. See also the KFEM homepage, http://www.kfem.or.kr, South Korea, accessed January 10, 2013.
4. Presidents Kim Dae-jung (1998–2000) and Roh Moo-hyun (2003–2008) came from liberal parties.
5. It should be noted that it is the South Korean case that is unusual here, not that of Taiwan. No KFEM-type national environmental advocacy organization is found in mainland China, Japan, Malaysia, Philippines, Laos, or Thailand.
6. Reardon-Anderson, J. 1997. *Pollution, Politics, and Foreign Investment in Taiwan: The Lukang Rebellion.* 91–92. Awards include an Environmental Excellence award from the National Forum for Environment & Health in Pakistan in 2010 (http://nfeh.org/award-winner-2010.htm, accessed January 20, 2013); a Green Supplier of the Year award from Yazaki in 2011 (http://www.benzinga.com/content/1850747/yazaki-north-america-grants-dupont-two-prestigious-environmental-awards, accessed January 20, 2013); and the 2012 Environmental Respect Award (http://www.environmentalrespect.com, accessed January 20, 2013). Note, however, that it is also the leading emitter of toxic air pollutants in the United States (Ash, M., J. et al. 2009. "Justice in the Air: Tracking Toxic Pollution from America's Industries and Companies to our States, Cities, and Neighborhoods." Political Economy Research Institute: University of Massachusetts Amherst, 10).

References

Aldrich, Daniel P. 2008. *Site Fights: Divisive Facilities and Civil Society in Japan and the West.* Ithaca, NY: Cornell University Press.

American Institute of Taiwan. Accessed January 12, 2013. http://www.ait.org.tw/en/about-us.html.

Armstrong, C., ed. 2002. *South Korean Society: Civil Society, Democracy and the State.* New York: Taylor & Francis.

Ash, M. et al. 2009. *Justice in the Air: Tracking Toxic Pollution from America's Industries and Companies to our States, Cities, and Neighborhoods.* Political Economy Research Institute: University of Massachusetts Amherst.

Broadbent, J. 1998. *Environmental Politics in Japan: Networks of Power and Protest.* New York: Cambridge University Press.

Caprio, M. E. 2009. *Japanese Assimilation Policies in Colonial South Korea, 1910–1945.* Seattle: University of Washington Press.

Chang, Y.-B., J. K. Han, and W. H. Kim. 2011. "Green Growth and Green New Deal Policies in South Korea: Are They Creating Decent Green Jobs?" GURN/ITUC workshop on A Green Economy that Works for Social Progress, October 24–25. Brussels, Belgium. Accessed October 31, 2014. http://www.ituc-csi.org/IMG/pdf/Green_Growth_and_Green_New_Deal_Policies_in_Korea_ECPI_.pdf.

Choi, J. J. 2010. "The Democratic State Engulfing Civil Society: The Ironies of South Korean Democracy." *South Korean Studies* 34: 1–24.

Eckstein, H. 1975. "Case Study and Theory in Political Science." In *Strategies of Inquiry,* edited by F. I. Greenstein and N. W. Polsby, 79–138. Reading, MA: Addison-Wesley.

"Green Energy, Green Growth." *Taiwan Review,* November 1, 2009. Accessed January 29, 2013. http://taiwanreview.nat.gov.tw/ct.asp?xItem=69656&CtNode=1337.

Haddad, M. A. 2012. *Building Democracy in Japan.* New York: Cambridge University Press.

———. 2013. "Paradoxes of Democratization: Environmental Politics in East Asia." In *Routledge Handbook of East Asia and the Environment,* edited by P. G. Harris and G. Lang, 86–104. New York: Routledge.

Hildebrandt, T., and J. Turner. 2009. "Green Activism? Reassessing the Role of Environmental NGOs in China." In *State and Society Responses to Social Welfare Needs in China: Serving the People,* edited by J. Schwartz and S. Shieh, 88–110. New York: Routledge.

Ho, M. 2013. "Lukang anti-DuPont movement (Taiwan)." In *The Wiley-Blackwell Encyclopedia of Social and Political Movements,* edited by D. Snow, D. dellaPorta, B. Klandermans and D. McAdams. Indianapolis: Wiley-Blackwell. Accessed October 31, 2014. http://homepage.ntu.edu.tw/~msho/book.files/B18.pdf.

Ho, P. and R. Edmonds, eds. 2007. *China's Embedded Activism: Opportunities and Constraints of a Social Movement.* New York: Routledge.

Hsiao, H.-H. M. 1999. "Environmental Movements in Taiwan." In *Asia's Environmental Movements: Comparative Perspectives,* edited by Y.-S. F. Lee and A. Y. So, 31–54. New York: ME Sharpe.

Interviews in Seoul and Taipei, November 2010.

Interview with Echo Lin of the Taiwan Environmental Action Network (TEAN) and Kuang-Jung (Gloria) Hsu, Professor of Atmospheric Sciences of Taiwan National

University and former chair of Taiwan Environmental Protection Union (TEPU) in Taipei, November 2010.

Johnson, C. 1982. *MITI and the Japanese Miracle: The Growth of Industrial Policy 1925–1975.* Menlo Park, CA: Stanford University Press.

Kan, S. A. 2012. "Taiwan: Major U.S. Arms Sales Since 1990." *CRS Report for Congress.* Washington, DC: Congressional Research Service.

Kim, S. 2000. *Politics of Democratization in South Korea: the Role of Civil Society,* Pittsburgh, PA: University of Pittsburgh Press.

Kim, H.-R. 2004. "Dilemmas in the Making of Civil Society in South Korean Political Reform." *Journal of Contemporary Asia* 34: 55–69.

Kim, E. 2009a. "The Limits of NGO-Government Relations in South Korea." *Asian Survey* 49: 873–94.

Kim, S. 2009b. "Civic Engagement and Democracy in South Korea." *South Korean Observer,* 40, 1–26.

Kim, H.-R. 2010. "The State and Civil Society in Transition: The Role of Non-Governmental Organizations in South Korea." *The Pacific Review* 13: 595–613.

Kingston, J. 2004. *Japan's Quiet Transformation: Social Change and Civil Society in the Twenty-first Century.* New York: Routledge Curzon.

Ku, D. 1996. "The Structural Change of the Korean Environmental Movement." *Korea Journal of Population and Development.* 25: 155–80.

———. 2002. "Environmental Movement and Policies During High Economic Growth in South Korea." In *Environment and Our Sustainability in the 21st Century: Understanding and Cooperation between Developed and Developing Countries,* edited by Y. Arayama, 65–87. Nagoya, Japan: Nagoya University.

———. 2011. "The South Korean Environmental Movement: Green Politics Through Social Movement." In *East Asian Social Movements,* edited by J. Broadbent and V. Brockman, 205–35. New York: Springer.

Leblanc, R. M. 1999. *Bicycle Citizens: The Political World of the Japanese Housewife.* Berkeley: University of California Press.

Lee, S.-H. 1999. "Environmental Movements in South Korea." In *Asia's Environmental Movements: Comparative Perspectives,* edited by Y.-S. F. Lee and A. Y. So, 90–119. New York: ME Sharpe.

Lee, S.-J. 2000. "The Environmental Movement and Its Political Empowerment." *South Korea Journal* 40: 131–60.

———. 2010. *RE: Interview—KFEM.* November 26.

Lyons, D. 2009. "The Two-headed Dragon: Environmental Policy and Progress under Rising Democracy in Taiwan." *East Asia* 26: 57–76.

Maclachlan, P. L. 2002. *Consumer Politics in Postwar Japan: The Institutional Boundaries of Citizen Activism.* New York: Columbia University Press.

Manyin, M., E. Chantlett-Avery, M. B. Nikitin, and M. A. Taylor. 2010. "U.S.-South Korea Relations." *CRS Report to Congress.* Washington, DC: Congressional Research Service.

Mertha, A. 2008. *China's Water Warriors: Citizen Action and Policy Change,* Ithaca, NY: Cornell University Press.

Myers, R. and M. Peattle, eds. 1987. *The Japanese Colonial Empire, 1895–1945.* Princeton, NJ: Princeton University Press.

O'Brien, K. 1996. "Rightful Resistance." *World Politics* 49: 31–55.

Oh, J. S. 2012. "Strong State and Strong Civil Society in Contemporary South Korea: Challenges to Democratic Governance." *Asian Survey* 52: 528–49.

Official ROC Foreign Relations overview. 2013. Accessed January 12, 2014. http://www.taiwan.gov.tw/ct.asp?xItem=27190&ctNode=1922&mp=1001.

Penn Data Tables. 2012. Accessed December 12, 2014. https://pwt.sas.upenn.edu/php_site/pwt71/pwt71_retrieve.php.

Reardon-Anderson, J. 1997. *Pollution, Politics, and Foreign Investment in Taiwan: The Lukang Rebellion*. New York: M.E. Sharpe.

Reimann, K. 2009. *The Rise of Japanese NGOs*. New York: Routledge.

Schwartz, J. 2004. "Environmental NGOs in China: Roles and Limits." *Pacific Affairs* 77: 28–49.

Takao, Y. 2007. *Reinventing Japan: From Merchant Nation to Civic Nation*. New York: Palgrave Macmillan.

Tang, D. T.-C. 1997. "New Developments in Environmental Law and Policy in Taiwan." *Pacific Rim Law & Policy Journal* 6: 245–46.

Tang, S.-Y. and C.-P. Tang. 1997. "Democratization and Environmental Politics in Taiwan." *Asian Survey* 37: 281–94.

Tsai, L. 2007. *Accountability without Democracy: How Solidarity Groups Provide Public Goods in Rural China*. New York: Cambridge University Press.

Tsurumi, E. P. 1977. *Japanese Colonial Education in Taiwan, 1895–1945*. Cambridge, MA: Harvard University Press.

U.S. Department of State Office of the Historian. "A Guide to the United States' History of Recognition, Diplomatic, and Consular Relations, By Country, Since 1776: China." Accessed January 12, 2013. http://history.state.gov/countries/china.

Weller, R. P. 1999. *Alternate Civilities: Democracy and Culture in China and Taiwan*. Boulder, CO: Westview Press.

Woo-Cummings, M., ed. 1999. *The Developmental State*. Ithaca, NY: Cornell University Press.

Xie, L. 2009. *Environmental Activism in China*. New York: Routledge.

CONCLUSION

NIMBY is Beautiful

How Local Environmental Protests Are Changing the World

Mary Alice Haddad

Citizens around the world increasingly face life-threatening environmental challenges. Unfortunately, local, national, and international policy-making structures are often ill-equipped to cope with the complexity of these economic, political, social, and ecological challenges. Thus far, social science literature and public rhetoric have often belittled NIMBY protests as parochial, shortsighted, and destructive to progress. In contrast to this conventional wisdom, this volume has demonstrated that NIMBY environmental protests often serve the public interest, have positive long-term effects, and promote progress on broader issues facing society. Drawing on cases of grassroots environmental protest from around the world, we have shown not only the numerous ways in which NIMBY is contributing to the improvement of environmental outcomes for particular communities, but also how it is transforming broader social and political landscapes across the developed, developing, democratic, and nondemocratic worlds.

This volume turns the conventional wisdom—conflict is bad for politics, and NIMBY protesters are uninformed, obstructionist citizens preventing progress toward the public good—on its head. It argues instead, through both large-n analysis and detailed case studies, that local conflict about environmental issues can be a positive and productive part of the political process. Conflict about local environmental issues can empower previously ignored or disempowered citizens, it can diversify knowledge and technology, it can facilitate creative solutions to difficult problems, and it can promote a more responsive governance structure.

Thus far, most studies of NIMBY have focused on the short-term outcomes of individual protests, but we show that those short-term outcomes are much less important than the process of the conflicts and the long-term social, political, and technological innovations that often emerge as a result of them. We do not argue that NIMBY battles should be studied because protesters usually "win." Consistent with the dominant literature, we have found that NIMBY protesters do not generally win. Of the sixty cases studied by Helen Poulos in chapter 1, only nineteen were clearly successful in obtaining their original aims. This means that a potential NIMBY protester has only a one-in-three chance of success measured this way. Since obtaining a specific goal is usually the main motivator for those engaged in such protests, these odds are not very encouraging.

We argue, however, that these protests are worthy of study not because protesters usually win, but rather because *NIMBY environmental protests often generate positive innovation irrespective of whether or not they are successful* in achieving the original aim of the protest. Using those same data from Poulos, a majority of NIMBY protests—thirty-four of sixty cases—resulted in some form of social, political, or technological innovation. The prospect for innovation emerging from NIMBY protests is even stronger within democratic countries;[1] although fewer than half of NIMBY protesters in the democracies in Poulos's data attain their original goals (seventeen of forty cases), the chances that a NIMBY protest will generate some form of innovation are nearly two-to-one (twenty-six cases of innovation, only fourteen without any innovation).[2] Thus, although NIMBY protesters usually lose, they also usually contribute positively to political and social processes that reach beyond their own localities. Therefore, studying the process of NIMBY protests is likely more important than studying their immediate outcomes.

This volume argues that, rather than atypical, non-generalizable, parochial skirmishes, NIMBY protests are important research locations where scholars can study politics in developed, developing, democratic, democratizing, and nondemocratic countries. No matter where they occur, NIMBY battles illuminate how well political channels are functioning and reveal the processes through which political discord is resolved (or not). They highlight, often dramatically, issues and groups that have been ignored and oppressed by current political and social systems. Communities fighting for their own backyards create spaces in which the definitions of the public and the public good are developed and redefined. They become schools of governance in which both citizens and governments can learn to work productively, or at least less destructively, with one another. NIMBY battlegrounds are places where local, national, international, and global forces interact, creating positive and negative dynamics: where global norms can influence local behavior, where local battles can transform global norms, and where the boundaries of national power can be reformed.

This conclusion aims to offer an overview of the findings of the volume. Drawing from the conclusions of the previous chapters, it will distill the main factors that lead NIMBY protests to generate innovative outcomes. It will also articulate the different types of positive outcomes that have been found to emerge from NIMBY protests. NIMBY environmental protests can sometimes be parochial, destructive, and shortsighted, but we aim to show some of the ways in which they can be broad and productive, and contribute to long-lasting, positive transformations that improve not just the ecology of the planet, but the societies and individual well-being of the humans who inhabit it.

Factors Leading to Innovation

In her large-n analysis of grassroots environmental protests (chapter 1), Helen Poulos identified three factors that contributed to innovations resulting from NIMBY protests. The most important factor was the duration of the protests: protests that lasted less than a year and a half did not result in innovation. In some cases, those protests were short because the government or company shut down the offending factory or changed siting plans quickly, a "win" for the protesters who opposed the project. However, without the time to forge social and political connections or to develop extensive counter-expertise, the activists remained confined to the narrow, local issue that was the initial focus of their protest, and quickly disbanded. Thus, even if they "won" their desired outcome, short NIMBY protests did not generate any innovation.

A second important factor determining innovation was whether or not the government responded in some way to the protest. When it responded positively, innovation almost always resulted. Although governments sometimes respond in ways that are negative, such as repressing protesters, according to the large-n analysis governmental response usually resulted in innovation. Furthermore, even if the initial governmental response was negative, innovation can occur when the NIMBY protest is viewed from a longer-term perspective. Gaining a governmental response—whether it was local or national—helped ensure that the legacy of the NIMBY action lived beyond the specific issue that had generated the protest. Finally, even if the government did not respond, if the protesters were able to engage external connections, international organizations or other groups who were outside the locality of the conflict, they were also often successful in creating innovative outcomes.

These factors are very helpful in illuminating some of the broad characteristics of NIMBY protests that generate innovative outcomes, but they can do very little to help us understand the process through which innovation emerges. How do protesters sustain their protest beyond a year and a half (indeed, sometimes through decades)? How do they induce the government to take action? How to they make, sustain, and use external connections? The answers to these process questions can only be answered through the case studies.

The case studies revealed four main factors that helped determine whether a local NIMBY action would be able to generate innovation: timing, political savvy, shifting the frame of debate, and the introduction of counter-expertise. The first two of these factors, timing and political savvy, are consistent with the extensive literature on the importance of political opportunity structure and social movements. Pioneered by Sidney Tarrow and refined by Charles Tilly and others, this literature highlights the importance of taking advantage of openings created by external events and shifts in political structure in the development of social movements.

Nearly every successful NIMBY group under examination in this volume was able to connect its protest to some other event that had created a political opening for the action. Often, this was a major environmental catastrophe that occurred just prior to the protest, so interest in the issues related to the protest was already high in the minds of the public. Protesters were able to link their specific, local protest to broader issues that were already of public concern. Examples include the ways in which the anti-nuclear movements in Germany and the United States were able to use public fears raised by the disasters in Chernobyl and Fukushima to protest expansion of nuclear power. Taiwanese activists protesting a new DuPont chemical plant could tap into the fears caused by the proximate Union Carbide gas tragedy in Bhopal, India that killed thousands and injured hundreds of thousands of people.

Activists were also able to take advantage of timing in other ways. American, Chinese, German, Japanese, Korean, Taiwanese, and Russian activists took advantage of political openings to push their agendas. Rising public interest in greater transparency and accountability of government was easily transferred to public demands for transparency and accountability on specific local issues. In this way, a particular community's fight became the fight of the whole country. Often, if any particular NIMBY protest were to have been held earlier or later, it would have been crushed or ignored. As James Reardon-Anderson wrote of the protest in Lukang, Taiwan, when the timing of a NIMBY protest is right, it can focus the attention of an entire country on a small provincial town, raise national consciousness about threats to the natural environment, and challenge the rules that government officials and industrial leaders had come to take for granted (Reardon-Anderson 1997: x).

Timing can also kill a NIMBY movement. When other issues become more important to the public than a small locality's environmental worries, the movement cannot gain traction outside that one community and cannot generate much innovation. As Plantan writes of the Baikal protest in chapter 5, "[T]he timing of this environmental battle, during a recession ... was fatal for the environmental movement. Economic issues trumped environmental concerns, and the factory reopened."

A second important factor for generating innovation was the political savvy of the leaders of the NIMBY movement, in particular their ability to calculate correctly how to manage center-local politics as well as inter-ministerial conflict. This calculation was country- and timing- specific. In several cases, such as the fight against nuclear power in Germany, the opposition to the oil pipeline near Lake Baikal in Russia, and anti-pollution campaigns in Korea, advocates were very successful in targeting the central government. They used a variety of methods to link their local NIMBY fight to national political issues that gained broader salience among the public and, ultimately, received political attention and action from top political authorities.

In contrast, in several cases, including the fight against DuPont in Taiwan, air pollution battles in Japan, and Chinese opposition to pollution in Dalian and a dam in Dujiangyan, activists were conscious to target only local officials and not central political authorities. Keeping their fight local helped ensure that central government officials did not shut down the protest. In fact, advocates often portrayed their position as being consistent with central government policy, arguing that it was the local officials who were violating the directives of the central government. Advocates were also often able to take advantage of intra-governmental divides by pitting one ministry (e.g., environmental and cultural ministries) against another (e.g., economic development or construction). This strategy commonly involved shifting the frame of the debate away from issues in the purview of government authorities whose position was inconsistent with the advocates' goals and toward issues in the purview of authorities whose position was in line with their goals.

Numerous studies have identified the importance of venue shopping and framing for successful environmental advocacy. David Snow et al. (1986) identified the important role that issue framing plays in mobilizing participation, and Robert Futrell (2003) refines this theoretical framework for the NIMBY context. In the cases in this volume, Russian and Chinese advocates successfully shifted the frame of discussion away from economic development and toward cultural preservation, and that shift helped promote a positive outcome for the protesters.

Americans, Germans, and Taiwanese shifted the frame of debate away from the technical specificity of site location characteristics toward the legitimacy of the policy making processes and the justice and equity implications of siting choices made according to dominant corporate and central government criteria. In contrast, clean air advocates in Japan selected almost the polar opposite strategy, electing to keep their advocacy focused on the specific technical issues, thereby avoiding having their environmental advocacy subsumed by partisan politics. Koreans consciously linked local environmental advocacy to national democratic governance issues; while that strategy was effective during the 1990s and early 2000s when the democratic transition was new and liberal political parties were in power, the strategy backfired when conservative parties regained control of the government. One of the most important lessons highlighted by the NIMBY cases examined in this volume is that no single frame is universally successful for environmental protests. Selecting a frame that is appropriate to the particular context of time and place is critical for successful innovation.

One of the common themes that can be found across nearly all of the cases is the ways in which advocates used local cultural resources to help make the connection between a specific time and place and their broader environmental concern. They used cultural symbols, such as selecting a local folk art festival as the location for their protest (Taiwan). They engaged religious leaders to help highlight the moral and ethical frame of their environmental advocacy and shore up the legitimacy of their protest (Germany, Korea). In some cases, such as with Lake Baikal and Dujiangyan, cultural preservation became the core of the protest, with the environmental issues taking a backseat in favor of a cultural frame.

Finally, NIMBY protesters often used counter-expertise as a method by which to innovate new technology and also offer a counter-narrative to the dominant one being presented by corporations and central government. Along with Alan Irwin (1995), John Dryzek et al. (2003), and others, we have found that developing and presenting counter-expertise is a common method to promote both outcome success and innovation in NIMBY movements. The counter-expertise in our cases took two very different forms. One common form was recruiting elite scientists and other high-status individuals to the NIMBY cause. This strategy was used by the NIMBY protests related to energy use: oil (Russia), nuclear (Germany and the United States), hydro (China), and renewable (Germany and the United States). We also saw elite non-governmental experts form their own think tank (Korea), institute (Germany), and advisory committees (Japan).

Another common form of counter-expert is not elite, university-educated individuals, but rather "ordinary" people who use their local knowledge about the environmental conditions of their locality and others near them to present an alternative narrative about the consequences of the objectionable project. In Taiwan, fishermen presented data and anecdotes about their catches and those of their neighbors, taking study tours of other areas where similar developments had taken place (Haddad). Chinese citizens followed this example, leading local leaders on visits to communities that had been displaced and flooded as a result of other dams

(Plantan). American activists argued that a different kind of expertise should be sought—experts on social justice were promoted over scientists testifying to the safety of nuclear waste facilities (Sherman).

Taken together, the chapters in this volume show that rather than being obstructionist and counter-productive, NIMBY environmental protests often have innovative outcomes, even if protesters do not generally win their specific battles. Four factors—timing, political savvy, framing, and counter-expertise—were especially important in facilitating innovative outcomes from NIMBY disputes. The next section shifts from the factors that lead to innovation to the positive outcomes that can emerge from NIMBY environmental protests.

Positive Outcomes Emerging from NIMBY Environmental Protests

Irrespective of whether a particular set of NIMBY protesters succeeds in winning a local battle, the process of organizing citizens in a particular place to object to an environmental threat has numerous benefits. In particular, it can lead to technological, social, and political innovation that can benefit not only the local protesters, but also their wider polity (Devine-Wright 2010; Aldrich 2008).

NIMBY politics creates technological innovation because it holds scientific/technical knowledge and the people who present it accountable, and creates incentives for the development of new, more environmentally friendly technologies (McAvoy 1999). Scientific information presented by the centers of power, whether they are government or corporate, is often portrayed as the only authoritative account of the environmental issue at stake. NIMBY protesters often engage a different set of scientists, those with equal standing in the academy, to present equally authoritative scientific evidence that offers an alternative interpretation of the environmental issues under dispute. Additionally, NIMBY protesters often present alternative forms of scientific evidence that are gathered from the field from local farmers, fishers, and other residents about changes in their environment as they have experienced them. Thus, NIMBY protests can create a venue for local knowledge to be introduced into public discourse and into policy-making processes. Additionally, as can be seen in the DuPont case in Taiwan, the renewable energy cases in Germany and the United States, and the clean air case in Japan, NIMBY protests also create political and market incentives for companies to develop more environmentally friendly products and production processes, which leads to safer products and factories that not only benefit the local producing population, but also consumers around the world.

NIMBY politics can lead to social innovation in two main ways: First, it may draw broad public attention to people and issues that have been ignored by the center of politics. Second, it can create a venue in which those who have been historically marginalized by the political system can become engaged in politics. NIMBY politics commonly raises issues of equity and justice because environmental issues that become the focal points of NIMBY protests often involve marginalized populations. In Poulos's study (chapter 1), about one quarter of all of the grassroots environmental actions around the world involved marginalized or indigenous populations.[3] In the cases examined in more detail in this book, the local farmers and fishers in China, Korea, Russia, and Taiwan were key instigators of the NIMBY battles in their countries. In Japan, the United States, and Germany, urban residents from poorer populations objected to their communities being subjected to higher rates of environmental damage than their compatriots living in other parts of the country. Of all the cases, those fighting against nuclear waste in the United States were perhaps the most overt in framing their NIMBY battle as one that was fundamentally about social and political justice and only secondarily about environmental damage.

Through the process of mobilizing their communities around a NIMBY issue, protesters often create venues in which those adversely affected by environmental issues can have their knowledge and concerns legitimized, respected, and included in the conversation. From this perspective, the value of the NIMBY protest lies less in the issues that it brings to the public agenda than in the people whom it engages. In all the cases studied here, people who usually would not be particularly engaged in politics not only participate, they often become the leaders of the fight. These ordinary citizens band together to make themselves heard. Even when those at the center of power ignore or overrun their concerns, the experience of becoming politically engaged and the organizations that they form have long-lasting implications for the politics and societies in which the NIMBY battles are fought. The most direct example of this is when the local leaders of a particular NIMBY protest continue to be engaged with environmental issues and emerge as leaders of the environmental movement. It is also common for organizations created to fight a particular NIMBY battle to remain intact and grow even after that specific NIMBY fight has been resolved.

NIMBY protests usually occur only when regular political and bureaucratic channels have been blocked (see the Introduction). Therefore, it should not be surprising that one of the most important contributions of NIMBY protests that we found from our studies is that they create new channels through which citizens can influence their governments and their governments can work with their citizens to improve policymaking.

These channels can be created inside the governmental bureaucracy, by political parties, or among citizen organizations. In nearly all the countries examined in this volume, Ministries of the Environment or their equivalents were created in direct response to public concern about environmental degradation as expressed through NIMBY protests (among other methods).

Political innovations in electoral politics occurred in Germany, Korea, Taiwan, and the United States. German politics was fundamentally transformed with the introduction of the Green Party, the creation of several non-governmental environmental organizations including the Eco-Institute, and new citizen-business collaborations around environmental issues. In Korea and Taiwan, NIMBY environmental protests and their organizations became deeply connected with the democracy movements sweeping both countries that ultimately brought an end to the countries' military dictatorships and ushered in entirely new political systems. In the United States, the environment and associated social-justice issues became legitimate and electorally expedient political issues.

Finally, NIMBY-generated innovations are often disseminated nationally and internationally, creating a new set of repertoires and organizations that can empower local citizens and their governments to address pressing environmental problems. We have seen this nationally—local NIMBY activists in the United States, Germany, Japan, and Korea networked with each other in order to influence national environmental policy change. We have also seen it regionally: cross-border protest activity not only helped German groups develop new forms of participation, but innovations generated in Germany also subsequently aided the activities of environmental movements in other European countries. Policy, organizational, and social innovation generated in Japan has spread to Korea and Taiwan and also to China. Finally, political repertoires and technological solutions emerging from a local battle on one side of the globe are now commonly adopted on the other side (e.g., anti-nuclear activists in Europe and the EU are learning from the experience of activists in Japan and vice versa). The dissemination of political, social, and technological innovations that emerge from NIMBY environmental protests help not only improve the natural environment of the planet, they are also promoting more participatory government in democratic and non-democratic political systems alike.

Conclusion

NIMBY politics can be narrow and destructive, but it need not always be so. Through a combination of a large-n analysis and a series of case studies drawn from around the world, this volume has highlighted some of the positive outcomes that often emerge from grassroots action in environmental issues. Communities that organize to protect their own backyards from environmental damage are certainly acting out of self-interest: they want to preserve their own health and safety and those of their families. News coverage and academic research about these protests has commonly focused on the parochial nature of their concerns without recognizing that these local battles often engage issues that extend far beyond the boundaries of their neighborhoods and *often* result in positive political, social, and technological innovations.

This volume has called into question many of the prevailing assumptions about NIMBY politics. It is not the case that conflict should always be avoided and collaboration should be the goal. We have found that NIMBY conflicts serve as an important corrective to flawed political processes that ignore certain voices and block access to decision making. The process of local environmental conflict reveals the underlying problems in governance and can help generate creative solutions to those problems. In nearly every case in the volume, conflict emerged because there was consensus among elites, but the reason for the initial consensus was that voices that might object could not be heard. In nearly every case study examined, the conflict that emerged broke apart that consensus in useful and productive ways and helped forge a new path toward more inclusive governance structures.

It is not the case that the facilities targeted by NIMBY protests generally promote the broader good, such that the main issue is one of finding an appropriate location rather than the more profound question about whether the project is, in fact, in the public interest. In several of the cases (e.g., Germany, Japan, the United States), NIMBY protests revealed that proposed projects were often unnecessary and that environmental standards deemed impossible to achieve were not only possible, they were profitable.

It is not the case that government and industry always have better technological solutions than citizens. In nearly every case, NIMBY conflicts created opportunities for counter-elites to propose alternative technologies and also to legitimize local forms of knowledge. Koreans formed an independent think tank when they did not trust government reports about water contamination levels. Germans promoted new alternative energy options that had not previously existed.

NIMBY legacies do not end with a final "win" or "loss." Revealed most compellingly in the larger-n analysis by Helen Poulos, but also highlighted in the cases of Taiwan, Korea, China, Germany, and the United States, NIMBY legacies can be long and powerful. The social, political, and technological innovations that emerge from NIMBY fights live much longer than the controversies that gave birth to them.

NIMBY protests that are able to take advantage of timing, those that are politically savvy in the ways that they navigate center-local relations and inter-ministerial conflict, those that can shift the frame of the debate away from frames that empower the central policy makers in favor of frames that empower local communities, and those that are able to mobilize counter-expertise can generate innovation from their local protests. This is true even when protesters lose the specific battle around which they organized, and even when the protests occur in non-democratic contexts.

NIMBY environmental action often generates a wide range of positive outcomes. It commonly raises public awareness of issues that have been ignored by the centers of power. It offers a method by which marginalized people who are usually indifferent to or disengaged from politics can become empowered; it gives them a venue to develop political expertise and legitimizes them as important participants in politics. NIMBY politics is a mechanism to keep technical and scientific experts accountable by introducing counter-expertise and local knowledge about the environment. Finally, NIMBY conflicts serve as important models for other communities struggling with similar environmental issues. Citizens, governments, and corporations can learn from their own experience as well as from the experiences of similarly situated communities about better ways to work together toward common goals of economic development and environmental sustainability.

This volume has revealed that NIMBY protests can often result in valuable, long-term, positive outcomes. This volume has also demonstrated that NIMBY protests offer important areas for social science research. NIMBY protests are useful research locations in which to examine what happens when a group of citizens strongly objects to public policy regarding the citizens' community. As research locations, NIMBY protests can illuminate the fissures in political and social systems that are often obscured by status quo politics, whether that status quo allows citizens voice in political decision making or ruthlessly represses and co-opts groups of citizens to prevent discord from becoming visible. These conflicts can raise the profile of groups and issues that have been ignored by the center of politics, creating useful locations in which to begin new research agendas.

NIMBY politics is also a place in which fundamental political values are debated and often transformed. Which people constitute the public? What constitutes the public good? Who has a voice in politics? What is the process through which governments gain the consent of the governed? These are all questions that are frequently at the heart of NIMBY battles, making those battles excellent places to examine how core political values are renewed, reinforced, and revised over time. The groups that form to organize the protests and those that are created to resolve the conflict establish places where citizens and government officials can learn to work productively, or at least less harmfully, with one another. De Tocqueville's "schools of democracy" often emerge from NIMBY conflicts. Researching the conditions under which citizens can transform a negative interaction with their government into better governance structures could lend great insight into political development in non-democracies, transitioning democracies, and mature democracies alike.

Finally, NIMBY battles today are no longer limited to a single backyard. Globalization means that neighborhood groups have the option to tap into global resources when mounting their NIMBY fights. They can leverage rich and powerful international organizations to generate publicity, finance activities, and lend legitimacy. Alternatively, local groups can consciously elect to decline external assistance and resist reaching outside their borders in order to retain control over their movements and mitigate external political pressure. Global environmental movements and norms are also effected by local NIMBY battles. Transnational organizations can use a local fight in one country to help motivate and organize protesters in another. They may revise their missions or their global strategy based on the experience of a local community. Even without working with an established international organization, NIMBY protesters can mimic and refine strategies and techniques used by people on the other side of the globe.

Thus, NIMBY protests are places where researchers can tease out the limits of Keck and Sikkink's (1998) boomerang effect, identifying the conditions under which international involvement in a local NIMBY conflict can help, can hurt, is sought after, or is refused. Furthermore, NIMBY battles are often places in which it is possible to examine exactly how states are managing local-global conflicts, where the boundaries of national power have become more curtailed, and where states are finding ways to gain new forms of power. Although "my backyard" is always at the heart of a NIMBY protest, the connections among backyards and the links among a single backyard and its country, region, and globe are among the most fascinating and important aspects of contemporary NIMBY politics.

This volume has argued that NIMBY can be beautiful. As environmental challenges grow in scope and intensity, scholars, policy makers, and advocates can learn a great deal from the experience of individual communities that are fighting to improve the environment of their own backyards. A closer and more comprehensive examination of NIMBY movements may help point the way to a greener and more just planet.

Notes

1. Those who rank "free" in Freedom House Data, which can be found at http://freedomhouse.org, accessed March 12, 2013.
2. Full success is one in which protesters get what they ask for—the facility is not sited, the factory is closed, and so forth. Of the forty NIMBY cases in Poulos's sample from democratic countries, seventeen were successful, eight had partial success, five failed, and ten are too recent to determine the outcome. As Poulos acknowledges, these results likely underplay the longer-term and more subtle effects of NIMBY that are not captured in journalistic accounts of the conflicts.
3. Poulos, unpublished data.

References

Aldrich, Daniel. 2008. *Site Fights: Divisive Facilities and Civil Society in Japan and the West.* Ithaca, NY: Cornell University Press.

De Toqueville, Alexis. 2003. *Democracy in America.* New York: Penguin Classics.

Devine-Wright, Patrick, ed. 2010. *Renewable Energy and the Public: From NIMBY to Participation.* London: Earthscan.

Dryzek, John et al. 2003. *Green States and Social Movements: Environmentalism in the United States, United Kingdom, Germany and Norway.* Oxford: Oxford University Press.

Futrell, Robert. 2003. "Framing Processes, Cognitive Liberation, and NIMBY Protest in the U.S. Chemical-Weapons Disposal Conflict." *Sociological Inquiry* 73(3): 359–86.

Irwin, Alan. 1995. *Citizen Science: A Study of People, Expertise and Sustainable Development.* New York: Routledge.

Keck, Margaret and Kathryn Sikkink. 1998. *Activists Beyond Borders: Advocacy Networks in International Politics.* Ithaca, NY: Cornell University Press.

McAvoy, Gregory E. 1999. *Controlling Technocracy: Citizen Rationality and the NIMBY Syndrome.* Washington, DC: Georgetown University Press.

Reardon-Anderson, James. 1997. *Pollution, Politics, and Foreign Investment in Taiwan: The Lukang Rebellion.* New York: M.E. Sharpe.

Snow, David A., E. Burke Rochford, Jr., Steve Worden, and Robert D. Benford. 1986. "Frame Alignment Processes, Micromobilization, and Movement Participation." *American Sociological Review* 51: 464–81.

Tarrow, Sidney. 1998. *Power in Movement: Social Movements and Contentious Politics.* Second ed. Ithaca, NY: Cornell University Press.

Tilly, Charles, and Sidney Tarrow. 2006. *Contentious Politics.* New York: Paradigm.

Contributors

Mike Gunter, Jr. (Ph.D., University of Kentucky) is a Cornell Distinguished Professor at Rollins College in Winter Park, Florida, where he also directs the Rollins International Relations Program. He is the author of *Building the Next Ark: How NGOs Work to Protect Biodiversity* (2004/2006) with Dartmouth College and University Press of New England and specializes in issues of sustainable development.

Mary Alice Haddad (Ph.D., University of Washington) is an Associate Professor of Government at Wesleyan University. Her publications include *Politics and Volunteering in Japan* (Cambridge 2007), *Building Democracy in Japan* (Cambridge 2012), and articles in journals such as *Comparative Political Studies, Democratization, Journal of Asian Studies,* and *Nonprofit and Voluntary Sector Quarterly.*

Carol Hager (Ph.D., University of California, San Diego) is a Professor and Chair of the Political Science Department and Director of the Center for Social Sciences at Bryn Mawr College. She is the author of *Technological Democracy: Bureaucracy and Citizenry in the German Energy Debate* (Michigan 1995) and articles in journals such as *German Politics, German Studies Review,* and the *International Journal of Urban and Regional Research.* She is interested in how lay citizens participate in policy areas with high technical content.

Takashi Kanatsu (Ph.D., Columbia University) is an Associate Professor of Political Science at Hofstra University. His research interest is in the political economy of East Asia and Latin America, particularly in the role of government in high-technology industrial development. He is the author of *Asian Politics: Tradition, Transformation, and Future* (Linus 2008) and numerous articles.

Dörte Ohlhorst (Ph.D., Free University of Berlin) is project manager at the Environmental Policy Research Center, Free University of Berlin. She formerly headed the Department of Climate and Energy at the Center for Technology and Society, Technical University of Berlin. She served as a research associate at the German Advisory Council on the Environment (SRU) from 2009 to 2012. She is co-author of *Renewable Energies in Germany's Electricity Market: A Biography of the Innovation Process* (Springer 2011).

Elizabeth Plantan is a Ph.D. student in Government at Cornell University. She was the Byrnes Fellow at Indiana University's Russian & East European Institute, where she completed her M.A. in Russian Studies. She holds a B.A. in Government and Russian and East European Studies from Wesleyan University.

Helen M. Poulos (Ph.D., Yale School of Forestry and Environmental Studies) is a Mellon Postdoctoral Fellow at Wesleyan University's College of the Environment. She has published over twenty peer-reviewed papers on a wide range of environmental topics including forest ecology, water management, and human-environment interactions.

Miranda Schreurs (Ph.D., University of Michigan) became Director of the Environmental Policy Research Center and a Professor of Comparative Politics at the Free University of Berlin in 2007. She is a member of the German Advisory Council on the Environment, has chaired the European Environment and Sustainable Development Advisory Council, and was a Fulbright New Century Scholars Distinguished Scholar Leader. She is author of *Environmental Politics in Japan, Germany, and the United States* (Cambridge 2002, Japanese translation 2007) and co-editor of *TransAtlantic Energy and Environmental Politics: Comparative and International Perspectives* (Ashgate 2009), among many other books and articles.

Daniel J. Sherman (Ph.D., Cornell University) studies environmental politics, policy, and sustainability. He is the Luce-funded Professor of Environmental Policy and Decision Making at the University of Puget Sound and Director of the Sound Policy Institute in Tacoma, Washington. He is the author of *Not Here, Not There, Not Anywhere: Politics, Social Movements and the Disposal of Low-level Radioactive Waste* (Resources for the Future 2011). He also focuses on sustainability efforts in higher education. His work in this area is represented in two recent articles: "Sustainability: What's the Big Idea?" and "Uncovering Sustainability in the Curriculum."

Index